Using Shadow Prices

USING SHADOW PRICES

edited by
I. M. D. Little
and
M. FG. Scott

 HOLMES & MEIER PUBLISHERS, INC.
IMPORT DIVISION
101 Fifth Avenue, New York, N. Y. 10003

Heinemann Educational Books Ltd

LONDON   EDINBURGH   MELBOURNE   AUCKLAND   TORONTO
HONG KONG   SINGAPORE   KUALA LUMPUR
IBADAN   NAIROBI   LUSAKA
JOHANNESBURG   NEW DELHI   KINGSTON

ISBN 0 435 84465 2
© I. M. D. Little and M. FG. Scott 1976
First published 1976

Published by
Heinemann Educational Books Ltd
48 Charles Street, London W1X 8AH
Printed and bound in Great Britain
at The Pitman Press, Bath

Contents

Notes on the Contributors

I. M. D. Little's best known work is *A Critique of Welfare Economics* (1950). Since 1958 he has specialized in the economics of developing countries, and now professes that subject at Nuffield College, Oxford. He has been Vice-President of the O.E.C.D. Development Centre, and is a member of the U.N. Committee for Development Planning. He is co-author with Professor J. A. Mirrlees of *Project Appraisal and Planning for Developing Countries* (1974).

M. FG. Scott has worked as an economist for the British Government and international organizations. He collaborated with I. M. D. Little and T. Scitovsky in writing *Industry and Trade in some Developing Countries* (1970), and with J. D. MacArthur and D. M. G. Newbery in writing *Project Appraisal in Practice: the Little–Mirrlees Method Applied in Kenya*. He has helped to evaluate projects in India, Mauritius, and Pakistan, as well as Kenya, and recently served on an economic mission to the Philippines. He is a Fellow of Nuffield College, Oxford.

Anne Forbes went to St Anne's College, Oxford, to study for a B.Litt. in Economics after several years working for the Development Assistance Committee of the O.E.C.D. in Paris. She is now a Research Officer in the Department of the Environment, Leeds.

G. A. Hughes is a lecturer in the Faculty of Economics and Politics, Cambridge, and a Fellow of Christ's College. He has written on the problems of housing policy in Britain as well as Kenya. He has also collaborated with A. F. Robertson in a research project to examine the links between the domestic organization and economic performance of family farmers in Uganda, the results of which are published in *The Family Farm*.

John Page Jr. has undertaken field research in both Latin America and West Africa. He has served as a consultant to the US Agency for International Development and the International Bank for Reconstruction and Development (World Bank). He has recently completed a number of studies of industrial investments in Ghana, on which Chapter 4 is based and which also form the basis of his doctoral thesis in Economics at Oxford.

David Newbery has worked as an economist for the Tanzanian Treasury, and since his appointment to the Faculty of Economics at

Cambridge University in 1966 has visited Kenya several times to work on project evaluation, and to work as a consultant of the F.A.O. at the Kenya Beef Research Station. He has published articles in learned journals on social cost–benefit analysis, development and beef production in the tropics. He is a Fellow of Churchill College, Cambridge.

David Bevan has worked as an economist for the British and Kenya Governments, advising on energy policy and the East African Community respectively. He has been a research officer at the Transport Studies Unit, Oxford University, and is a Fellow of St. John's College, Oxford.

D. W. Soskice is a Fellow of University College, Oxford. He has worked as an economist for the U.K. Treasury.

Ian G. Heggie is Director of the Transport Studies Unit at Oxford University. A qualified engineer and economist, he has participated in numerous overseas studies in an executive as well as in an operational capacity. He also acts as economic consultant to Freeman Fox and Associates. He is the author of *Transport Engineering Economics* (1972).

List of Tables

Note: a dash, "–", indicates nil or negligible, throughout the tables;
two dots, ". .", indicate not available or not applicable.

CHAPTER ONE

INTRODUCTION

This book is an outcome of research, sponsored by Nuffield College, and largely financed by the Leverhulme Trust, whose main aim was to develop the methods of project appraisal originally put forward in Little and Mirrlees, 1968 (the *Manual*). These methods were first applied to industrial projects, as the *Manual* was written for them, and the results of 17 such case-studies are summarized in Little, Scitovsky and Scott, 1970, Chapter 5, Section VII[1]. However, a wider field of application seemed both appropriate and desirable, and so some 25 other case-studies were undertaken during the years 1969–1973, and these (whether published or not) are listed at the end of this chapter. It may be seen that the studies include projects in agriculture, roads, irrigation, housing and tourism, as well as the estimation of shadow prices of labour, of private investment and of goods and services in general. Work has been done in over 15 different countries in Africa, Asia and Latin America.

What has emerged from all this work? One result has been the adoption of the method by several aid agencies and by the planning offices of a few developing countries. Another has been the rewriting of the original *Manual* (Little and Mirrlees, 1974). Some of the case-studies have also been published. This volume contains some more. It is not, we hope, by any means the end of the story. On the contrary, as further experience is gained with the method, it will evolve. The scope for improvement is great. Nevertheless, as our own direct involvement in the work is lessening, we take this opportunity to reflect on what we have learned so far. A recurring theme is the relevance of shadow pricing to many more economic policy questions than just project appraisal, and we draw our illustrations mainly from the studies presented in this volume.

---

[1] A great many other industrial studies, using broadly the same methods, have now been done as the method is in fairly general use. For published examples see Lal, 1975, and Streeten and Lall, 1973.

PRACTICAL PROBLEMS OF ESTIMATING ACCOUNTING PRICES

Accounting prices have been estimated for a wide range of countries, goods and services. This has been done at a cost in terms of man-hours which is very small indeed in relation to those involved in other aspects of the projects concerned, and also in relation to the effort involved in preparing national plans. The estimates for Mauritius,[1] for example, took less than three man-months. This was perhaps a particularly straightforward case, and the estimates for Kenya,[2] which were more ambitious in scope, probably took about one man-year, although the actual work was spread over four years.

The quality of the estimates which could be achieved in the above sort of time depended heavily on several factors. First, where the main method of government intervention in trade, or in the economy generally, was through taxes and subsidies, it was much easier to make estimates than where direct controls were widely used (as in India, for example). In the latter case, the estimates were very unreliable unless they referred to the actual prices of traded goods. Second, the stability of accounting ratios (that is, the ratios of accounting to market prices) also depended on the system of intervention. With unchanging tax or subsidy rates, most accounting ratios would be roughly constant. With direct controls, however, accounting ratios could be expected to fluctuate considerably, and any usable estimates would need to refer to an average situation. Third, in some countries (for example, Kenya) there was a relatively good supply of official statistics and also of empirical studies, made by economists on the spot, of such matters as the rural or urban labour market, rates of effective protection, the pattern of consumers' expenditure and farm or company accounts. Without this sort of information, the element of guesswork in the estimates became rather great. Fourth, in countries other than Chile, inflation was moderate when the studies were undertaken. Faster inflation since then has undoubtedly increased the difficulty of producing reliable up-to-date estimates. Finally, it is much easier to estimate accounting prices for a small island economy than for, say, India. Many more items are traded, transport and distribution margins are smaller, and the country's ability to influence world prices for its exports or imports is normally less. Most of these remarks apply, it should be emphasized,

---

[1] See Chapter 5.
[2] Scott, MacArthur and Newbery, 1976, Part I.

to *any* system of project appraisal which uses prices at all—even market prices.

Even though the time required to produce rough estimates (which are nevertheless better than nothing) is rather short, it would be much better if they were made by the governments of the countries concerned rather than by consultants for each project. Their overhead cost could then be spread over a large number of projects, they could be continuously improved and updated and they would carry more weight. Furthermore, the task should have a salutory effect on government policies concerned with a very wide range of economic affairs. Some of these are discussed below.

EMPLOYMENT, INCOME DISTRIBUTION, AND THE SHADOW WAGE

Attention has shifted increasingly towards the topics covered by the heading. The World Employment Programme sponsored by the I.L.O. has, amongst other things, led to a series of reports on policies to increase employment opportunities and improve the distribution of income in particular countries.[1] The World Bank is much concerned with fostering development which benefits the poor.[2] One way of giving effect to this desire is to design and implement projects with due regard to their effects on the incomes of the poor. To do this consistently and efficiently, one needs to use shadow prices, and in particular shadow wages, which allow for these effects.

The new version of the *Manual* gives much more explicit attention to income distribution than did the original one. Of the already published case-studies, those on shadow wages in Chile,[3] shadow wages and land settlement in Kenya,[4] small-holder tea in Kenya,[5] wells in India,[6] and palm-oil in Malaysia,[7] are especially relevant. They discuss the problems of estimating shadow wages and of valuing income benefits accruing to different groups and show, in most cases, that just how this is done can make a very big difference to the

---

[1] ILO, 1970, 1971, 1972, 1973, 1974.
[2] McNamara, 1972, 1973. See also Chenery *et al.*, 1974, Ch. II, where use is made of income weights which are similar to those described in Chapter 5 of this volume and in Little and Mirrlees, 1974, Chapter XIII.
[3] Seton, 1972.
[4] Scott, MacArthur and Newbery, 1976.
[5] Stern, 1972.
[6] Lal, 1972.
[7] Little and Tipping, 1972.

project's rate of return. This is in contrast to the earlier case-studies of industrial projects, where it seldom made much difference to their acceptability whether one took a shadow wage equal to the market wage or only half as great.[1] There is clearly an important difference between industrial and agricultural projects in this respect. The projects where potentially large beneficial effects on the incomes of the poor are most likely to be neglected if investment criteria are solely based on market prices lie in agriculture rather than in industry.

They may also lie in housing, road-building and harbours. Chapter 3, on low-cost housing in Kenya, shows, first, that the use of a proper social cost–benefit analysis, instead of a conventional financial analysis of the revenues and expenses of the Nairobi City Council, greatly increases the estimated net present value of the project. Second, the benefit is sensitive to the weights given to gains accruing to the parties involved: the City Council, the landlords and the tenants. Third, although housebuilding requires unskilled labour, it also requires, directly or indirectly, a great deal of skilled labour and foreign exchange. Hence any housing scheme must ensure that these complementary inputs are provided—it is not just a question of raising the effective demand for housing, one also needs to cut down other demands to set free the necessary complementary resources. Roads and sewers are more unskilled-labour-intensive than housing, but the same basic point applies.

Chapter 5, on shadow wages for Mauritius, illustrates one way of estimating income weights. These are important in determining the shadow wage, which in turn is an important determinant of the relative social profitability of different kinds of port improvement in Mauritius—for example, the choice between the old-fashioned labour-intensive method of loading sugar by lighters, and the modern labour-saving method of a bulk-sugar terminal. Some problems resulting from the use of shadow prices in redesigning the port are discussed in Chapter 8, of which more below. We merely make the point here that this is the type of project in which the level of shadow wages matters.

A further point illustrated by this case-study is the way in which macroeconomic factors impinge on the design of particular projects, and how a consistent system of shadow-pricing draws attention to this. After the study was undertaken, there was a tremendous increase

---

[1] Little, Scitovsky and Scott, 1970, p. 195.

in the price of sugar, Mauritius's chief export, and source of income and government revenue. At the same time, world inflation reduced the real rates of return available to the government on investment abroad. The government therefore found its revenue much increased, and one of the main outlets for its savings made much less attractive. Both factors should have raised the base level of income (this is the level which is so low that the government believes that subsidies paid to persons at that level are as socially valuable as other forms of government expenditure—see Chapter 5). This has implications for sickness benefits and other welfare payments; but also for the shadow wage, which should *fall*, thus encouraging, for example, greater expenditure on labour-intensive public works. The only offsetting consideration is the rise in the marginal product of labour on the sugar estates. It is unlikely, however, that a great deal of the unemployed in Mauritius could be absorbed there without driving down the marginal product to its former level.

THE RATE OF DISCOUNT

In most of the case-studies the rate of discount (or accounting rate of interest, ARI, in *Manual* terminology) where it is estimated at all[1] is only a little better than a crude guess. In the original Mauritius study, reference was made to rates of return on investment abroad, and, in the Kenya and Trinidad studies, both to this and to the cost of borrowing from abroad, and these set rather wide limits between which the ARI should lie. The Kenya study finally settled on a round figure of 10% per annum.[2] The study of wells in India estimated the ARI by reference to the ratio of profits to capital stock in Indian manufacturing, the ratio being calculated, in principle, at accounting prices.[3]

Chapters 6 and 7 give more careful attention to this problem. In Chapter 6 a minimum estimate of the ARI is derived from the social profitability of money in the hands of companies, together with governmental behaviour towards companies. If a benevolent government is behaving consistently in taxing companies, it cannot

---

[1] In the Malaysian palm-oil study, for example, the internal rate of return of the project was estimated without any explicit estimate of the ARI.
[2] Scott, MacArthur and Newbery, 1976, Chapter 2.
[3] Lal, 1972, Appendix II.

also believe that the social benefit arising from a gift of $1 from itself to a private company is greater than, or even equal to, $1. Now the higher the ARI, the lower the present social value, i.e. the social benefit, of the returns to this hand-out. So the ARI implied by consistent governmental behaviour must be high enough to reduce the social value of a gift of $1 to industry below $1. In other words, a consistent government must believe that the social cost (= 1 − social benefit) of such a gift is positive. For Kenya, the evidence given in Chapter 6 suggests that the above-mentioned figure of 10% per annum is on the low side—12^1/$_2$% or even 15% might be better.

However, as was argued in the Kenya study,[1] even an ARI as high as 10% per annum encounters the following difficulty. First, define base-level income (or consumption) as on p. 5. Then a consistent government should ensure that the social value of marginal benefits to persons at base-level income falls at the rate given by the ARI. The rate of fall of the social value of such marginal benefits may in turn be thought to depend on three things: the rate of increase of base-level income, g; the elasticity of the marginal social utility of income with respect to income, n; and the rate of pure time preference, p, as in the following equation:

$$ARI = g \, n + p.$$

If g is taken as the rate of increase of income of agricultural wage-earners, outside the big estates, it seems unlikely that it has been higher than about 2% per annum in recent years. This may not be the right way to measure g,[2] but there is little evidence that other, more relevant, classes of income have increased faster. Since n in the Kenya study was put at one, the implication is that the Kenya Government, if consistent, has a very high rate of pure time preference, perhaps of the order of 8% per annum, or even more if the ARI exceeds 10% per annum.

Of course, there are alternative explanations (e.g. *n might* be much higher than one, although this would indicate a greater concern for

---

[1] Scott, MacArthur and Newbery, 1976, Chapter 2.

[2] We really need to know the rate of increase of incomes which the Government would be prepared to subsidize at the margin, if subsidization had no other costs than the direct transfer of resources. Since, inevitably, there are other costs, and since the Kenya Government has not systematically subsidized poor people, the required information is not available.

equality than seems plausible), and the Government, never having viewed the matter in this way, may not appreciate the apparent inconsistency of its different policies. Were it to do so, it might increase subsidies to very poor persons, or it might reduce taxes on companies, and there are doubtless other possibilities. Here is another example of the way in which estimates of shadow prices can bring out implications for a variety of economic policies.

Chapter 7 illustrates a different method of attacking the problem of estimating the ARI, namely, by using a dynamic model of the whole economy (the Seychelles, in this case). The overall investment programme which would maximize the present value of utility for an assumed rate of pure time preference is first calculated. This yields rates of growth of the components of consumption, which together with the assumed utility function produce an estimate of n for each moment of time. Hence, the essential ingredients for estimates of the ARI (g, n, and p) are either assumed (p), or calculated from a macroeconomic model together with a utility function (g and n). Four different phases of growth are distinguished, each having a different formula for the ARI, which is finally intended for use in the evaluation of the composition and details of the investment programme. Clearly, with this kind of procedure, iteration is necessary if the final evaluations yield rates of return which are far from those assumed for the rate of return of the whole programme.

Despite the theoretical attraction of this method, there are very real practical difficulties, which are discussed in Chapter 7. It remains to be seen whether it can provide a workable solution, even for economies as small and relatively simple as the Seychelles.

PRIVATE INVESTMENT, INCLUDING INVESTMENT BY FOREIGNERS

Lal, 1975, and Chapter 6 are both concerned with the general problems of appraising private investment projects, the former with private foreign investment in Kenya and India, the latter with both foreign and domestic investment in Kenya. Little and Tipping, 1972, examined a quasi-private foreign investment in palm-oil in Malaysia. Chapter 2, on the Trinidad Hilton Hotel, concerns a public sector project, but with some foreign private finance and foreign management. Chapter 4, on logging and wood-processing industries in Ghana, is an analysis of the social efficiency of these industries, and domestic and foreign private firms are considered and compared. Other case-studies involve a mixture of private and public sector projects; for example, the small-holder tea in Stern, 1972, the private settlement farms in Scott, MacArthur and Newbery, 1976, the housing in Chapter 3, and the hotels in Chapter 7.

These studies exemplify a large number of different approaches, and it is clear that there is a great deal more work to be done in this field. It is, in many ways, at the centre of the development problem, since most investment in developing countries is private. It is also highly relevant to the controversies over the gains and losses to the recipient country from private foreign investment. While our studies are too few to justify firm generalizations, they nevertheless contain some highly interesting and suggestive results.

For example, investments in industries with low, zero or negative effective protection have been socially very profitable. This is often the case with export industries (palm-oil in Malaysia; logging, sawmilling and plywood in Ghana; the Trinidad Hilton Hotel; small-holder tea in Kenya), and occurs despite various factors which reduced efficiency and *private* profitability considerably (e.g. the emergency in Malaysia, some too small-scale firms and relatively weak management in Ghana, and a possible low occupancy ratio in the Trinidad Hilton).

The method of finance is often crucial. This point has long been neglected by economists, who have tended to regard only 'real' magnitudes as important, and finance as essentially a transfer with little economic significance. Bankers and businessmen, by contrast, have always been aware of its importance. It is clearly brought out in Chapter 6,[1] where it is estimated that the social rate of return on a typical Kenyan manufacturing investment (concerned, therefore, mainly with moderately protected import substitution), is about 35% per annum where a substantial proportion of the finance comes from private domestic capitalists' consumption, and as high as 120% per annum where it comes from abroad. By contrast, it is only equal to the ARI (12¹/₂%) if it is diverted from similar investments elsewhere. It is, unfortunately, not easy to ensure that private investment 'comes out of' capitalists' consumption, but at least the social desirability of increasing private savings is made clear.

---

[1] See also Little and Mirrlees, 1974, Chapter XI; and Scott, MacArthur and Newbery, 1976, Chapters 6 and 11.

Private foreign investment is more likely to be an *additional* source of investment, and the fact that it apparently yields a very high *social* return in Kenya, even with some albeit moderate protection, must provide food for thought. Much of the debate on this kind of investment has been conducted in terms of generalities and ingenious externalities, both beneficial and harmful.[1] David Newbery's estimate for Kenya neglects many of the alleged side-effects, but does it not quantify the most important effects, especially those on tax payments and employment? It is, of course, quite consistent with his estimate to argue that *particular* foreign investments can be and have been socially very costly. But this has been mainly because of the neglect of the tax and employment aspects. Had a proper evaluation been done, the government would have discovered that heavy subsidies were being paid for doubtful 'externalities'.

Chapter 3 brings out the importance of charges (or prices) as determinants of social profitability. The net present social value of the housing scheme considered depends heavily on the charges levied by the Nairobi City Council for the sites and services it provides. In effect, if the scheme can be used as a vehicle for raising more tax revenue (and assuming that this revenue will be wisely used!) its social value is much increased.

Chapter 4 analyses the social profitability of both foreign and domestic firms in the timber industries in Ghana. Since data for only one year were available, the measure used (social profit per unit of output) is, perforce, an approximation. Several interesting conclusions emerge. The furniture industry, producing mainly substitutes for imports, contains much the highest proportion of firms with negative social profits. Cheap loans and other incentives have been used to encourage small and capital-intensive firms in logging, where, unfortunately, economies of scale are important, so there have been adverse effects on social profitability. Capacity utilization, not surprisingly, is closely related to social profitability, but managerial experience apparently is not. A specially constructed index of managerial *efficiency* (not the same as experience) does, however, explain a significant part of the variation in social profitability between firms. Once allowance is made for other factors (e.g. size of firm in logging), differences in ownership are not significantly related to social profitability. Foreign firms remit profits abroad, unlike

---

[1] For a list, see Streeten and Lall, 1973.

Ghanaian firms, but also provide foreign exchange for the initial investment. Hence the policy of Ghanaianization need not, in principle, have been socially costly (nor, perhaps, especially beneficial); but the actual policies followed, which resulted in a large number of small, capital-intensive firms in logging, were undoubtedly so.

MANAGEMENT OF PUBLIC ENTERPRISES

Shadow pricing is usually considered in the context of investment appraisal, and the arguments for using it for this purpose have been frequently deployed.[1] Problems arise, however, when a public enterprise which has used them in designing and selecting its major investments comes to operate them. If shadow prices make any difference at all, they will lead to costs which are higher at actual prices (though lower at shadow prices) than they need have been, so customers will complain if charges are based on actual costs. Competitors, on the other hand, will complain of subsidization. The Ministry of Finance will also complain if it has to pay subsidies, although such complaints may, in fact, have little justification since shadow pricing should often *increase* governmental revenues compared with a short-sighted application of market criteria. These and similar problems are discussed in Chapter 8, where the illustrations are taken from the Mauritius Port development project for which the shadow prices in Chapter 5 were estimated. The problems are, however, very general, and relate to the continuing debate on price and output policies of public enterprises.

CONCLUSION

In searching for a title for this book, the one which first leapt to mind was 'Case Studies in Project Appraisal'. On reflection, however, this seemed too narrow. True, some of the chapters are well described by this. But some of them do not refer to particular projects at all, and all of them contain implications for a series of economic policies which transcend the selection and design of particular projects—important though that may be in its own right. Hence we chose a more ambitious, but, we believe, more accurate, title.

---

[1] Little and Mirrlees, 1974, Chapter II.

There are some who reject economic analysis, believing that it has little relevance to development. This book is not for them. There are also some economists who are impatient with the niceties of shadow pricing. Is it really worth all the labour involved? Would we not be better employed in advocating measures which will improve the actual price system, instead of building this dim and shadowy construction with its seemingly elaborate, even labyrinthine, structure of argument? We certainly believe in the importance of getting actual prices right. But we also believe that shadow pricing has a part to play, not only in designing and selecting projects in the period before that millenium is reached, but also in revealing the ways in which actual prices need to be changed. As evidence, we point to the chapters which follow.

List of Case Studies[1]

Authors	Country	Topic	Details of publication
D. L. Bevan and D. W. Soskice	Seychelles	Tourism	See Chapter 7.
A. Chakravarti	India	Workers' training	The Social Profitability of Training Unskilled Workers in the Public Sector in India, *Oxford Economic Papers, March 1972.*
A. Chakravarti	India	Industry and Training	*The Social Profitability of Selected Public Sector Projects in India—An Application of the Little–Mirrlees Method,* B.Phil. thesis, Oxford, 1972.
E. V. K. Fitzgerald	Central and South America	Public infrastructure	*Problems in the Application of the Manual to Infrastructure Investment in Latin America,* Cambridge (mimeo.), 1974.
A. M. Forbes	Trinidad	Hotel	See Chapter 2.
G. A. Hughes	Kenya	Housing	See Chapter 3.
V. R. and H. E. Joshi	India	Labour market	*Surplus Labour and the City: A Study of Bombay,* O.U.P. (India), 1975.
H. E. Joshi	Algeria	Petrochemicals	*The Use of the Little–Mirrlees Criterion for Project Evaluation in Developing Countries: an Algerian Case-Study.* B.Litt. thesis, Oxford, 1971.
A. R. Khan	Bangladesh	Planning model	*The Economy of Bangladesh,* London, 1972, Chapter 10.
A. R. Khan and J. A. Mirrlees	Bangladesh	Industrial sectors	*Optimal Prices for a Developing Economy,* typescript, Nuffield College, Oxford, 1972.
R. L. Kitchen	Zambia	Housing	*Social Cost–Benefit Analysis of Low-Cost Housing in Zambia,* University of Bradford (mimeo.), 1974.
D. Lal	India	Wells	*Wells and Welfare,* O.E.C.D., Paris, 1972.
D. Lal	India and Kenya	Foreign private investment	*Appraising Foreign Investment in Developing Countries,* London, 1975.
D. Lal and P. Duane	India	Large-scale irrigation	*A Reappraisal of the Purna Irrigation Project in Maharashtra, India* (mimeo.), Washington D.C., December 1972.

I. M. D. Little and D. G. Tipping	Western Malaysia	Oil palm	A Social Cost-Benefit Analysis of the Kulai Oil Palm Estate, O.E.C.D., Paris, 1972.
A. K. Nath	India	Marginal product of farm labour	'Estimating the seasonal marginal product of labour in agriculture', Oxford Economic Papers, November 1974.
D. M. G. Newbery	Kenya	Private investment	See Chapter 6.
J. M. Page	Ghana	Timber industries	See Chapter 4.
M. A. Parsonage	Zambia	Shadow wages	Employment, Wages and Shadow Wages in Zambia (mimeo.), 1974.
P. G. Sadler	Ethiopia	Coffee processing	A Social Cost-Benefit Analysis of a Proposed Regional Development Project for Washed Coffee Production in Ethiopia, University College of North Wales (mimeo.), 1974.
M. FG. Scott	Mauritius	Shadow prices	See Chapter 5.
M. FG. Scott, J. D. MacArthur and D. M. G. Newbery	Kenya	Shadow prices; Land settlement; Beef fattening	Project Appraisal in Practice: the Little-Mirrlees Method Applied in Kenya, London, 1976.
F. Seton	Chile	Shadow wages	Shadow Wages in the Chilean Economy, O.E.C.D., Paris, 1972.
L. A. Squire	Thailand	Roads	The Social Cost-Benefit Analysis of Road Projects in Developing Countries, Ph.D. thesis, Cambridge, 1974.
N. H. Stern	Kenya	Tea	An Appraisal of Tea Production on Small-Holdings in Kenya, O.E.C.D., Paris, 1972.
K. P. Teh	Western Malaysia	Investment incentives	The role of protection and fiscal incentives in the industrial development and employment of a small developing economy: W. Malaysia since independence in 1951, thesis to be submitted for a D.Phil. at Oxford.
D. G. Tipping	Sri Lanka	Irrigation and shadow prices	Project Evaluation in Ceylon, Nuffield College, Oxford (mimeo.), 1971.
D. G. Tipping	Tanzania	Shadow prices	Project Evaluation in Tanzania, Nuffield College, Oxford (mimeo.), 1971.

[1] The list includes studies partly or wholly financed by the grant to Nuffield College from the Leverhulme Trust, or those for which 'intellectual support' was given by members of the College.

OTHER REFERENCES

H. Chenery, M. S. Ahluwalia, C. L. G. Bell, J. H. Duloy and R. Jolly, *Redistribution with Growth*, World Bank and Institute of Development Studies, London, 1974.

International Labour Office,
Towards Full Employment, a Programme for Colombia, Geneva, 1970.
Matching Employment Opportunities and Expectations, a Programme of Action for Ceylon, Geneva, 1971.
Employment Incomes and Equality in Kenya, Geneva, 1972.
Employment and Income Policies for Iran, Geneva, 1973.
Sharing in Development in the Philippines, Geneva, 1974.

I. M. D. Little and J. A. Mirrlees, *Manual of Industrial Project Analysis in Developing Countries*, O.E.C.D. Development Centre, Paris, 1968.
Project Appraisal and Planning for Developing Countries, Heinemann, London, 1974.

I. M. D. Little, T. Scitovsky, and M. FG. Scott, *Industry and Trade in some Developing Countries*, O.E.C.D., O.U.P., London, 1970.

R. S. McNamara, *Address to the Board of Governors of the World Bank Group at Washington on September 25th 1972*, I.B.R.D., Washington, 1972.
Address to the Board of Governors of the World Bank Group at Nairobi on September 24th 1973, I.B.R.D., Washington, 1973.

P. P. Streeten and S. Lall, *The Flow of Financial Resources: Private Foreign Investment*, UNCTAD (mimeo.), TB/B/C.3/111 and TD/B/C.3 (VI)/Misc. 6 and 7, May 1973.

CHAPTER TWO

The Trinidad Hilton:
A Cost–Benefit Study of a Luxury Hotel
Anne M. Forbes

The original study on which this chapter is based was carried out in 1970.[1] As well as a detailed analysis of the Trinidad Hilton Hotel's costs and revenues, it contained an examination of various facets of management policy, such as employment structure, tariff levels, purchasing patterns and training. Here, however, the emphasis is on the cost–benefit methodology used and the difficulties that emerged which relate specifically to the appraisal of a tourist project. Section 1 discusses the application of the Little–Mirrlees method; Section 2 describes the results at market and shadow prices; and Section 3 attempts to evaluate the relevance of the method of appraisal to this type of project.

INTRODUCTION

Tourism in Trinidad is still in its infancy. Officially the Government is eager to develop the sector in order to diversify foreign exchange earnings which are at present heavily dependent on petrol and petrochemical products. With 15% of the labour force in 'open' unemployment it is also imperative that job opportunities should expand. Yet at the same time there is some reluctance to press ahead with tourist development when Trinidadians look at the social problems that expansion of the sector has brought to some of the more northerly Caribbean islands. The Government is trying to avoid these problems by being selective about the type of tourism that is encouraged and by stringent measures to preserve the rights of the

---

[1] This was submitted to Oxford University in 1972 as a B.Litt. Thesis, 'Trinidad Hilton Hotel: a cost–benefit study using the Little–Mirrlees method'. My thanks are due to the Overseas Development Administration who financed my visit to Trinidad and helped me in other ways; to my supervisor, Mr Maurice Scott, Nuffield College; and to Mr Frank Rampersad (Ministry of Finance), Mr Bernard Primus (Industrial Development Corporation) and Mr Braune (Hilton International Co.) in Trinidad.

local citizens. The Third Five-Year Plan[1] describes the guiding social principles behind official tourist policy as follows:

(1) the preservation of the dignity of the local people, whatever their colour;
(2) the banning of casinos, which experience has shown can lead to the influx of organized crime syndicates;
(3) the prevention of the alienation of a disproportionate amount of the country's land to foreigners.

The Trinidad Hilton, opened in June 1962, was the first international-standard hotel to be built on the island. It was thought necessary to have such a hotel because the advent of independence, the creation of the Federation of the West Indies and the growth of world travel were bringing increasing numbers of visitors to the capital, Port-of-Spain. These numbered just under 50,000 in 1962 but ten years later had reached 100,000.

The hotel is situated on a 25-acre hillside site outside the town (formerly the residence of the Governor-General of the island). Its design, mainly glass and grey stone, helps it to blend quite successfully into the woods and hills behind, and the interior furnishings create a certain Caribbean style. There are 261 guest rooms in the main building and 180 in the extension which was opened in 1971. Facilities include two swimming pools, three restaurants and a shopping arcade. Since its opening, it has been considered to be a successful venture in that room occupancy rates have risen each year. By 1970 they had reached an annual average of 81%, and more than half the visitors came from the United States.

The hotel is owned by the Industrial Development Corporation (I.D.C.) of the Government of Trinidad and is managed under contract by Hilton International Corporation. The initial construction and equipment costs of 13·2 million Trinidadian dollars[2] were covered by a government grant of $8·7 million and by a loan of $4·5 million from Barclays D.C.O. The extension costs of $5 million were also covered by a government grant. All the necessary materials, furnishings and equipment were imported tax-free.

---

[1] Government of Trinidad and Tobago, 1969.

[2] The ruling exchange rate was two Trinidadian dollars to one U.S. dollar. All succeeding references in this chapter to dollars are to Trinidadian dollars.

In 1959, prior to the construction of the hotel, an agreement was signed between the Industrial Development Corporation and Hilton International Co., whereby the latter would manage and operate the hotel in return for one-third of the gross operating profits, the remaining two-thirds to go to the I.D.C.[1] In order to carry out their contract, Hilton International Co. supply a General Manager and a Food/Beverage Manager who in return are responsible for the recruitment of other staff in order to maintain the accepted Hilton level of service. It is at their own discretion whether they employ local or foreign staff (subject to the availability of work permits). The hotel is run on a standardized system that has been developed by the company; most of the furnishings, operating equipment, china, glass, etc., are purchased through the central purchasing office in New York; some food is obtained locally and some flown in from the U.S.A. At the time of the writer's visit the hotel did not appear to be overstaffed but the management claimed that the plentiful supply of local labour had pushed the staff/room ratio above the level acceptable in hotels in the United States. Factors such as purchasing and employment policy are not discussed in this chapter but they are an important element in the final assessment of the impact on Trinidad of the presence of a luxury hotel.[2]

1. APPLICATION OF THE LITTLE–MIRRLEES METHOD IN TRINIDAD

The analysis of the hotel's costs and receipts was in five stages. To summarize:

(i)   An input–output matrix was constructed which described the composition of all direct and indirect inputs into the building and operation of the hotel.

(ii) Factors derived from this matrix were applied to the individual cost items of the hotel to convert them to values at shadow prices, the numéraire being foreign exchange in the hands of the government.

(iii) Labour was separated from other cost items, the shadow wage estimated and consumption revalued at world prices.

---

[1] See *Industrial Development Corporation, Annual Reports*. Government of Trinidad and Tobago.

[2] The author hopes to publish an article which considers in more detail the policy conclusions that emerge from this study.

(iv) Those benefits were identified which could be directly attributable to the hotel, as opposed to those which would have accrued to the economy even if the Hilton had not been constructed, and these net benefits were valued at shadow prices.

(v) Shadow costs were deducted from shadow benefits to give a cash flow which was subsequently discounted to show the net present value and internal rate of return.

1.1 *Matrix of direct and indirect inputs*

Fifty individual items were identified from the construction and operating costs of the hotel and set out in a matrix which showed their composition. There were 14 non-tradeable items and 36 tradeable items. The direct cost composition of each of these items in terms of five 'primary' inputs—scarce and unscarce labour, professional salaries, tradeables and non-costs (mainly or entirely taxes), all discussed more fully below—was determined. By inverting the matrix, the direct and indirect primary content of each of the 50 items was calculated. After working out the accounting ratio for each of the five primary inputs, it was then possible to work out the shadow prices for each of the 50 items.[1] Although this was a lengthy process, as it necessitated finding or estimating a breakdown of the components of each of the 50 items, once the matrix had been worked out it could be used to calculate the shadow prices of other projects in Trinidad and could be regularly updated.

1.2 *Application of matrix factors to the Trinidad Hilton cost items*

Total construction, equipment and furnishing costs of the main building of the hotel came to approximately $13·2 million. In order to convert this to shadow prices, the tradeable component and different labour components of each of the individual items (e.g. kitchen equipment, office expenses, landscaping, etc.) were worked out from the matrix described above. These are summarized in Table 2·1 where it can be seen that tradeables accounted for 58% of the construction costs and 51% of the operating costs in the latest year (1969) for which information was available when the study was carried out. Table 2·1 also shows that the management fee paid to

---

[1] See Scott, MacArthur and Newbery, 1976, Chapters 1 and 10, for a fuller explanation of the method.

Hilton International Co. was treated as entirely tradeable because almost all of it was repatriated. However, the exact ratio of shadow prices to market prices could not be determined until the accounting ratios for the first three primary inputs had been estimated (see below). The ratio for tradeables was one, and that for non-cost items (taxes) zero.

These percentage breakdowns for 1969 were applied to each year's operating costs so that a breakdown between tradeables, different labour categories and non-cost items was derived for the period 1962–1988. Ideally it would have been preferable to work out the breakdown for each year separately from the component items but this would have been a lengthy process and it is unlikely that the annual variations in the categories would have significantly affected the results.

1.3 *The shadow wage rate*

First of all, a brief explanation is needed about the division of the categories of labour into scarce, unscarce and professional. The more usual division is into 'skilled' and 'unskilled' when labour markets in developing countries are being examined, but in the case of Trinidad and Tobago this distinction does not reflect the real shortages and surpluses; the standard of general education is relatively high and a significant percentage of those seeking work could be said to be skilled. It is more helpful to divide the labour force into those who could find alternative employment if the need arose, i.e. 'scarce' labour, and those who could not. Of the wage-earning employees at the Hilton, only the chef and his assistants, certain maintenance men and some administrative staff come into this scarce category. With the exception of the salaried professionals, all other employees are considered to be 'unscarce'. The few professional staff are almost all foreigners engaged directly or indirectly on the Hilton project, either at the stage of construction or operation, e.g. the general manager, food/beverage manager, architect, designer, etc.

The social cost of these three categories of labour varies. Theoretically the cost of employing scarce labour is the alternative product that could have been produced elsewhere in the economy by those involved directly or indirectly in the construction and operation of the hotel. In the case of *unscarce* workers the alternative product foregone is zero as by definition they have no alternative product; they are drawn from the pool of unemployed labour in the urban areas

Table 2·1   Analysis of construction and operating costs of the main building into five primary factors ($thousand*)

	Total at market prices	Direct and indirect primary factor content				
		Unscarce labour	Scarce labour	Professional salaries	Tradeables	Non-costs (taxes, etc.)
I. CONSTRUCTION COSTS						
1. General costs	8,615	2,944	144	89	3,745	1,694
2. Furnishings	811	25	1	3	779	3
3. Equipment	1,062	18	3	—	1,032	8
4. Expenses incurred by Hilton and I.D.C.	634	32	54	50	435	63
5. Professional fees and expenses	1,092	—	—	—	1,092	—
6. Contingency and additional expense	981	231	—	—	648	102
TOTAL (I)	13,195	3,250	202	142	7,731	1,870
Shares of each category in total	100%	24·8%	1·6%	1·1%	58·0%	14·5%
II. OPERATING COSTS IN 1969						
7. Rooms	538	309	21	—	157	51
8. Food/beverage	1,784	679	75	—	750	280
9. General administration	364	196	73	15	63	17
10. Advertising	254	8	8	42	173	23
11. Heat, light, power	239	69	22	21	95	32
12. Repairs and maintenance	319	150	46	—	92	31
13. Other operating depts.	218	62	8	—	121	28
14. Management fee	768	—	—	—	768	—
15. Rates	50	15	4	—	23	8
16. Insurance	25	9	—	—	11	4
17. Additions and replacements	191	2	2	—	149	38
TOTAL (II)	4,750	1,499	259	78	2,402	512
Shares of each category in total	100%	31·6%	5·4%	1·6%	50·6%	10·7%

*Trinidadian dollars, as are the dollars referred to in all subsequent tables in this chapter.

around Port-of-Spain. The main cost to the economy in employing such a worker is the increase in his consumption because of his new wage. The shadow price of this consumption depends on the extent to which the Government views it mainly as a welfare benefit; this will be discussed later. With regard to *scarce labour*, a standard conversion factor of 0·8 was used in order to find the cost in foreign exchange, or the valuation at border prices of the alternative product. A rather higher conversion factor was used for *professionals* to allow for the fact that almost all were expatriates who probably repatriated a significant percentage of their earnings.

Shadow wage rate for unscarce labour
On the basis of the definition of unscarce labour just described, and using the *Manual*[1] formula for the calculation of the shadow wage rate:

$$SWR = C - \frac{1}{S}(C - M)$$

where C = consumption
M = alternative marginal product of labour
S = the ratio of the value of foreign exchange in the hands of the government to the value of workers' consumption.

M is taken as zero for the case of Trinidad. As registered unemployment is running at about 15% of the labour force, and is considerably higher in the 15–25 age group, it is unlikely that any loss of production is felt elsewhere in the economy when an additional job is created.

But although the social opportunity cost of labour may be zero, this does not mean that additional employment will not bring other costs to the economy in its wake. Just because a man is unemployed it does not mean that there is no welfare loss to him if he takes a job. He may have to work in unpleasant conditions, give up his leisure, sometimes move from the countryside to urban areas. In Trinidad the situation has arisen whereby those of the unemployed who have received a secondary education are selective about the type of job they accept. In the Third Plan[2] it is stated that the incidence of unemployment is highest amongst those who have attended Secondary School but have

---

[1] Little and Mirrlees, 1968; and Little and Mirrlees, 1974, Chapter 14.
[2] Government of Trinidad and Tobago, 1969.

not passed the G.C.E. Ordinary Level Examination, and lowest (3%) amongst those with absolutely no formal education. Somehow these social costs to the individual, the price of his effort, have to be introduced into the above Little–Mirrlees formula.

In addition, there is the consideration of how the Government views the extra consumption generated by the new project (in this case the hotel) and the importance that is attached to the potential use of these flows for its own purposes, including investment. The notation S expresses how many units of workers' consumption are, in the Government's view, equal to one unit of its own expenditure. To find the value of S is difficult in practice. Questions to Government officials yield few answers as the choices involved in this type of decision are rarely made explicit.

In this particular study S seems to have a value of unity; that is, an additional unit of workers' consumption is considered as beneficial to Trinidad as an additional unit of Government expenditure. There are two main reasons for thinking that at the margin the Government is indifferent between the two. The first reason relates to the discovery in 1970 of further oil reserves off the coast of Trinidad, and the second to the fact that the creation of employment is one of the three stated aims of the Third Plan (the other aims being diversification and increased self-reliance). With growing social unrest on the island it seemed at the time of this study in 1970 to be as important that consumption (i.e. jobs) be given to the present generation as it was to save and invest for future generations who, given the oil discovery, were likely to be well provided for anyway. The recent very significant rises in the price of oil have served to strengthen this argument.

If, however, the value of unity for S is accepted, and the alternative marginal product for unscarce labour is zero, then the solution of:

$$SWR = C - \frac{1}{S}(C-M)$$

gives a shadow wage rate of zero, i.e. the additional consumption generated by the project is considered to be costless to the economy. The difficulty in accepting that unscarce labour is really costless lies in the various costs incurred by the individual when he takes up a job, and in certain cases by the Government. Some of these have been mentioned already: the value of leisure, disagreeable work, etc. But there may also be further costs incurred by the authorities, e.g. new housing or more schools in the urban areas where the jobs are being created. Some part of these costs may be borne by the workers but the major contribution for social amenities is likely to come from the Government. Indeed in Trinidad in 1970 there were considerable demands for further Government housing in the capital, Port-of-Spain, as urban growth had created severe accommodation problems.

As it was difficult to put a value on these extra costs of employment, there was uncertainty about the true social cost of unscarce labour. For the purposes of this case-study four alternative valuations of the shadow wage rate were taken. It was decided to experiment with:

$$SWR = \text{consumption cost (market wage)}$$
$$SWR = \tfrac{1}{2} \text{ consumption cost}$$
$$SWR = \tfrac{1}{4} \text{ consumption cost}$$
$$SWR = \text{zero}$$

in order to see whether these variations had a significant effect on the net present values and internal rates of return of the hotel. In addition, this cost to the economy had to be revalued in terms of consumption at border prices, again with the help of the matrix described earlier. After revaluation, these four alternatives equalled 78%, 34%, 16% and 0% of the market wage respectively.

Finally, these four alternative sets of labour costs were added to the tradeable component of the capital and operating costs for each year, as well as the shadow costs of professional salaries and of scarce labour. These four cost streams were then subtracted from the benefit stream to give four alternative net cash flows at shadow prices.

1.4 *Shadow pricing of the benefits from the Trinidad Hilton Hotel*
The most difficult problem was that of assessing how many extra visitors came to the island *because of the hotel,* visitors who would not have come had the Hilton not been constructed. In addition one had to allow for the fact that the visitors who would have come to the island anyway may have had a different spending pattern because they were staying at the Hilton. Had they stayed at one of the other first-class hotels, the Queen's Park or the Normandie, they might have spent less and the costs to the island of accommodating them might have been less. Finally an estimate had to be made of the expenditure of the visitors outside the hotel.

(i)   Estimates of the number of visitors who would not have otherwise come to Trinidad

The assumption was made that a visitor who stayed at the Hilton would not have stayed at any alternative hotel in Trinidad except one of the two other first-class hotels open in 1970. This may seem a rather strong assumption, but it was probably almost correct for holiday visitors. Some businessmen might have been obliged to come to the island regardless of the level of accommodation available, but the Hilton management claimed that the availability of international-standard hotel accommodation was a factor in stimulating the interest of foreign businesses in the economy.

The method used consisted in assessing the number of room nights 'sold' at the Hilton in each year and deducting from them the number of guests who could have been accommodated in one of the other two hotels, taking the actual occupancy rates of the two hotels into account. An example will clarify.

In 1967 the Hilton average occupancy rate was 75%, i.e., 71,449 room nights were 'sold'. In the same year the Normandie had an occupancy rate of 64%, so that 36% of its room nights were not sold, and the Queen's Park had 40% of its room nights unsold. These total:

Normandie: (36% × 365 nights × 56 rooms)   7,358
Queen's Park: (40% × 365 nights × 100 rooms) 14,600
                                                          21,958 room nights
                                                                    available.

If these 21,958 available room nights are deducted from the 71,449 room nights sold at the Hilton, there remain 49,491 room nights sold at the Hilton whose occupants could not have been accommodated in any other first-class hotel on the island, i.e. 69% $\left(\frac{49,491}{71,449}\right)$ of total Hilton room nights sold in 1967. Similar calculations for other years yielded the percentage shown in Table 2·2 of room nights which could not have been sold if the Hilton or a similar hotel had not been constructed. These percentages represented the most conservative estimate of the benefits directly attributable to the Hilton presence. In reality a certain proportion of those who could have been accommodated in other first-class hotels would not have accepted to stay in them. This was particularly true of holiday visitors touring the Caribbean and staying at Hilton hotels at each stop. For them to have stayed at one of the other hotels, it is claimed, would have meant a

Table 2·2   Percentage of room nights sold attributable to the presence of the Hilton or a similar hotel

1963	1964	1965	1966	1967	1968	1969
38%	40%	53%	63%	69%	76%	74%

marked loss of comfort and amenities; a certain attractiveness is attributed to the Trinidad Hilton itself as a focus for at least this type of visitor. The Hilton's world-wide booking system enables these guests to be sure of a room in a particular city without difficulty and without having to find out the name of a reliable first-class hotel. At the other extreme, the least conservative estimate, it could be claimed that all visitors to the hotel only came because of its name and the type of accommodation it offers. This is unlikely to be correct, firstly because of the businessmen who account for 30% of all visitors to the hotel and of whom at least some must come to the island regardless of the accommodation available; and secondly because the Normandie and the Queen's Park suffered decreases in their occupancy rates when the Hilton opened. This seems to indicate that some of their guests moved to the new hotel, and therefore that some of the visitors at the new hotel were regular visitors to the island.

It was difficult to decide where between the extremes the most realistic estimate lay. Finally, for want of better information, it was decided to use the conservative calculation based on alternative available accommodation. Even under these modest assumptions the project proved to have a high internal rate of return and a positive net present value.

(ii)   Extra spending by 'necessary' visitors to Trinidad
Having decided what percentage of guests would not have come to the island if the Hilton had not been constructed, account had also to be taken of the extra spending incurred by those Hilton guests who would have come anyway but whose expenditure pattern was affected by the higher prices charged by the hotel. In 1970 Hilton charges for both rooms and food/beverage exceeded those of the other first-class hotels by about 50%. It was therefore assumed that those guests who would have come to the island whether there was a luxury hotel there or not were obliged to spend approximately 50% more when they stayed at the Hilton. In addition the accommodation at the hotel of

these guests who would have come anyway also meant an increase in the hotel's total costs because of the difference in expenditure patterns, as well as a decline in the costs and the receipts of the Queen's Park and the Normandie. These are all included in the discussion of the net benefit stream.

(iii)   Benefits from expenditure outside the hotel

In order to calculate the *net* benefits from spending outside the hotel, total spending per person per day in 1970, estimated at $24 (excluding hotel costs), was valued at shadow prices. The analysis in terms of five primary factors using the matrix was as shown in Table 2·3. The net social benefit to Trinidad from this daily spending was calculated as the difference between the spending at market price ($24) and the cost at shadow prices. This cost at shadow prices varied according to which of the four valuations of the shadow wage rate was used, so that the net benefit was either: $5, $7·7, $8·7 or $9·7. In the sequel, a best guess of $8 was taken. These net benefits were only attributable to those guests who would not have come to the island if the Hilton had not been built (e.g. 69% of total arrivals in 1967).

1.5   *Calculation of the net benefit stream at market prices and at shadow prices.*

(i)   At market prices. This private cost–benefit analysis was concerned with those items of the hotel's accounts which represented a direct financial cost or a direct financial gain to its statutory owners, the Industrial Development Corporation; that is, the private costs and benefits to the company rather than the social costs and benefits to the Trinidadian economy. The items included in the analysis were:

Costs	*Benefits*
Construction	
Operation	Revenue from: hotel departments
Additions and replacements	shop rentals
Hilton management fee	Loans from Barclays D.C.O.
Amortization and interest	
Repayments to Barclays D.C.O.	

and the net benefits for each year were reached by deducting total costs from total benefits. In addition to the calculation of the cash flow using the items listed above, three other cash flows were also worked out at market prices: first, the items above with the exclusion of the

Table 2·3 Analysis of outside expenditure (1970) in terms of five primary factors

Dollars

	Market value	Unscarce labour	Scarce labour	Professional salaries	Tradeables	Non-Costs (taxes, etc.)
1. Tours and transport	5	1·4	0·4	—	2·9	0·3
2. Shopping	5	0·1	—	—	4·8	—
3. Entertainment, of which: food $5 alcohol $5	10	3·8	0·4	—	4·2	1·6
4. Profit on all items*	4	0·7	0·1	—	1·7	1·5
Total	24	6·0	0·9		13·6	3·4
% of total		25%	4%		57%	14%

Theoretically this should be divided between depreciation, interest and monopoly profit (if any) going to the entrepreneur. However, as in this case it was a relatively unimportant item, the analysis for personal consumption, derived from the matrix, was used.

27

bank loans and the corresponding interest and amortization payments; this showed the rate of return on the hotel if it had been financed entirely from Government resources: second, all the items listed with the exception of the Hilton management fee; this was in order to show the possible rate of return if the Government ran the hotel itself (and makes the strong, and doubtful, assumption that an equal number of guests would have arrived and that costs would have remained at the same level): third, the items listed above with the exception of both the management fee and the financing in order to give a general idea of the potential rate of return on the operation of a luxury hotel such as this.

All four cash flows covered the period 1959 to 1988, using historical data up to 1969 and projected data from 1970 onwards. Three sets of projections were made. First, under the optimistic assumption that the predictions of the Third Plan would be realized, the projected increase in holiday visitors was 18% per annum and business visitors was 10%. This implied that the hotel reached full occupancy by 1976. However, the political disturbances in the Caribbean and the increasing attraction of Europe as a holiday destination for United States residents made it seem unlikely that the number of visitors to Trinidad and Tobago would expand as rapidly as the Plan predicted. A more reasonable rate of growth was 10% per annum for holiday visitors and 5% for businessmen staying at the Hilton, giving an average growth rate of 8% for all guests. These seemed the most likely projections, and if they were accurate then the hotel would reach full occupancy in 1979, three years later than under the optimistic projections. However, there was also the third alternative, namely that further disturbances and riots would cause a serious drop in tourism, and that Trinidad and Tobago would acquire the reputation of a destination to be avoided. Interestingly enough, even under these pessimistic assumptions and with an occupancy rate of only 37%, the hotel still had a positive net present value, as will be shown later. All projections went, in principle, to infinity, it being assumed that the conditions ruling in the year in which full occupancy was achieved would remain constant or, in the pessimistic alternative, that the 37% occupancy rate would be maintained. Given the 8% per annum discount rate, the precise assumptions made for later years were not crucial.

(ii)   At shadow prices.   The Little–Mirrlees method seeks to identify

the costs and benefits to the whole economy rather than those directly related to the owners of the hotel, the Industrial Development Corporation. In this particular case, three main adjustments were made to the cost/benefit streams, besides their conversion into shadow prices:

(a) Only the revenue and costs attributable to those guests who came to the island because of the presence of the Hilton hotel were included (these are subsequently referred to as 'Hilton-only' guests). In 1963, for example, these amounted to 38% of the total.

(b) Of the Hilton guests who would have visited the island irrespective of the luxury accommodation available, it was assumed that their spending at the Hilton was 50% higher than it would have been elsewhere (i.e. one-third of their spending was due to the Hilton presence), and that the costs incurred by this hotel were 33·3% higher than those of any other first-class hotel (i.e. 25% of the costs of this category of guest were attributable to Hilton). This meant that 21% of the Hilton's total revenue and 15% of its costs were in this category in 1963.

(c) The net social benefit resulting from spending outside the hotel by 'Hilton-only' guests was included in the cash flow.

When these three adjustments had been made to the cost/benefit streams at market prices under the three sets of assumptions about the future of Trinidadian tourism, the components were then converted into shadow prices using the methodology just described; total annual costs at shadow prices were deducted from total benefits and the net benefits discounted to give the net present values and the internal rates of return (see Table 2·5 for an example of the calculations in 1963). To summarize:

The *Benefit* Stream comprised:
1. a percentage attributable to 'Hilton-only' guests of the annual revenue from the hotel departments and shop rentals;
2. 33·3% of the revenue from other guests;
3. outside spending (net) of 'Hilton-only' guests, based on the 'best guess' of $8 per person per day in 1970;
4. Barclays Bank loans.

The *Cost* stream comprised:
1. total construction costs;
2. total financing costs;
3. percentage of the operating costs attributable to 'Hilton-only' guests;
4. extra costs incurred in accommodating those who would have come to the island anyway.

All the cost streams have four alternate valuations to correspond to the four values of the shadow wage rate.

Net Benefits comprised: four annual cost streams deducted from the one annual revenue stream which in turn had three sets of projections. Thus there were twelve sets of results (see Table 2·4) which are discussed below.

Unlike the cash flows at market prices, all those at shadow prices in Table 2·4 included the costs of financing and the management fees. For one additional set of calculations not in Table 2·4 (in which the 'most likely' assumptions about future trends were used and the shadow wage rate was valued at half the market rate) these two items were excluded; the results of this exercise are discussed in the next section.

2. THE RESULTS: INTERNAL RATES OF RETURN AND NET PRESENT VALUES AT MARKET PRICES AND SHADOW PRICES

The rationale underlying the Little–Mirrlees method springs from a concern that market prices when used to evaluate projects might fail to reveal social benefits and costs because of distortions in the price mechanism. An examination of the net present values of the Trinidad Hilton cash flows when discounted at 8%, as in Table 2·4, revealed very marked differences in social profit according to whether market prices or shadow prices were used. In all cases there was a positive net present value but when shadow prices were used this was two or three times as high as that calculated at market prices, the exact amount depending on the shadow wage rate used. A discount rate of 8% was chosen which at the time the study was being carried out (1970) was higher than the rate the Government could have earned abroad if it had invested in, for example, U.S. Federal Funds, which were then paying 7·17%. As inflation was running at about 3% per annum, this

Table 2.4 Internal Rates of Return and Net Present Values

	Internal rates of return	Net present value (discounted at 8%) $ mill
Optimistic Assumptions		
1. Market prices (including fee and finance)	15·1	23·6
2. Market prices (less finance)	13·4	22·5
3. Market prices (less fee to Hilton)	18·1	40·2
4. Market prices (less fee and finance)	16·0	39·1
5. Shadow prices: zero shadow wage rate (including fee and finance)	··	69·1
6. Shadow prices: 16% shadow wage rate	··	65·8
7. Shadow prices: 34% shadow wage rate	··	60·9
8. Shadow prices: 78% shadow wage rate	··	52·7
Most Likely Assumptions		
9. Market prices (including fee and finance)	13·5	15·7
10. Market prices (less finance)	12·0	14·6
11. Market prices (less fee to Hilton)	16·9	28·6
12. Market prices (less fee and finance)	14·6	27·4
13. Shadow prices: zero shadow wage rate (including fee and finance)	··	54·4
14. Shadow prices: 16% shadow wage rate	··	51·0
15. Shadow prices: 34% shadow wage rate	··	45·8
16. Shadow prices: 78% shadow wage rate	··	38·6
Pessimistic Assumptions		
17. Market prices (including fee and finance)	9·7	4·2
18. Market prices (less finance)	9·0	3·1
19. Market prices (less fee)	12·0	12·4
20. Market prices (less fee and finance)	11·2	10·7
21. Shadow prices: zero shadow wage rate (including fee and finance)	··	29·8
22. Shadow prices: 16% shadow wage rate	··	27·7
23. Shadow prices: 34% shadow wage rate	··	25·3
24. Shadow prices: 78% shadow wage rate	··	19·6

meant a return in constant prices of about 4% p.a. On the other hand, the real *marginal* cost of borrowing from abroad for the Trinidad Government was probably more than 8% p.a. While Trinidad has been a borrower from overseas in the past, the oil discoveries may result in its becoming a net lender. If so, the discount rate used in this study may prove to have been too high, and the net present value of the investment in the hotel may have been understated for this reason.

Using this discount rate, the results at market prices showed that the hotel was a satisfactory investment for the Industrial Development Corporation. The internal rates of return ranged from 13% to 18% under optimistic assumptions, and 12%–17% under 'most likely' assumptions, to 9%–12% under pessimistic assumptions. If the financing arrangements were excluded from the D.C.F., the returns dropped slightly, and they increased when the management fee was left out.

When the results using shadow prices were analysed it became evident that the hotel was much more profitable 'socially' than had previously been thought. Under all three sets of assumptions the net social profit was more than double the present value at market prices, and the lower the shadow wage rate the higher the social profit. When the shadow wage rate equalled zero the social profit was more than three times as great as the private profit to the Industrial Development Corporation.

The question then arose of identifying those sections of the Trinidadian community who were benefiting from this large social profit. Conversion from market prices to shadow prices of the 1963 data (see Table 2·5), together with certain other adjustments, transformed a financial loss into a social profit and one wanted to know to whom this had accrued.

Obvious beneficiaries were those employed in unscarce labouring jobs directly and indirectly associated with the hotel and who were being paid a market wage whilst the social valuation of their labour, according to the 'best guess', was only 34% of what they were earning. The Government benefited as tradeables did not cost the economy as much as their market prices would indicate, i.e. the non-cost items represented the extra tax revenue accruing on expenditure. The presence of the hotel seems to have ensured that more visitors came to the island and encouraged those who would have come irrespective of Hilton to spend more than they would have done otherwise.

Table 2.3 Conversion from market to shadow prices of 1963 costs

$ thousand

	Market prices	Conversion factors	Shadow prices
1. Operating costs:	2,290		
of which:			
tradeables		942×1	942
scarce labour		149×0·8	119
professional		46×0·9	41
unscarce labour		858×0·34	292
non-cost items		295×0	0
2. Amortization and interest	514	514×1	514
3. Management fee	257	257×1	257
4. Construction costs	373		
of which:			
tradeables		218×1	218
scarce labour		5×0·8	4
professional		5×0·9	5
unscarce labour		92×0·34	31
non-cost items		54×0	0
Total costs	3,434	Total above	2,423
		of which 53% attributable to Hilton presence[1]	1,284
Total revenue	3,196	'Hilton-only' guests	1,214
		Other guests	661
		Outside spending	155
			2,030
Net cash flow	−238 at market prices		+746 at shadow prices

[1]53% is composed of the 38% of total costs accounted for in 1963 by 'Hilton-only' guests and the 15% of extra spending by guests who would have come to the island anyway (see p.29).

33

On the other hand there were some offsetting economic costs, especially in the early years. Other first-class hotels on the island suffered a loss of revenue as guests whom they could have accommodated stayed instead at the Hilton. The operating costs of these hotels were reduced but so were their revenues. There was a consequent loss not only to their owners but also to the Government as taxable income declined.

There were also other effects on Trinidad which related to the establishment of an international hotel and which have not been described in this methodological survey. In particular the hotel's purchasing policy was found to rely very heavily on imported goods; its staff/room ratio was lower than might have been expected in view of the surplus labour available; and there was a divergence in pricing policy according to whether shadow or market costs were being considered and which revealed a potential source of conflict between the company and the owners. The effect of all these policies, particularly those relating to purchasing and employment, are important and have to be taken into account, as well as the net social benefit, when an assessment is being made of the potential contribution to development in Trinidad of this type of luxury hotel.

3. CONCLUSIONS: USE OF THE LITTLE–MIRRLEES METHOD IN EVALUATING THE TRINIDAD HILTON

Before discussing the special features and difficulties of the methodology as revealed by this examination of a tourist project, it is useful to comment on the suitability or otherwise of the Trinidad economy for an exercise of this type. Much of the discussion about the use of the Little–Mirrlees method[1] has centred not only on the theoretical framework of the analysis but also on the question of whether the structure of the economy in many developing countries is such that the method can be applied without too many modifications and complex calculations. This study was fortunate in that Trinidad has an open, well-integrated economy which is documented by fairly reliable statistical information so that the basic assumptions underlying the straightforward application of the method approximate quite closely to reality, and the divergences between private and social values that the authors believe exist in most

[1] See *B.O.U.I.E.S.*, February 1972.

developing countries are indeed to be found. The three most usual divergences are that:

(a)   prices of goods may be out of line with their social value, either because of distortions in factor markets and/or because of Government interference with the market mechanisms (taxes, subsidies, controls on foreign trade);

(b)   wage rates in the 'modern' sector may overstate the opportunity cost of labour which is usually drawn from the agricultural sector;

(c)   aggregate savings and investment in the economy may be less than the level that is socially desirable.

The recommendations that Little and Mirrlees make about how these divergences can be estimated and allowed for in an analysis are at the core of their method of evaluation. In this particular study they were tackled as follows:

3.1   *Valuation of goods*
In Trinidad divergences between the private and the social cost of goods is quite marked. Import tariffs are levied on almost all categories (manufactured goods 25%, food 20%, motor vehicles and parts 30%), and imported goods equalled 55%-60% of gross domestic product at market prices between 1965 and 1968, thus causing a significant distortion in the pricing of direct and indirect inputs into the operation of the hotel and of indirect inputs for construction; direct inputs for construction and equipment were allowed duty-free entry. On the annual operating costs of the hotel the residual item (i.e. direct and indirect taxes) represented 12.8% of total operating costs, so the extent of the distortion in the pricing of goods was not inconsiderable.

Less easy than the valuation at 'border' prices of tradeable inputs was the decomposition of non-tradeable goods. Fortunately a detailed breakdown on construction was available, but for other items such as transport and electricity extremely tentative estimates had to be made. However, the share of the latter in total costs was relatively minor so their impact on the accounting prices was not very marked.

3.2   *Shadow wage rates*
These were much more difficult to evaluate than the physical inputs

described above. Although it was apparent that the true shadow wage rate was considerably lower than the market rate, its exact value was hard to assess and the range of NPVs shows that the project is fairly sensitive to the shadow wage rate used.

The argument in favour of some revaluation of the wage rate at accounting prices was based on the high percentage of the labour force out of work and seeking employment, on the fact that most of the unemployed lived in Port-of-Spain, where in general they contributed little or nothing to national income, and on the seeming incompatibility between this large number of job-seekers and the high wages earned by those in employment, especially those in the oil industry who were highly unionized and earning almost 60% more than the national average wage. These high wages, when costed at market prices in the evaluation of a project, gave a distorted picture of the cost to the economy of using labour. The real cost of employing one more man is the value of his alternative production foregone plus his extra consumption resulting from his higher wages, minus the value of the latter in terms of the numéraire. These three aspects Little and Mirrlees link together in their formula for the shadow wage as described earlier, and not surprisingly the results of revaluing the Hilton labour and inputs at shadow prices were reflected in the much higher social profits. The actual value of the shadow wage rate, depending as it does on the size of S (i.e. the ratio of the value of the numéraire, which is foreign exchange in the hands of the Government, to the value of consumption), was difficult to determine since the value of S depended on a complex of political and economic factors. In practice four alternative values were taken which, when revalued to account for consumption at border prices, gave a shadow wage equal to 78%, 34%, 16% and 0% of the market wage.

3.3 *Optimality of Government savings*

In Trinidad it is less apparent than in many other developing countries that the level of savings is sub-optimal, so S could well be one although the estimates also allow it to be greater than one. What this means is that, given the increase in Government resources due to the new petroleum discoveries and taking account of the climate of political discontent that emanates in part from the high rate of unemployment, the Government should be indifferent between an additional unit of its own expenditure, including amounts saved and invested, and an additional unit of workers' consumption.[1] This situation may be rare (although Little and Tipping, 1972, came to a similar conclusion in Malaysia) but it reflects in part Trinidad's place as one of the wealthier countries in the Caribbean.

One common problem occurred in the estimates of all three sets of divergences, namely what assumptions could one make about future Government policy? In the original *Manual*, the authors appear to assume that the evaluator can himself influence policy to some degree (although his exact role and that of the Central Office of Project Evaluation are left very unclear). In the 'Reply to Criticisms' by Little and Mirrlees[2] they clarify and modify this position a little by saying that 'if there is reason to expect the government to make mistakes in a systematic way (for example by favouring certain kinds of domestic production, although the benefiting groups could be more cheaply provided for in other ways), the application of the basic criteria must be modified'.

In Trinidad the objectives of the Government are stated as being diversification, increased employment and self-reliance. These objectives are not very precise, and are not weighted so as to form a single valued function. It would therefore be difficult to know whether a certain policy—e.g. making at home all those items on the list of prohibited imports—was a mistake or not in the light of these accepted objectives, and if a mistake, whether the Government would effectively recognize this. In fact almost all inputs in the present case were directly traded, and the non-traded items, such as construction and transport, were very clearly defined. It was assumed that the freely traded items would not in the relevant future become restricted, so the problem of the treatment of non-traded but tradeable items was deemed not to arise. However, it would be likely to arise with other projects in Trinidad if the Government continued to place emphasis on self-reliance and to define the type of external dependence that they wish to avoid as 'a marked orientation of the production structure towards exports, with concomitant dependence on imports for many goods and services which could be produced locally'.[3] As

---

[1] In principle, S could even be less than one if, for example, direct subsidies to the unemployed were thought to be less good than paying them for work of very low value because, say, the former destroyed the will to work.

[2] *B.O.U.I.E.S.*, February 1972.

[3] Government of Trinidad and Tobago, 1969.

always, however, the analyst can pass the buck by using sensitivity analysis and valuing the doubtful items as both traded and non-traded.

3.4 *Other problems in the evaluation of a tourist project*

Definitely the most difficult other problem which arose was that of estimating how many guests came to Trinidad who would not have visited the island if the Hilton hotel had not been built. Of course this problem would have arisen whatever method of cost–benefit analysis were being used, but its answer is crucial to the whole study. If the guests staying at the Hilton are people who have merely transferred from another hotel on the island then their net benefit to the economy of Trinidad is relatively unimportant. One might have attempted to answer the question by carrying out a sample survey of Hilton guests over a fairly representative period, asking them their exact reasons for visiting the island and that particular hotel. However, the replies obtained would have been unreliable, and in any case this approach was not feasible as part of this case-study. Consequently the (unsatisfactory) assumption was made that only those guests who could not have found first-class accommodation elsewhere on the island would be counted as 'Hilton-only' guests. This estimate undoubtedly understates the number of guests who came as a result of either Hilton advertising, Hilton renown or the efficiency of the company's booking service, but it was thought better to work out the social profit on the basis of moderate benefits which were lower than reality rather than to be open to a charge of exaggeration. Our conclusion that the hotel was socially profitable holds *a fortiori*.

A second problem was related to the valuation of the externalities which result from the Hilton presence on the island. Amongst these can be included the training in the hotel trade that is given to the staff who work for the company, the 'demonstration effect' of a luxury hotel on local consumption, and the effect on local production of an increased demand for tourist souvenirs, local food, beverages and equipment. These may be of considerable significance, and the problem for the evaluator is either to fit them into his quantifiable scheme or at least to describe their effects in general terms. Because there was no empirical evidence available on the impact of these externalities in Trinidad one had to be content with describing their possible value and impact on the economy. In the future, though, when Harewood[1] has finished his socio-economic study of Tobago, in which he is tracing the impact of the expansion of tourism on the lives, attitudes and consumption patterns of the inhabitants by means of a continuous survey, it may be possible to give a more accurate assessment of the importance of these externalities.

Unlike certain industrial projects, the valuation of benefits (revenues) to the hotel from the spending of foreign visitors holds no special difficulty, except that associated with identifying 'Hilton-only' guests and allowing for the extra spending of those guests who would have come to the island anyway. As the numéraire in the Little–Mirrlees method is 'foreign exchange in the hands of the government' there is no problem of conversion as this accurately described receipts from spending by non-Trinidadian visitors in a Government hotel. The only potential problem arises with the valuation of spending by domestic tourists. In this case expenditure at the hotel by Trinidadians was valued in the same way as receipts from foreign tourists. No information is available on its exact amount but it was not thought to represent more than 20% of total revenue and the resulting overstatement of total receipts at shadow prices was probably only a couple of per cent, and was offset by the conservative assumptions we made elsewhere. But one can envisage hotels where domestic spending is a significant proportion of total revenue and some attention would have to be given to the problem of how best to value this in terms of the numéraire. One might, for example, multiply these receipts by the consumption conversion factor, on the assumption that extra spending by Trinidadians at the hotel reduced their average consumption elsewhere by the same amount, so that it was the foreign exchange value of this that was saved.

The final question one has to ask when examining the application of the Little–Mirrlees method to a tourist project is: does the use of the method bring to light aspects or ramifications of the project that would not appear otherwise?

The construction of the 50×50 matrix giving the direct and indirect inputs into the most important items facilitated the analysis of tourist spending, pricing policy and job creation, as well as the direct inputs into the hotel. With the aid of the matrix it was possible to evaluate the net social profit on outside spending by applying the conversion

[1] Mr Jack Harewood, Head of the Central Statistical Office, Port-of-Spain, Trinidad, is conducting a five-year socio-economic study into the effect of tourism on the pattern of life on Tobago. The study began in 1970.

factors to the cost items; similarly the marginal social cost per room night 'sold' and marginal social revenue received could be identified and an alternative optimization level to that suggested by market prices decided upon. When the labour costs of any item such as outside spending have been valued the approximate number of jobs (direct and indirect) created can be calculated by dividing the total by the average wage rate. These and other aspects can be elucidated once the matrix has been prepared but this preparation can be quite lengthy. In his account of his experience using the Little–Mirrlees method, Stern[1] points out that his use of Scott's calculation for another project reduced his work considerably, and experience on the Trinidad study strengthens the view this this method would be better used by a National Office of Project Evaluation and the results made available to the individual consultant as necessary.

Ultimately, of course, the Little–Mirrlees method is designed to assist project choice and not just to examine *ex post* an existing enterprise, as happened in this case. When several comparable projects are being investigated—for example, a range of different hotels—then the method can be used more speedily as one set of shadow prices will apply to all hotels and wide-ranging comparison can be made. This in fact is what ought to be carried out in Trinidad and Tobago as a sequel to this study; now that a luxury hotel has been examined in detail a similar examination should be carried out on different categories of hotel to see which type contributes most to the economic development of the islands.

BIBLIOGRAPHY AND LIST OF REFERENCES

Artus, J., *The Effect of Revaluation on the Foreign Travel Balance of Germany,* I.M.F. Staff Papers, November 1970.

Bryden, J., *Tourism and Development,* Cambridge University Press, 1973.

Bryden, J. and Faber, M., *Multiplying the Tourist Multiplier,* Social and Economic Studies (West Indies), March 1971.

Bulletin of the Oxford University Institute of Economics and Statistics (B.O.U.I.E.S.) 'Symposium on the Little–Mirrlees method of project analysis', February 1972.

Commonwealth Secretariat, *Organisation of the Tourist Industry in Commonwealth Countries as at December 1969,* London, July 1970.

---

[1] *B.O.U.I.E.S.,* February 1972.

Cumper, G., *Personal Consumption in the West Indies,* Social and Economic Studies (West Indies), 1958, No. 2.
Tourist Expenditure in Jamaica in 1958, Social and Economic Studies (West Indies), 1959, No. 3.

Demas, W. G., *The Economics of Development in Small Countries with Special Reference to the Caribbean,* McGill University Press, 1965.

Diamond, P., *On the Economics of Tourism,* Institute for Development Studies, University of Nairobi, January 1969.

Economist Intelligence Unit, *International Tourism,* Quarterly Economic Review, Special No. 7, 1970.

Gerakis, A., *Effects of Exchange-Rate Devaluations and Revaluations on Receipts from Tourism,* I.M.F. Staff Papers, November 1965.

Government of Trinidad and Tobago, Central Statistical Office:
Third Five-Year Plan 1969-1973, 1969.
Annual Abstract of Statistics.
Balance of Payments Reports (various issues).
Industrial Development Corporation, Annual Reports.
Labour Force Sample Survey (LF 2-3).
Continuous Sample Survey of Population.

Henry, J., *A Report on International Tourism in Trinidad and Tobago,* sponsored by Peat, Marwick, Mitchell & Co., Trinidad, April 1970.

International Union of Official Travel Organisations (I.U.O.T.O.), *International Travel Statistics,* Geneva, annual.

Little, I. M. D. and Mirrlees, J. A., *Manual of Industrial Project Analysis in Developing Countries, Vol. II,* O.E.C.D. Development Centre, Paris, 1968.
Shadow Pricing as a Method of Project Selection, Nuffield College, Oxford (mimeo.), 1970.
Project Appraisal and Planning for Developing Countries, Heinemann, 1974.

Little, I. M. D. and Tipping, D., *A Social Cost–Benefit Analysis of the Kulai Oil Palm Estate, W. Malaysia,* O.E.C.D. Development Centre, Paris, 1972.

Matthews and Andic (eds.), *Politics and Economics in the Caribbean,* Institute of Caribbean Studies, University of Puerto Rico, 1971.

Mitchell, F., *Costs and Benefits of Tourism in Kenya,* Report prepared for the Kenya Tourist Development Corporation, November 1968.

O.E.C.D., *International Tourism and Tourism Policy in O.E.C.D. Member Countries,* annual.

Peters, M., *International Tourism,* Hutchinson, 1969.

Ross, D. F., *The Costs and Benefits of Puerto Rico's Programme,* Social and Economic Studies (West Indies), 1957, No. 3.

Scott, M. FG., *The Estimation of Accounting Prices for some Non-Tradeable and Tradeable Goods in Kenya,* Nuffield College, Oxford (mimeo.), March 1970.

Scott, M. FG., MacArthur, J. D. and Newbery, D. M. G., *Project Appraisal in Practice: the Little–Mirrlees Method Applied in Kenya,* Heinemann, 1976.

Seers, D., *A Step Towards Political Economy of Development, Illustrated by the Case of Trinidad and Tobago,* Social and Economic Studies (West Indies), September 1969.

Using Shadow Prices

Seton, F., *Shadow Wages in the Chilean Economy,* O.E.C.D. Development Centre, Paris, 1972.

Stern, N. H., *An Appraisal of Small-Holder Tea in Kenya,* O.E.C.D. Development Centre, Paris, 1972.

Tripartite Economic Survey of the Eastern Caribbean, Governments of Canada, United Kingdom and United States, London, 1966.

U.N.I.D.O., *Guidelines for Project Evaluation,* New York, 1972.

Williams, E., *From Columbus to Castro: A History of the Caribbean,* André Deutsch, 1970.

Zinder, H. & Associates, *The Future of Tourism in the Eastern Caribbean,* Washington, 1969.

CHAPTER THREE

Low-Income Housing: A Kenyan Case Study[1]

Gordon Hughes

1. INTRODUCTION

This paper discusses the application of the Little–Mirrlees method of social cost–benefit analysis to low-income housing projects. It focuses on low-income housing in Nairobi, Kenya, but the fundamental approach and many of the conclusions will be equally valid for urban low-income housing in other less developed countries—especially in Africa and Latin America.

Section 2 outlines the procedure followed in estimating the accounting ratios used to convert the money project costs to social costs. One particular building material—cement—has a rather low accounting ratio in Kenya due to the special features of the cement industry; this seems to be of wider relevance, so it has been discussed specifically. The method of cost analysis provides figures of the total demand—direct and indirect—for various primary factors induced by expenditure on the various house types and social infrastructure. These primary factors include foreign exchange, and skilled and unskilled labour, so that it is possible to examine the full effects as regards employment and trade of many items of public and private investment.

In Section 3 the problems of estimating the benefits of housing are considered. In view of the alternative assumptions which might be made about the operation of the housing market and the effects of a housing project two methods of estimation are suggested. These set upper and lower limits to the value of social benefits with the actual outcome falling between them, closer to one or the other depending upon which set of assumptions more accurately represents the behaviour of the market.

[1] I am grateful to Maurice Scott, Ian Little, David Newbery and John MacArthur for their comments, and to Brian Waters and members of the Nairobi Urban Study Group for their assistance in collecting the data on which this study is based.

Finally, in Section 4 the material discussed in the preceding sections is used to evaluate the specific project in Nairobi. This is the Dandora Community Development Project Site and Service Scheme (called the Dandora Project) which was prepared during 1973 for submission for a World Bank loan by the Nairobi City Council. The Dandora project is evaluated using both methods of social benefit estimation. The project itself is quite profitable in social terms, but could be improved by levying higher charges on those allotted the scheme's plots than those specified in the proposal. The analysis shows that the transfer benefits of income redistribution brought about by an increase in the supply of housing form a significant proportion of the project's gross benefits. Further, the response of the net present value of the project to changes in various assumptions and parameter values is discussed, and also the variance of the results due to uncertainty concerning some of the estimates on which the evaluation is based.

As a background to the discussion a brief outline of the Nairobi housing situation will be useful. The city has been growing rapidly since independence in 1964, and especially post-1968. The overall rate of population growth is now thought to be between 6% and 8%, of which about 3% is natural growth and the rest is migration—mostly from rural areas. In principle it was government policy to provide sufficient housing of all kinds to cater for this growth in a controlled manner through the Nairobi City Council, the government housing agency, and private building. In practice the amount of housing officially built, though quite large relative to the past record, was totally inadequate in relation to the city's growth. Furthermore almost all of it was built to standards of housing provision and cost substantially above what could be afforded by most of the population. Thus a large private housing market developed in which entrepreneurs built and let rooms (the room is the basic housing unit), while owner-occupiers and council tenants sublet part of their houses, so that most of the population live in privately let accommodation. Much of the new building constituted uncontrolled development because building regulations were not followed and land was often occupied by squatting. Recently the City Council has accepted that it does not have the resources to implement its previous policies, and has been considering site and service schemes for providing low cost housing. In these the Council does not build housing, but instead prepares plots and provides basic service units—with water and toilets—before letting the plots to individuals who are required to build on them within a certain time period.

The material upon which this paper is based was collected in March–April 1973, and except for the Dandora project all figures are given in terms of 1972 prices. The work reported here represents only a part of a much fuller analysis of housing markets and policy in Kenya and other developing countries. Complete details of the empirical and analytical work underpinning the present discussion may be found in the full study.[1]

2. THE SOCIAL COST OF HOUSING

2.1 *General approach*

The analysis of the social cost of investment in housing and related expenditures presents no fundamental problems in the application of the Little–Mirrlees method. It does, however, provide useful information on the wider impact of construction activity in the economy and on a number of specific issues which are of particular importance in the housing sector. The general approach to the derivation of accounting prices adopted in the study was to construct a pair of input matrices A, B giving unit input requirements of goods and primary factors for each of the outputs. The $i, j th$ element of A, a_{ij}, gives the value of good i required as a direct input to produce £1 of good j, while b_{hj} is the value of factor h required as a direct input to produce £1 of good j. Let us denote the primary factor accounting ratios by v_h ($h = 1, \ldots, m$) and the goods accounting ratios by w_j ($j = 1, \ldots, n$). Then we have:

$$w = Aw + Bv,$$

where $v = (v1, \ldots, v_m)$ and $w = (w1, \ldots, w_n)$.

Rearranging this equation gives:

$$w = [I-A]^{-1}Bv$$

$$\text{or} \quad w = Rv$$

$$\text{in which } R = [I-A]^{-1}B.$$

R is the matrix of total direct and indirect primary factor input requirements.

---

[1] Hughes, 1975.

Specifying the problem in this way enables us to relate the accounting price of goods or the whole project directly to the accounting prices of primary factors. This is useful because it enables us to assess the sensitivity of crucial accounting ratios to changes in the assumptions concerning primary factor accounting ratios. In addition the input–output formulation makes it possible to predict the demand for various factors—e.g. unskilled labour, foreign exchange—generated by expenditure on housing or on various other types of construction. The cost of this extra information is the rather laborious work involved in preparing the data needed to build up the two input matrices. In many cases this might not be worthwhile, but as housing represents such an important aspect of gross investment and government expenditure in most economies[1] it is valuable in the present case. Further, the work was simplified by the use of Scott's estimates for various of the minor inputs utilized by the building sector—e.g. road and rail transport, machinery, bitumen.

The value of the information provided by this approach must depend upon the fineness of the classifications of goods and primary factors adopted when preparing the input matrices. In selecting material inputs to be distinguished, the principal criterion must be the importance of the input in the final output or in intermediate goods. A further consideration concerns the extent of differences in cost structure, which will lead to different accounting ratios for the inputs. In an economy such as Kenya's a large proportion of inputs may have very similar accounting ratios because they are imported goods subject to similar rates of import duty and costs of distribution. Most of the minor inputs used in building and construction have accounting ratios in the range 0·75 to 0·85; this implies that a certain amount of aggregation will make little difference to the final estimates. It enables us to focus on the major items—in particular non-traded goods and goods subject to rather special market conditions.

The input matrix **A** which was prepared was organized hierarchically so that no good required inputs of goods occurring later in the list, i.e. $a_{ij}=0$ for all $i>j$. This gave a triangular matrix which could be inverted much more easily than a full matrix of equivalent

---

[1] According to the Kenyan national accounts for 1971, building and construction accounts for 4·4% of monetary GDP, 83% of public capital formation and 46% of modern sector capital formation.

size. The term 'good' is slightly misleading since the items distinguished included such activities as various operations of roadbuilding, sewer and water pipelaying, house maintenance and the running costs of various services. Of the inputs included fifteen were directly taken from the work done by Scott, 1976; these were mostly of minor importance in total costs and they covered a wide range of goods. A further seven inputs were imported building materials—plywood, sanitary fittings—whose accounting ratio is determined by the costs of import duty, distribution and transport in the final price. The remainder of inputs required detailed cost analyses since they are either non-traded goods or traded goods subject to special factors. Broadly these inputs fall into three categories: (i) building materials and services; (ii) infrastructure construction, maintenance and running costs; (iii) house construction and maintenance. Each of these categories will be discussed in turn to elucidate special points of interest.

The choice of primary factors to be distinguished in the analysis is of fundamental importance, but there is a substantial degree of uncertainty about any distinctions which are adopted. Preliminary investigations of the building industry and the operation of the housing market showed that the most important categories were labour and profits. However, the significant variations between the accounting ratios for different types of labour (cf. Scott, 1976, Chapter 4) and for profits earned by enterprises or entrepreneurs in different situations (Newbery, Ch. 6) required a more detailed breakdown. For labour we use the two criteria of skilled or unskilled and formal sector or informal sector to give four types of urban labour. In the case of profits it was assumed that the accounting ratio is directly related to the scale of the enterprise since this determines the proportion of profits reinvested rather than consumed, the proportion of profits which should properly be regarded as payments for entrepreneurship—i.e. skilled labour—rather than pure profits, and the average tax rate. As we shall see, the problem of the division of nominal profits between payments for entrepreneurship and pure profits is a recurring one in this study. This approach gave four of the profits categories in the final classification of primary inputs (B.8–B.11 in Table 3·1), including informal sector profits. In addition a miscellaneous category was introduced to cover those cases where a reasonable assessment of the recipient of profit income could not be made; this explicitly recognizes the fact, which can be equally true for labour income as well, that it may not be possible to identify the ultimate beneficiary of certain expenditures on primary factors.

The primary factors used in the study and their accounting ratios are listed in Table 3·1. The accounting ratios mostly come directly or indirectly from Scott's work. The ones for labour are his estimates with the addition of the value of 0·75 for informal sector skilled labour. This last category principally covers informal sector entrepreneurs, and an accounting ratio of less than that for the formal sector seemed appropriate as they are in relatively elastic supply and their savings rate seems to be above the average for households. Turning to profits, Scott's figures (1976, Chapter 6) suggest a wide range of possibilities for the standard accounting ratio; he uses a figure of 0·2, noting that tax evasion would raise this substantially. Newbery's later figures give best estimates for the accounting ratios of extra income accruing to large companies of 0·1 for domestic companies and 0·4 for foreign ones (see Table 6·20). However, in the present study much of the income accruing to foreign companies goes to the cement producers. If Newbery's analysis is applied specifically to these companies the accounting ratio for their extra income is negative, because their profit at accounting prices as a fraction of market profit is much higher than the average for all foreign companies. Hence the accounting ratio of 0·2 used for B.8 is probably an over-estimate of the true accounting ratio. The accounting ratio adopted for medium-sized capitalists' income is a guess based on allowances for lower effective rates of tax for such firms plus a higher marginal propensity to consume out of profits.

The accounting ratios for small and informal sector capitalists' income are based on an assumed marginal propensity to save of 0·2, zero direct tax payments, and accounting ratios for urban consumption and savings of 0·8 and 0·3 respectively. The latter is somewhat lower than Scott's figure (1976, Chapter 8.3) because for urban households a higher proportion of savings is likely to go into money deposits than in rural areas and there will therefore be some extra direct tax revenue as a result of new saving. Finally the accounting ratios for extra income accruing to rich and poor households—in practice to landlords and tenants respectively—are derived in a similar manner. In both cases a savings rate of 10% was used, but in addition the estimates incorporate income weights measuring the social benefit of extra income accruing to households in each group. The income weight for poor urban households, w_h, was estimated as 0·3. This is the average income weight for households in Nairobi earning less than 420 Kenyan pounds[1] in 1968-69.[2] For rich households there are no good estimates of average incomes, but the income weight for households earning over £1,200 p.a. would be 0·048. Thus a suitable value for w_p—the income weight for landlords and rich urban consumers—is 0·05. On this basis the income weight for middle income urban households would be 0·10, though it is in fact not required.

Table 3·1   Primary factor accounting ratios

Ref.	Primary factor	Accounting ratio
B.1	Taxes and residual	0·0
B.2	Foreign exchange	1·0
B.3	Unskilled formal sector urban labour	0·68
B.4	Unskilled informal sector urban labour	0·75
B.5	Skilled formal sector urban labour	0·80
B.6	Skilled informal sector urban labour	0·75
B.7	Misc. capitalists' extra income	0·40
B.8	Large capitalists' extra income	0·20
B.9	Medium capitalists' extra income	0·50
B.10	Small capitalists' extra income	0·70
B.11	Informal sector capitalists' extra income	0·70
B.12	Extra income, poor urban households	0·45
B.13	Extra income, rich urban households	0·70
B.14	Non-traded agricultural output	0·85

One important point arising from the analysis of the costs of many goods and services used as inputs in building is the large share in total costs of the component covering profits and entrepreneurial income. In preparing the breakdown of costs, allowance was made for depreciation of equipment and a normal return on the firm's capital. Thus this component is either payment for the skills and contribution of entrepreneurs or it is pure profit. Since in many cases the difference between the relevant accounting ratios is quite large, the allocation of

---

[1] All succeeding references to pounds in this chapter are to Kenyan pounds.
[2] For full details of the estimates underlying these figures see Hughes, 1976, Chapter 4.6 and Scott, 1976, Chapter 3 and 4. The income weights given all incorporate the necessary conversion to accounting prices.

this component between primary factors is a matter of some importance. Some observations will clarify the issues involved. First, the existence of a large differential between the long-run marginal cost of production and the selling price of a good is strongly associated with under-utilization of capacity and monopolistic competition among producers. Typically the goods are ones whose production in Kenya has been encouraged by tariffs or other trade barriers. In some cases the spare capacity was prompted by the prospect of exports to the other East African countries. Whatever the cause of this overcapacity there seems to have been little downward movement in prices to narrow the gap between price and marginal cost. The firms seem to consider that they are making an adequate return on their investment and do not wish to compete with other firms by cutting prices. In such cases the differential between price and marginal cost must principally be allocated to profits.

The second point is that for Kenyan private manufacturing industry both the average rate of profit and its dispersion are relatively high. Newbery's estimates given an average of 18·4% for the rate of profit with a standard deviation of 11·4% (see Table 6·3). Further, the rewards expected for managerial and entrepreneurial services are large relative to urban incomes. Underlying both observations is the scarcity of entrepreneurs with the desire and ability to establish and run medium- or large-scale commercial and industrial enterprises. This is compounded by the insecurity felt by expatriate firms or individuals, who thus will only invest in or manage such enterprises if the returns are high. In other words, at least part of the apparently large pure profits must be treated as the opportunity cost of entrepreneurial services used by the firm. On the basis of income tax figures a notional income of £4,000 p.a. per entrepreneur was used to estimate the cost of skilled labour as a component of profits.

2.2 *Building materials and services*

The accounting ratios for the most important building materials and services are listed in Table 3·2. On the whole they are significantly lower than the median ratios for Scott's two categories of non-traded goods and services and urban goods and services, which are 0·77 and 0·80 respectively. This is because the proportion of foreign exchange in total costs is relatively small while both profits and unskilled formal sector urban labour form relatively large proportions.

Table 3·2 Accounting ratios for major building materials and services

Ref.	Building material service	Accounting ratio
A.23	Cement	0·55
A.24	Timber	0·92
A.27	Aggregates/ballast	0·71
A.29	Concrete blocks	0·64
A.30	Murram-cement blocks	0·67
A.31	Galvanized corrugated iron sheets	0·81
A.35	Exterior woodwork	0·82
A.36	Informal sector units	0·80
A.39	Builders' markup—1	0·70
A.40	Builders' markup—2	0·74
A.41	Builders' markup—3	0·73
A.42	Plumbing work	0·77

Note: see text for distinction between three builders' markup categories

The most important and atypical accounting ratio is the one for cement. As an input cement represents a significant proportion of the costs of many types of building. In addition the cement industry is in a unique position among Kenyan manufacturing industry both because of its importance as an exporter and because of the size of the profits it makes. The special features of the cement industry—enormous economies of scale, large transport costs and strong locational ties to its raw material—have resulted in quasi-monopoly market structures with price fixing and market-sharing in many parts of the world. The Kenyan industry follows the same pattern with the additional element of price discrimination which maintains a large differential between the ex-factory prices of domestically sold cement and that exported. Formally the industry consists of two firms—East African Portland Cement and Bamburi Portland Cement—but both are effectively controlled by the British firm Associated Portland Cement. They operate a market-sharing agreement by which E.A.P.C. supplies Nairobi, while Bamburi, much the larger of the two, supplies the rest of Kenya plus all exports. The lowest Mombasa f.o.b. price for cement exports in 1972 was Shs. 84·4 per tonne[1] while the ex-factory domestic price was Shs. 249·4 per tonne excluding the special cement tax. It is improbable that these exports were

---

[1] These exports went to Réunion which was Kenya's second largest customer outside East Africa. The average f.o.b. export price in 1972 was Shs. 105·5 per tonne.

unprofitable since Bamburi is almost doubling its capacity in order to supply its export markets. Hence cement for building in Nairobi was treated as an exportable good.

The largest item in the breakdown of cement costs is B.8—large capitalist's profits—which amounts to Shs. 114 out of a final price of Shs. 284 per tonne. As a result the accounting ratio of 0·55 is somewhat sensitive to the value taken for B.8's accounting ratio: a change of 0·1 in the latter would alter the former by 0·04. However, as argued earlier, the accounting ratio of 0·2 for B.8 is almost certainly an over-estimate of the appropriate value for profits accruing to the cement companies. The very low value for the cement accounting ratio is rather significant, especially when taken with the high value of 0·92 for the timber accounting ratio, since it implies that market prices may be a very poor guide to the appropriate choice of building material. In particular it is quite possible that the relative cheapness of timber houses at market prices compared with ones built from concrete blocks or other materials using cement may be reversed at accounting prices. Further, the general pattern of a cement accounting ratio substantially below that for timber is likely to hold in many underdeveloped countries because of the special features of the cement industry which have been pointed out. The accounting ratio for timber is likely to be high in most countries because it will almost always be a traded good whose foreign exchange content is high as a proportion of final cost.

Other general choices relating to building materials concern the use of modern, possibly capital-intensive, building materials or methods of production in comparison with traditional or labour-intensive techniques. In two cases the results of this study seem to be applicable to many other countries. The first is based on an examination of the costs at accounting prices of producing aggregates (i.e. crushed, graded stones of different sizes for making concrete or laying roadbeds and the like) using a rather highly mechanized quarry as compared with a labour-intensive quarry. Excluding the profit element it seems that the mechanized technique has the lower cost of production at current market prices in Kenya. However, both methods generate substantial profits at the present market price for aggregates, and, so long as this price remains above the level at which the labour-intensive quarry makes a loss, the accounting prices of crushed stone from each quarry are equal. In the long run the mechanized quarry represents the best technique at market prices and is no worse than the labour-intensive quarry at accounting prices. This advantage would be strengthened if multi-shift working was introduced in place of the present single shift operation.

The second choice is that between the use of concrete blocks and blocks of earth stabilized by cement (i.e. murram-cement blocks, ref. A.30). The latter have been promoted by a number of organizations as an 'intermediate technology' substitute for concrete blocks.[1] However, if they are made on a small scale as has been suggested, they would be both more expensive at market prices per square metre of wall and would have the higher accounting ratio. If a more mechanized method of production, similar to that used for concrete blocks, proved feasible, then they would be cheaper at both market and accounting prices.[2] This saving is largely due to the lower proportion of cement assumed necessary to stabilize the earth—5%—as compared with the amount used in concrete blocks. It is arguable that 10% cement should be used, in which case the advantage would be approximately halved. Further, if we examine the net savings at accounting prices from using the 5% cement blocks in place of concrete blocks, it amounts to between 4·5% and 9·5% of the total construction cost of a complete house depending on the house type.[3] These are certainly significant in terms of the house cost itself, but they are small in relation to total project costs because housing usually forms less than one-third of total project costs. It would seem worthwhile for the Government to encourage the use of murram-cement blocks based on relatively large-scale production, but too much should not be expected in terms of savings in building costs. In conclusion, both of these cases show clearly that simple rules of thumb relying on notions of labour-intensity may be seriously misleading when choosing the best technique of production.

The final aspect of building materials and services which we will consider is the role of the builder's markup and its associated accounting ratio. In costing building work it is usual to calculate the

---

[1] See Spence, 1970, for a full discussion of the use of soil-cement in building.

[2] The appropriate machinery for making these blocks on a large scale has not yet been perfected. However, if it were available the cost per m² of wall would be Shs. 8.4 for murram-cement blocks compared with Shs. 14.2 for concrete blocks and Shs. 15.2 for murram-cement blocks made on a small scale. The accounting ratios are 0.67, 0.64 and 0·69 respectively.

[3] This advantage would be offset if these blocks proved significantly less durable than concrete blocks, but Spence's tests suggest that this is not true of properly made murram-cement blocks.

direct costs of labour and materials for the operation under consideration and then to apply a standard markup or oncost percentage. This is intended to cover the overheads of the firm and to provide the margin of profit. The magnitude of the markup and the composition of the underlying costs is therefore a rather important element in determining the accounting ratios for building work. Discussion with quantity surveyors and others suggested a figure of 15% for the markup in 1972, but examination of data collected by the 1967 census of Industrial Production and annual Surveys of Industrial Production revealed substantial variations in the markup over time and between firms. The results are given in Table 3·3; the variation between years is largely due to the profit element in the markup. Thus in the late 1960s the building industry would seem to have been making very large profits; this is compatible with other evidence of substantial excess demand in the industry during this period—see Wells and Rado, 1968.

Table 3·3   Estimated markup on direct cost in building and construction

A. *Census of Industrial Production 1967*	*markup* (%)
Building, 5–19 employees	27·5
Building, 20–49 employees	21·8
Building, 50+ employees	25·4
B. *Surveys of Industrial Production*	
Building and other construction, 50+, 1967	23·3
Building and other construction, 50+, 1968	37·1
Building and other construction, 50+, 1969	21·2
Building and other construction, 50+, 1970	16·3

Source: Estimated from the Census of Industrial Production 1967, Tables 15 and 16, and from the Surveys of Industrial Production (*Statistical Digest,* annually).

Table 3·3 also shows significant differences between the markup for different sizes of firm. This is complemented by detailed analysis of the composition of the markup which indicates different markup accounting ratios for each size category. The reason for this variation lies partly in the different profit accounting ratios which are applied and partly in the fact that the type of work principally done by building firms differs between categories. Large housebuilding and construction contracts are usually taken by the large firms. They require relatively more entrepreneurial and managerial skill, and there are only a small number of firms capable of taking on such contracts. On the other hand medium sized firms compete strongly for contracts to build sewers, roads and similar work. Further, they may obtain housebuilding contracts if the markup of the large firms rises too much relative to their own. Finally the smallest groups of firms are involved in very minor works or small-scale housebuilding. Their markup tends to be high because they are often inexperienced and obtain jobs infrequently. Hence it was decided to distinguish three categories of builder's markup (A.39–A.41) corresponding to the division of firms by size and main type of work. The categories and their associated markup percentages are given in Table 3·4. The markups assumed are lower than those obtaining in the late 1960s on grounds that the industry is not in the same state of excess demand. There has also been expansion and new entry of firms which should have lowered profit margins.

Table 3·4   Categories for builder's markup

Ref.	Type of work	Size of firm (No. of employees)	markup (%)
A.39	Large housebuilding	Large (50+)	17·5
A.40	Infrastructure and services	Medium (20–49)	15·0
A.41	Small building	Small (<20)	20·0

2.3   Infrastructure and public services

There are a total of thirty-three items under this heading which cover all aspects of the provision and operation of social infrastructure and public services. They include roads, water supply, sewers, footpaths and electric lighting, refuse collection, etc. The accounting ratios for the most important items are given in Table 3·5. No particular difficulties or interesting features arise in estimating these accounting ratios. However, the stage of preparing estimates of the costs of these services associated with a project does introduce important issues. These relate to policy decisions concerning the density of housing, the organization of the supply of services—i.e. whether there should be communal or individual facilities—and the method of charging for such services.

Table 3·5   Accounting ratios for main infrastructure and public services inputs

Ref.		Accounting ratio
	Infrastructure: capital costs	
A.61	Footpaths with lighting	0·77
A.62	Main/secondary road	0·73
A.63	Tertiary road	0·72
A.64	Sewers	0·70
A.65	Water supply to plots	0·82
A.66	Communal water supply	0·81
	Public services: running costs	
A.67	Main/secondary road maintenance	0·77
A.69	Sewerage	0·76
A.70	Water supply	0·77
A.71	Refuse collection and misc. services	0·68

These questions link up with wider problems, as an example will show. To obtain cost estimates for the capital and running costs of water supply to a project we must examine three sets of questions: (*a*) How much water will be consumed by the average household in the project? What is the price elasticity of demand for water and how does water consumption vary as between plots with individual water supply and those with a communal supply? (*b*) How many households will there be in the project's housing? This may not be at all closely related to the official number of dwelling units if, for instance, households each occupy a room rather than a house. (*c*) To what extent will the demand generated by the project be an addition to the city's total water consumption? A considerable number of households in the project's housing may have moved from other parts of the city, so that we are only concerned with the increment in the cost of meeting the city's demand for water. To assess this we must estimate the wider impact of the project in terms of inducing migration to the city and so forth.

Many of these issues lead us to the general problem of what might be called 'optimal land-use'. In determining the density, location and other features of new housing it must be borne in mind that these decisions will strongly influence the subsequent character of urban development. Obviously this takes us into the whole field of land-use planning, but even within a rather simplified framework it suggests the need to introduce shadow prices for different patterns of land-use in order to take account of these long-run effects. There is not sufficient space in this chapter to explore these questions further, but the interested reader should refer to the full study for a more extended analysis and some estimates for Nairobi.

One particular aspect of public services which should be noted is the contribution made by charges to the revenue of the local council. It is a moot point for Nairobi as to whether this revenue should be treated as if it were equivalent to general government revenue. Under the terms of a World Bank loan for a large new water scheme the Water and Sewerage Department of the City Council is required to operate commercially as if it were independent of the N.C.C. However, the extent of internal transfers and joint planning led us to assume equivalence for the purpose of weighting revenue. The marginal costs of water supply amount to approximately 14% of the water charges, while for sewerage marginal costs are approximately 23% of sewerage charges. Thus schemes in which the plot-holder or the householder is charged for his use of these services (in Nairobi both charges are based on the amount of water used) will generate substantial revenue for the government. The transfer of income from the typical household to the government will produce a net gain at accounting prices. As a result charging for services may significantly improve the present social value of a project. For instance the net surplus from water and sewerage charges from a scheme of a thousand low-income houses studied would be over £45,000 p.a. at the current density of occupation. This amounts to one-third of the total annual equivalent of the present cost of the project.

2.4   *House construction and maintenance*
The major problem encountered in preparing estimates of the accounting ratios for house construction was lack of data. In part this arises because there is such a wide variety of house types, methods of construction and alternative building materials. If we focus the analysis on a number of representative house types, this need not be too serious a problem. However, even after the selection has been made it is often extremely difficult to ascertain the composition of the costs of building a particular house. As one might expect, this is especially true of houses built in the informal sector for which the builder has but the haziest notion of his expenditure on materials, let alone the inputs of labour. Many such houses are built by their owners over a considerable period of time, contracting with specialist

workers to do particular jobs such as roofing or block-laying. On the other hand, for houses built by large contractors there is no shortage of figures based on tenders and quantity surveyors' estimates. Unfortunately this data is not particularly helpful for our purpose because it gives costs for different building operations but no indication of the composition of these costs. In most developed countries there are detailed books on builders' estimating which give full breakdowns of cost. Similar material for various underdeveloped countries would be very useful for builders and quantity surveyors as well as economists. In the meantime the figures used are based on information provided by builders concerning the labour/materials breakdown of the direct costs of various building operations.

The cost per room and accounting ratio for house construction of various house types is given in Table 3·6. We define a room as a living room, typically with a floor area of about 12 square metres (i.e. 130 square feet), which forms the basic unit of accommodation for low income households. As well as house costs Table 3·6 includes the cost per room of various types of toilet and washing facilities where these are provided separately from the house itself, i.e. for house types A.81–A.85. In categorizing house type the term 'rooms' implies that the building design is simply a back-to-back set of rooms for individual occupation with no other facilities, while a 'house' includes a kitchen, store-room, and usually a shower and toilet. 'Houses' are designed for occupation by a single household—often with rooms on three sides of a courtyard—though the separate rooms may in practice be sublet. All the units are single storey buildings. A Swahili mud and wattle house is a high quality traditional building made basically from mud and wattle but with cemented floors and plastered walls so that it has a fairly long life span. The term 'core house' is used for a housing unit built on part of one site and service scheme in Nairobi which was intended to provide basic accommodation for a household and to allow scope for extension as and when this could be afforded by the family.

Clearly the house types listed in Table 3·6 will have very different expected life-spans. One way of taking account of this is to assume a life-span for a house type, e.g. 10 years for the timber rooms, and then include in the cost calculation the replacement cost required at the end of each ten-year period. This method, however, is not entirely satisfactory because whether or not replacement is allowed for in the total project cost will depend on the length of the time horizon for the whole project. The method adopted here, which allows a fairer comparison between house types, is to add to the annual expenditure on regular maintenance the annual equivalent of the replacement cost using the accounting rate of interest in calculating this sum. Another annual cost which must be included along with maintenance and replacement is the management cost of running the project. This may be considered at two levels. First, there is the straightforward cost of government/local authority administrative work relating to the project as a unit over and above that incorporated in estimates of public services costs. Second, there is the micro-level cost of managing the letting of houses or rooms. In as far as the project is one of local authority houses let directly to individuals with no subletting, then this cost is simply the operating cost of the appropriate section of the local authority. However, in most cases the structure will be substantially more complicated with co-operatives, companies or private landlords playing some managerial role.

Table 3·6   House costs and accounting ratios

Ref.	Type	Life span (years)	Capital cost per room (£*)	Accounting ratio
	Sanitary Facilities			
A.77	Pit latrines	(a)	8·9	0·74
A.78	Individual plot services unit	40	26·6	0·74
A.79	Communal services unit	40	13·1	0·74
	Houses			
A.81	Basic mud and wattle rooms	5	40·0	0·80
A.82	Swahili mud and wattle house	25	89·6	0·71
A.83	Timber rooms	10	48·3	0·76
A.84	Concrete block rooms	40	80·9	0·72
A.85	Murram—cement rooms	40	72·5	0·73
A.86	3 room core house	50	251·0	0·73
A.88	3 room N.C.C. house	50	322·8	0·74
A.89	3 room private house	50	381·5	0·71

Note: (a) No life span can be given since it depends on use, type and other factors.
*Kenyan pounds, as are the pounds referred to in all subsequent tables in this chapter.

Co-operatives and companies can be treated in much the same way as local authority managerial services. For individual landlords it will usually be necessary to impute a management charge. The only source of information on this is a study of housing built by private companies in the uncontrolled areas of Nairobi (Richards, 1970). There it is noted that a manager for one company was paid Shs. 400 per month to look after 26 rooms—i.e. just over Shs. 15 per room. Adding an allowance for other managerial and entrepreneurial services performed by the company or individual owners gives an estimate of Shs. 20 per month per room. The company housing was all either timber or concrete block rooms whose rent is approximately twice that of mud and wattle rooms, so that in relation to the rent of the latter the management charge seems excessively high. Further, it is likely that the owner of a mud and wattle house will live in one of its rooms and will provide less in the way of general managerial services *qua* landlord. Hence a figure of Shs. 10 per room per month was used for these houses. These imputed management charges are large relative both to rents and to the total costs of the whole project. With respect to rents they amount to between one-third and one-fifth of the rent per room. Taking the present values of management and total project costs for schemes in which houses are owned and let by private landlords, management forms about 25% of the total for mud and wattle units and about 40% for timber or concrete block ones. This is treated as income to informal sector skilled labour, whereas if no management charges are imputed the corresponding amount would represent profits accruing to informal sector capitalists. The accounting ratios for these two primary inputs are close so that in practice the exact allocation of management charges is not crucial.

2.5   *Primary factor use*
In this section we use the information provided by the primary factor requirement matrix **R** to assess the total demand for different primary factors generated by expenditure on housing and public infrastructure. This is an important question because it has been suggested by some planners—e.g. Currie, 1971, p. 893f.—that investment in housing and urban infrastructure would be an appropriate way to increase employment in underdeveloped countries. Alternatively it has been argued by the I.L.O. Mission to Kenya—I.L.O., 1972, pp. 196–201—that the choice of different housing types for public investment would increase employment as well as match public housing provision more closely with demand.

The results of this analysis are given in Table 3·7. As a basis of comparison we might take the induced demands generated by an extra £1 million spent on the road transport of goods. From Scott's figures this would result in the expenditure of £425,000 on foreign exchange, £241,000 on unskilled labour and £184,000 on skilled labour. Beside this we see that most housing and infrastructure investments require less foreign exchange than road transport but considerably more skilled labour. Indeed the notable feature about the figures in Table 3.7 is that they indicate that the building activities studied tend to be more skilled labour-intensive than unskilled labour-intensive. The only exceptions to this are the traditional types of houses built of mud and wattle. As a result the scope for creating new employment in the short run by public works of this kind is fundamentally limited by the supply of skilled labour and entrepreneurs in the industry. Over the longer run public expenditure should increase the supply of skilled labour as a result of on-the-job training so that the constraint is essentially a short-term one. In this light the experience of the late 1960s, when a building boom resulted in a large increase in building prices, may be readily explained by reference to the scarcity of the skilled labour needed to complement the other inputs.

Table 3·7 also shows that the demand for foreign exchange generated by housing and infrastructure is by no means especially small. Excepting the traditional houses, it is the items of infrastructure investment—roads, sewers—which have both the highest demand for unskilled labour and the lowest for skilled labour and foreign exchange. Thus in terms of generating employment the Kenyan Government would clearly meet given goals at least cost by expenditure on these types of social infrastructure. Note that the figures relate to expenditures on the items in urban areas such as Nairobi. It is quite probable that the employment-generating benefits of expenditure on rural social infrastructure would be even more marked. If we restrict the comparison to the different types of housing, the argument that simpler, less expensive types of houses generate more employment may be seen to be only partially correct. Only the basic mud and wattle huts induce expenditure on unskilled labour exceeding that induced by the usual N.C.C. housing. As earnings are lower in the informal sector and a considerable proportion of the unskilled labour income generated by Swahili mud houses and timber rooms goes to this sector, these two types result in a slightly higher total demand for unskilled labour measured in terms of man-years than the more expensive houses. Further, if we examine the foreign exchange cost of the more expensive house we see that they

Table 3·7 Demand for primary factors induced by housing and infrastructure expenditure
Total direct and indirect demand induced by £1 million expenditure in 1972 on listed items

Expenditure on:(a)	Foreign Exchange (£'000)	Unskilled labour				Total skilled labour(d)		Accounting ratio	No. of units constructed for expenditure of £1 million in 1972
		Formal sector(b)		Informal sector(c)					
		£'000	Man-years	£'000	Man-years	£'000	Man-years		
Footpaths with lighting	365·2	225·8	1673	—	—	276·6	395	0·77	165·6 km
Main/secondary roads	237·2	388·0	2874	—	—	263·5	376	0·73	22·5 km(e)
Tertiary road	225·9	361·8	2680	—	—	281·5	402	0·72	50·5 km
Sewers	193·1	422·9	3133	—	—	249·5	356	0·70	30,670 plots(f)
Water supply to plots	469·6	218·5	1619	—	—	256·5	366	0·82	121,200 plots
Communal water supply	427·9	295·2	2187	—	—	227·3	325	0·81	220,750 plots
Plot services unit	291·6	231·9	1718	—	—	328·8	470	0·74	37,590 plots
Mud and wattle rooms	288·8	50·1	371	297·0	2970	88·9	127	0·80	25,000 rooms
Swahili mud house	117·7	32·4	240	144·0	1440	248·8	355	0·71	11,160 rooms
Timber rooms	397·8	98·1	727	97·1	971	185·5	265	0·76	20,700 rooms
Concrete block rooms	345·3	101·2	748	19·0	190	314·3	449	0·72	12,360 rooms
Murram-cement rooms	341·8	106·9	792	21·0	210	339·5	485	0·73	13,790 rooms
Core house	310·0	198·0	1466	—	—	317·6	454	0·73	1,325 houses
N.C.C. house	330·3	208·9	1547	—	—	291·0	416	0·74	1,030 houses
Private house	306·7	204·5	1515	—	—	285·1	407	0·71	870 houses

Notes: (a) For full details of items of expenditure see Tables 3.5 and 3.6.
(b) Average annual wage £135 p.a.
(c) Average annual wage £100 p.a.
(d) Average annual wage £700 p.a.
(e) Main roads; 27·9 km of secondary roads.
(f) Assuming separate service units on each plot.

are no more costly than the other permanent house types. In other words the standard stereotype of middle-income housing generating little employment for unskilled labour but large expenditures on foreign exchange and skilled labour is far from an accurate reflection of reality. Only the traditional mud and wattle houses have a clear advantage on these criteria. Against this must be set their possible lack of permanency and of acceptability to Government officials and potential occupants.

3. THE SOCIAL BENEFITS OF HOUSING

It has been suggested that techniques of cost–benefit analysis cannot properly be applied to 'social' investments such as housing because of the difficulty of assessing the benefits generated. The problems encountered in measuring the benefits of a housing project are not fundamentally different from those encountered in many other projects, but it is possible that they are sufficiently serious to make any estimates almost valueless. There seem to be three principal problems involved:

(i)   The quality of housing cannot be measured at all easily, nor can the quantity provided by a particular unit or project. Housing has many features—floor area, access to sanitary facilities, building materials, location and so on—which are valued in different ways by different households. Linked to this is the problem of discreteness, that is to say the fact that a household can usually only live in one unit so that the preferred combination of features cannot be obtained by mixing units of several types.

(ii) There may not be a wide, genuine market for housing because of the effect of government intervention either in the form of rent control, or by the large-scale provision of public housing let at non-market rents. Further, the housing market may be very imperfect, segmented as between household or house types, and rather slow to adjust. As a result it may be difficult to establish any kind of demand function for housing.

(iii) Housing has external effects on such social variables as health, crime and the general amenities of the city, which may be significant but extremely difficult to estimate with reasonable accuracy.

For Nairobi and for most other cities in underdeveloped countries these problems are not insurmountable from an analytical point of view. It is possible that the shortage of good quantitative data may prove more troublesome, but usually this can be overcome with some ingenuity plus, if necessary, a limited amount of new data collection. It is worth making the point that the dominant approach underlying government attitudes to housing both in Kenya and elsewhere tends to deflect their attention and data collection away from many important questions. The approach is based on analysing the housing stock in terms of household 'housing needs' defined in some conventional manner rather than assessing the determinants and composition of demand for housing. Underlying this seems to be a reluctance to treat the housing market as a genuine market, perhaps with special features, but subject to the usual operation of supply and demand.

The first problem concerning the differences between houses may be dealt with by adopting a 'characteristics' approach to the analysis of the housing market (c.f. Lancaster, 1971). In this we treat a particular house as a particular combination of different characteristics which are demanded by households. Thus the price of the house—or the rent where we are concerned with a rental market—is the sum of the prices of the characteristic supplied by the house. In other words if the rent for a standard room was £20 p.a. and two houses were the same in all respects except that one has one less room than the other, then the smaller house would have a rent of £20 p.a. less than that of the larger. By analysing the rents of houses with different characteristics throughout Nairobi it was possible to estimate the rents associated with the relevant characteristics for our study. The indivisibilities associated with the consumption of housing do not invalidate this procedure when it is used to examine the consequences of large schemes for which one is relying on the average outcome.

Once the existing pattern of rents has been analysed in the manner outlined the direct social benefits of a housing project may be assessed using either or both of two methods depending upon one's assumptions about the operation of the housing market. Method A assumes that the market does not operate as a competitive market and the rent level charged for units in the project is different from (in practice below) the market-clearing rent level. Method B is based on the assumption of a reasonably competitive market using an estimated value for the elasticity of rents with respect to the stock of housing.

The direct benefits may be most generally analysed on the assumption that the Government lets the project's housing or plots at a charge equivalent to £r per room to landlords who sublet—to themselves or others—at the market rent of £p per room. Further, we suppose that the landlords' cost for maintenance, management and replacement of the houses plus interest on capital invested amount to £d per room ($r+d\leqslant p$). Then the gross annual social benefit, *SB*, of a project providing x new rooms is the sum of four components:

(i)   The payment of £r per room to the Government represents a net reduction in the disposal income of households for expenditure on consumption or saving. As a result the social cost of gross consumption and saving will be lowered by this amount weighted by the accounting ratio for the marginal expenditure of the typical tenant household. In Kenya the accounting ratios for average and marginal urban consumers' expenditure is very close,[1] so that we have

$$SB_1=\{v_c(1-s_h)+v_ss_h\}rx,$$

where v_c, v_s=the accounting ratios for consumption and savings respectively, and s_h=the marginal savings rate of households.

(ii)   The landlord's net income per room after paying the Government charge and his costs is £$(p-r-d)$. This income represents a reduction in the expenditure of tenant households which is offset by the increase in the expenditure of landlords. The net social benefit per unit of extra income will be equal to the income weight for landlords plus the net reduction in expenditure at accounting prices as a result of the transfer. This gives the benefit as:

$$SB_2=\{w_p+(v_c-v_s)(s_p-s_h)\}(p-r-d)x,$$

where w_p=the income weight for landlords and s_p=the marginal savings rate of landlords. The term $(v_c-v_s)(s_p-s_h)$ measures the net benefit per unit of income transferred from households to landlords. It will be positive if landlords save more than tenants and it vanishes if there are no landlords.

---

[1] Cf. Scott, 1976, Chapter 8.

(iii) The third component measures the social benefit associated with the portion of the tenants' rent payments which cover the landlords' expenses. Clearly this represents a reduction in the expenditure of tenants. On the other side we have already included the resource cost of expenditure on maintenance, management and replacement in the estimates of the project's total social cost. The other element of landlords' expenses is the interest due upon the capital invested in the houses. Insofar as this capital has been diverted from other investments, these interest payments do not lead to any net increase in expenditure. Thus it is necessary to include only the social cost of expenditure out of interest payments on new saving directly brought about by the project. We will suppose that this item amounts to £f per room.[1] Its cost is equal to the cost at accounting prices of extra income accruing to the people who provided the additional saving. In practice it is virtually impossible to identify this last group of people, so we will assume that they are similar to the landlords in their incomes and consumption behaviour. Thus for the third component of the social benefit we obtain:

$$SB_3 = \{v_c(1-s_h) + v_s s_h\}dx - \{v_c(1-s_p) + v_s s_p - w_p\}fx.$$

Note that the same final result would be reached by defining the landlords' costs as $d' = d - f$ and using:

$$SB_2' = \{w_p + (v_c - v_s)(s_p - s_h)\}(p - r - d')x,$$

$$SB_3' = \{v_c(1-s_h) + v_s s_h\}d'x.$$

(iv) The final component of benefits relates to the consumer surplus enjoyed by the occupants of the housing plus the net benefit of income redistribution caused by a fall in rents—if any—consequent upon an increase in the total stock of housing. It is here that we must distinguish between the two methods adopted for estimating total social benefits. Each is based on an extreme version of the alternative assumptions in order that the estimates based on them will define lower and upper limits for the total social benefits of a housing project.

---

[1] If the capital expenditure by landlords is £k_p per room of which a proportion γ comes from new saving directly induced by the project and the private profit rate is ρ, we get: $f = \gamma \rho k_p$.

In performing the evaluation of the Dandora project parameter values were also chosen so as to reinforce this role of the two estimates.

A.   This method assumes that the rent charged for a unit in the project is below the market clearing rent and that the project has a negligible effect on rents for other housing. This might be the case if the Government fixed rents charged for project housing and if the housing market was rather imperfect and slow to adjust. Alternatively the secondary effects of the project on migration into the city, other investment in new housing, demolition of housing linked to the project and other factors might hold the rent level for non-project housing above that in the project. Suppose that the difference between the original market-clearing rents and those in the project averages p_d. Then a reasonable estimate[1] of the consumer surplus at accounting prices is:

$$SB_4^A = \tfrac{1}{2} w_h p_d x.$$

B.   The alternative approach assumes that the market adjusts significantly and smoothly to the supply of new houses and that at all times the housing in the project is let at market clearing rents. Suppose that the market clearing rent prior to the project is p_b and that the elasticity of this rent with respect to the stock of housing is ε.[2] Then the initial rent in the project will be:

$$p = p_b \left(1 - \frac{\varepsilon x}{q}\right),$$

where q = total stock of housing at the start of the project. It will be assumed that the total housing stock is growing at a rate determined

---

[1] In estimating consumer surplus a triangle approximation is used for both methods A and B as this minimizes the data required. The formula for method A understates the true consumer surplus if a differential between market-clearing and project rents remains after the project is completed. The intention of this method is to provide a lower bound for our estimates of project benefits. This is assured by the formula used which eschews prediction of the fall in market rents due to the project and assumes no income transfers from landlords to tenants as a result of such a fall.

[2] For a complete analysis separate elasticities and stocks should be used for each of the characteristics, but adequate data to attempt this is not available so that the discussion is based on the assumption of equal proportional changes in the rents of each characteristic.

independently of the project. The fall in rents due to the project will generate benefits in the form of the consumer surplus of those occupying the new housing plus the distributional effects of lower rents transferring income from the landlords to the tenants of old housing. These may be estimated using:

$$SB_4^B = \frac{1}{2} \frac{\varepsilon x}{q} p_b \times w_h + \lambda \varepsilon x p_b \left\{ (w_h - w_p) - (v_c - v_s)(s_p - s_h) \right\}$$

where λ = the proportion of housing owned by landlords.

The gross annual social benefit is the sum of these four components, using the appropriate formulation for the fourth component. An examination of the formulae shows that the benefits are largely generated by the transfer effects of payments made by landlords/households to the government and by households to landlords. If we modify the assumption that the project's plots are taken by landlords who then let to tenants by assuming that the landlords are in fact poor families themselves, then the formula for SB_2 may be simplified by using $s_p = s_h$ and $w_p = w_h$. No change is required in the fourth component because this assumption does not affect the situation for the initial housing stock. If we compare methods A and B for estimating the benefits it is clear that the fundamental difference between them is B's inclusion of the transfer effects—on expenditure and income distribution—caused by the lowering of all rents because of the project's contribution to total housing supply. The total consumers' surplus under the two methods will probably be similar over the life-time of the project, so that we may take the difference between the two estimates as a measure of the net benefits of the redistributive effects of more housing.

Finally there are the indirect benefits of a housing project. The information on which estimates of these would be based—e.g. differences in crime rates and health variables between areas of the city—is even more inadequate than that relating to the direct benefits. In addition there seems little evidence to suggest that these indirect effects will be significant relative to the direct ones. No attempt is made here to estimate them.

Turning to the empirical material on which our benefit estimates are based, it was noted above that data on market rents in Nairobi is difficult to obtain. However, by combining figures collected in surveys by the Housing Research and Development Unit, 1971, with other surveys and estimates prepared by the Valuation Department of the Nairobi City Council it was possible to estimate rents for the various characteristics of houses occupied by low and middle income households. The resulting market rents for different house types are given in Table 3.8 together with the minimum rent which a landlord would require to make a normal profit assuming no government charges. The difference between these two indicates the maximum government plot and water charges at current rent levels. Since many landlords pay nothing for these at present it is clear that housing is an extremely profitable investment. The high level of rents observed has been sustained by the city council's actions to stop new building in the uncontrolled areas of housing development by demolishing a part of this illegal housing. Using the consequences of the large-scale demolitions which took place in 1970–71 as a basis, the elasticity of rents with respect to the housing stock was estimated as, very approximately, 2. There is almost no reliable evidence on the distribution of households by tenure on which to base an estimate of λ. Taking into account the fact that a significant proportion of the mud houses in uncontrolled areas are owner-occupied and the number of council units a figure of 0·5 was used for this parameter.

4. THE DANDORA SITE AND SERVICES SCHEME

In this section we will examine a scheme prepared by the Nairobi City Council and submitted to the I.B.R.D. for a loan (N.C.C., 1973). The project proposal was drawn up during 1973 and submitted at the end of that year, so that all quantities will be valued at 1973 prices. The full scheme is intended to provide a total of 6,000 site and service plots over a three-year period together with community facilities such as schools, health clinics and a community centre. In this evaluation we will consider only the housing element of the scheme (including all necessary complementary infrastructure) on the grounds that the community facilities are not a necessary part of a housing scheme and should be evaluated separately.

Each plot will be provided with a core services unit consisting of a w.c. and a shower. After being allotted his plot the holder will be required to complete within 18 months—either himself or by employing other workers—a permanent two-room house which

Table 3·8   Rents in Nairobi, 1972

Rents in Sh. per month per room

House Type (a)	Market Rent (1)	Landlord's Breakeven Rent (b) (2)	Max. Government Charge (c) (3)
Mud and wattle with pit latrines	60	28	32
Mud and wattle with communal services	75	28	47
Swahili mud and wattle with pit latrines	70	34	36
Timber and communal services	100	38	62
Concrete with communal services	105	40	65
Concrete with services on plot	110	40	70
Three-room core house	130	82	48
Three-room N.C.C. house	150	96	54

Notes: (a) The house is assumed to be located in the main central area of Africa low-income housing east of the central business district. The difference between communal and plot services is that the household density per w.c. or water tap for communal services is approximately twice that for plot services. With pit latrines water is not freely available but must be bought.

(b) This is the rent which would just allow the landlord to make a normal profit of 15% on his investment in the house, excluding any charge for the plot and services. .

(c) col. 3=col. 1—col. 2.

meets certain city building standards. A small number of house designs plus instructions and technical assistance will be provided; a number of houses will also be built by the project to demonstrate the designs. The principal house type will be constructed using concrete blocks and its specification is very close to the concrete block rooms (A.84) in Table 3·6. Thus in the evaluation the figures for this type will be used. Plotholders will be provided with a materials loan—that is, a loan given in the form of building materials rather than money—to cover the cost of the two-room house. It is expected that after the completion of the first two rooms during the first year and a half holders will add extra rooms at a rate of one a year up to an average house size of four rooms. As well as the living rooms the basic plans include a small storeroom and a kitchen. Allowing for a 10% increase in building costs over 1972–73 the final cost of a four-room house would be £450, not including the core unit, while the materials loan would be worth £140.

The plots would be allocated to households with incomes between £120 and £360 p.a. They would be required to pay a plot charge calculated to recoup the costs of the scheme over thirty years, while the materials loan would have to be repaid over ten years. Both payments would commence from the date of the final grant of tenure, which would be given on the completion of the minimum house. The proposal puts forward two sets of costs based on a high level and a low level of infrastructure facilities. The plot charges for the two alternatives would be Shs. 115 per month and Shs. 90 per month respectively while the materials loan payments would be Shs. 35 and Shs. 30 respectively. The plot charges would include charges for all services—water, sewerage, refuse collection. It is recognized that households within the income bracket specified might not be able to meet these charges themselves so there is no prohibition on sub-letting rooms. Clearly it is the intention that the plots should not be acquired by non-resident landlords and to prevent this there are restrictions on the transfer of plots. However, this was the intention for earlier site and service schemes in Nairobi and in practice it proved very difficult to prevent it happening. Thus two sets of estimates have been prepared for the assumptions:

(*a*) the plots will be all occupied by resident households sub-letting rooms;

(*b*) the plots will all be acquired by non-resident landlords.

71

Using Shadow Prices

The capital costs of the project are given in Table 3·9 by major item for the two alternatives. Since these are spread over three years the present value of the expenditure was calculated using the accounting rate of interest, 10%, as the discount rate. The second year of the project was taken as the date to which all sums were discounted since the first one thousand plots would be allotted for holders to build their houses at the beginning of this year. The actual year will be probably 1976. Table 3·9 shows that the plot-holders will have to contribute 36% and 44% of the total capital costs of the alternative projects while the cost of the houses plus core units represents 63% and 72% respectively of the total capital costs.

Table 3·9   Dandora project: present value of capital costs

Present value of capital costs at market prices in £'000

Item	High-level project	Low-level project
A. *Public capital*		
Site preparation	128	41
Water, sewerage and drains	504	458
Roads and paths	432	216
Misc. works	98	37
Core units and demonstration houses	531	468
Administration	444	283
Materials loans	663	568
Total public capital	2,801	2,071
B. *Private capital*		
House capital expenditure by holders	1,562	1,657
C. *Total capital cost*	4,363	3,728

In estimating the running costs of the project a different procedure from that used in the official project proposal was adopted. This also required a change of assumptions. The procedure was to include in the costs only the actual marginal costs of providing services to the project and not the notional charges for those services included in the project estimates. To estimate the costs of water and sewerage it was necessary to use figures on the population of the project in each year. In the proposal these were estimated by assuming a density of 2·5 people per room. This seems much too low a density since in all of the other areas of Nairobi with predominantly low income households the density lies between 4 and 5 people per room. Thus an average of 4·5 people per room was used to predict the population giving a level of

45,000 people by the fourth year and 108,000 people by the seventh. The present values of the project's running costs calculated on this basis are given in Table 3·10.

Table 3·10   Dandora project: present value of running costs
Present value of running costs at market prices in £'000

Item	High-level project	Low-level project
A. *Public costs*		
Water, sewerage and drains	340	330
Roads and paths	198	104
Lights and refuse collection	173	131
Administration	514	514
Total public costs	1,225	1,079
B. *Private costs*		
Maintenance and replacement of houses	519	519
Management	2,075	2,075
Total private costs	2,594	2,594
C. *Total running costs*	3,819	3,673

The total costs of the project were broken down into expenditures on the inputs included in the input matrix, and thus into expenditures on each of the primary factors. The results of the breakdown in the form of the percentage of total costs spent on each of the primary factors are given in Table 3·11. The difference between the 'resident' and 'landlords' figures for each project lies simply in the allocation of management charges to B.12 in the first case and B.6 in the second. The switch from the 'resident' basis to the 'landlord' basis significantly raises the social costs of the projects as is indicated by the accounting ratios for total costs given at the bottom of the table. If we examine the composition of total costs for each project and ignore the management element we see that for both the expenditure on all skilled labour is greater than that on all unskilled labour while the foreign exchange cost exceeds both. This reinforces our previous conclusion that housing projects cannot be considered a particularly good way of generating employment for unskilled workers unless there is a plentiful supply of the complementary skilled labour.

In order to calculate the benefits of the Dandora project we must assume values for the parameters introduced in Section 3. The most important are clearly the initial market clearing rent, p_b, the rent disequilibrium, p_d, and the fixed rent, p_a. In Table 3·8 the current

73

Table 3·11 Dandora project: primary factor analysis of total costs
Percentage of total cost spent on primary factor

Ref.	Primary factor	High-level		Low-level	
		Resident	Landlords	Resident	Landlords
B.1	Taxes and residual	5·8	5·8	5·7	5·7
B.2	Foreign exchange	22·4	22·4	21·8	21·8
B.3	Unskilled formal labour	15·6	15·6	13·6	13·6
B.4	Unskilled informal labour	3·4	3·4	3·7	3·7
B.5	Skilled formal labour	17·8	17·8	16·7	16·7
B.6	Skilled informal labour	4·3	29·7	4·7	32·7
B.7	Miscellaneous capitalists' extra income	0·0	0·0	0·0	0·0
B.8	Large capitalists' extra income	3·6	3·6	3·8	3·8
B.9	Medium capitalists' extra income	0·9	0·9	0·9	0·9
B.10	Small capitalists' extra income	0·9	0·9	1·0	1·0
B.11	Informal capitalists' extra income	0·0	0·0	0·0	0·0
B.12	Extra income, urban poor	25·4	0·0	28·0	0·0
B.13	Extra income, urban rich	0·0	0·0	0·0	0·0
B.14	Non-traded agric. output	0·0	0·0	0·0	0·0
	Accounting ratio for total costs	0·662	0·738	0·652	0·736

Notes: Resident = project plots held by resident householders;
Landlords = project plots held by non-resident landlords.

market rent for a room of the type to be provided by the project was Shs.110 per month in 1972. Now the location of the Dandora project is substantially further from the central business district and the industrial area of Nairobi than the houses considered in Table 3·8, so a deduction must be made to cover the cost of transport. An appropriate allowance would be Shs.15 per month which is derived from figures for an earlier site and services scheme, Kariobangi, which is similarly located. Against this must be put the increase in rents between early 1972 and the end of 1973 in order to put the benefits on the same valuation basis as the costs. Over the period January–June 1972 to July–December 1973 the general price index for low income households in Nairobi rose by 16·1%. Thus an allowance of Shs.15 per month was made for this factor, as no better information was available, giving a 1973 market clearing rent of Shs.110 per month. Turning to method A for estimating benefits, it is suggested in the project proposal that the Government might place a ceiling on the rent which a plot-holder could charge when sub-letting. It is doubtful whether this would in fact prove effective, but for present purposes we will assume a rent ceiling giving p_a=Shs.80 per month. This is similar to the rents charged by the City Council for equivalent accommodation in council houses. To go with this a value of Shs.10 per month was assumed for the rent disequilibrium, p_d, in order to give a conservative estimate of the benefits when using this method.

Table 3·12   Dandora Project: parameters for the benefits estimates

Fixed rent ceiling, p_a	Shs.80 p.m.
Rent disequilibrium, p_d	Shs.10 p.m.
Initial market rent, p_b	Shs.110 p.m.
Household marginal saving rate, s_h	0·10
Landlords' marginal saving rate, s_p	0·20
Household income weight, w_h	0·30
Landlords' income weight, w_p	0·05
Consumption A.R, v_c	0·80
Savings A.R, v_s	0·30
Rent elasticity, ϵ	2
Private profit rate	15%
Exogenous growth rate of city	7%
Initial housing stock, q	80,000

The values assumed for the other parameters are given in Table 3·12. They are mostly based on the work by Scott quoted earlier. A high marginal savings rate for landlords was used because it seemed probable that they would save a considerably higher proportion of their net business income than the average for all households.

Two further aspects of the benefits of the project must be introduced; both concern the financial features of the capital expenditure. Insofar as the finance for the project's capital is provided by parties other than the Government there may be additional benefits generated by the method of financing. First, part of the expenditure is made by private individuals in Kenya who divert funds from other investments or who reduce consumption to provide the funds, so that there is a social benefit because of the saving on other uses of primary factors. Funds diverted from other forms of household investment represent a net benefit of the sum multiplied by the savings AR. Similarly funds coming from reduced consumption give a net benefit of the sum multiplied by the consumption AR. Since v_c is much larger than v_s, the most conservative assumption is to assume that all private capital expenditure comes from other investments. This assumption was used. Had it been assumed that new saving formed one-half of all private expenditure the present value of the project would have been increased by £390,000 for the high level and £414,000 for the low level. These increases would make no significant difference to our conclusions.

The second aspect concerns the I.B.R.D. loan. In the main evaluation we will focus on the project's value, assuming that all public capital comes from the Kenyan Government. If, as is almost certain, the Kenyan Government receives a loan from the World Bank—or any other foreign donor—the value of this loan can be assessed separately and added to the main evaluation to give the final result. A formula to calculate the present value of a foreign loan may easily be worked out and is given below:

$$P.V \ of \ loan = K \left\{ 1 - \frac{r(1+m)}{m} \cdot \frac{(1+m)^T - 1}{(1+r)^T - 1} \cdot \left(\frac{1+r}{1+m} \right)^{S+T} \right\}$$

$$m = d + i + id,$$

where K = value of loan, d = real discount rate (i.e. the accounting rate of interest), r = interest rate on loan, S = number of years' grace at the beginning of the loan, and T = number of annual payments. The parameter i needs special explanation. If we assume that the loan is denominated in terms of a foreign currency, it is the rate of inflation in that country, since the real value of the basket of Kenyan goods required to generate the foreign exchange to make the loan payments will be falling at that rate. If the loan were denominated in Kenyan currency, then i would be the domestic Kenyan rate of inflation. The terms on which the World Bank will probably lend to the Kenyan Government for the Dandora project give the following parameter values:

$$K = £2·5 \text{ million}, \quad r = 0·75\% \text{ p.a.}, \quad d = 10\% \text{ p.a.}, \quad S = 3, \quad T = 50.$$

We can calculate the present value of the loan for alternative assumptions concerning the value of the inflation rate i. However, if $i=0$ the present value of the loan is 99·75% of the value of the loan itself, while for $i>0$ this proportion would be even higher, so that for all practical purposes we may treat the loan as a gift whose present value at accounting prices is £2·5 million. This should be added to the present values shown in Table 3·13 to give the total present value of the Dandora project with a World Bank loan on the terms specified.

This completes the preliminaries of our project evaluation. As well as performing the evaluation using the official plot charge the calculations were repeated for a number of other levels of the plot charge. These included no charge at all and the maximum plot charge compatible with allowing landlords a normal return on their investment. In addition the plot charge which would just give a zero net present value for the project was calculated; this is called the breakeven plot charge. The principal index of the value of the projects which we will use is their net present value. As an alternative, the payoff period for each project was computed to indicate the minimum time horizon to assure a zero discounted present value for the project. In calculating the full present values of the projects a time horizon of 30 years was used.

The results of the evaluations of the alternative schemes—including the effect of different plot charges—are presented in Tables 3·13 and 3·14. In interpreting these it must be remembered that method A should set a lower limit to the net present value for the project while method B should set an upper limit. The actual outcome will fall between these two with the net present value determined by the behaviour of rents in the housing market as a whole and by the extent of government control over rents for project housing. The

Table 3·13   Dandora Project: net present values of schemes

Net present values at accounting prices in £'000

Plot charge/Benefit method	High-level		Low-level	
	Resident	Landlords	Resident	Landlords
1. *Project plot charge*				
Method A	1,278	616	1,590	796
Method B	2,739	2,062	3,051	2,241
2. *Zero plot charge*				
Method A	−145	−1,440	475	−816
Method B	1,316	6	1,936	630
3. *Maximum plot charge—Shs.143 p.m.*				
Method A	1,622	1,112	2,241	1,736
Method B	3,083	2,558	3,703	3,182

Table 3·14.   Dandora Project: breakeven plot charges and payoff periods

	High-level		Low-level	
	Resident	Landlords	Resident	Landlords
A. *Breakeven plot charges** (Shs. per month)				
Method A	12	81	0	46
Method B	0	0	0	0
B. *Payback periods* (Years)				
1. Project plot charge				
Method A	16·9	21·9	14·8	19·9
Method B	11·9	13·8	10·8	12·8
2. Zero plot charge				
Method A	>30	>30	21·9	>30
Method B	15·9	30·0	12·9	19·9
3. Maximum plot charge				
Method A	15·0	18·0	12·8	14·9
Method B	11·0	12·8	9·8	10·8

*Where the project has a positive net present value with no plot charge the breakeven level is recorded as zero.

marked responsiveness of market rents to changes in the supply of housing in the recent past suggests that the probable outcome will be close to the method B estimates. However, in the tables of results we will give values for both methods. First, in Table 3·13 the net present values of the schemes are shown. As proposed the Dandora project is clearly profitable socially, even if landlords do acquire the plots. The net present value would be higher with resident plotholders, because the value of the extra income to poor households significantly outweighs the gain due to the higher savings rate of landlords.

This same point is reinforced by the considerable difference between the A and B estimates. As noted earlier, this primarily measures the distributional benefits of an increased housing supply. In this case they amount to approximately £1·4 m. out of a total social benefit of £7·7 m. under B. While both these points stress the gains linked with income redistribution from landlords to tenants, the value of the benefits generated as a result of landlords' saving should not be under-estimated. Consider the case of a zero plot charge; the method A gross benefits amount to £4·6 m. if the plots are taken by landlords. Approximately £0·5 m. of this is due to the investment of private capital, while the consumer surplus component amounts to about £0·4 m. This leaves £3·7 m. of benefits generated by landlords' savings, which shows that private investment in the housing market should not be hindered by Government action as it produces significant social gains either by lowering rents or by increasing savings.

Another point arising from Table 3·13 is that the Government would increase the social value of housing which it controls by charging the maximum possible rent, whether this be for a plot or for a council house. Thus, for instance, the gain from choosing the low-level rather than the high-level project because of its lower costs is considerably reduced by the intention to levy a lower plot charge. The difference between the two levels is at a maximum when equal plot charges are used for each, and the present value for any of the schemes is highest when the plot charges are set as high as possible. Nonetheless it is clear that the breakeven plot charges will mostly be low; this is confirmed by the results given in Table 3·14A. Table 3·14B gives the payoff periods for the schemes. They are not especially short by the standards of some industrial or agricultural projects, but since housing has an expected life of well over 25 years the payoff periods show reasonably high social rates of return on the schemes.

Table 3·15   Dandora Project: comparison of net present values at accounting and market prices

Net present values in £'000

Scheme with resident plotholders [a]	Accounting prices		Market prices [b]
	Method A	Method B	
1. *Project plot charge*			
High Level	1,278	2,739	−833
Low Level	1,590	3,051	−621
2. *Zero plot charge*			
High Level	−145	1,316	−4,026
Low Level	475	1,936	−3,150
3. *Maximum plot charge*			
High Level	1,622	3,083	−55
Low Level	2,241	3,703	821

Notes: (a) At market prices NPV is unaffected by whether the plots are taken by landlords or residents.

(b) The market price evaluation is a purely financial evaluation of public costs and revenue, so that the distinction between methods A and B in estimating benefits has no bearing on it.

To illustrate the significance of performing a full cost–benefit analysis at accounting prices rather than a straightforward financial evaluation Table 3·15 compares the net present values of the Dandora schemes at accounting prices and market prices. The market price net present value is simply the discounted present value of the revenue from plot charges minus the present value of public costs for the project. Using the proposed plot charges, the net present value for both high- and low-level schemes is negative because the evaluation uses a discount rate of 10%, whereas the City Council assumed an interest charge of 6% on the public capital cost when preparing the project.[1] The table shows that the use of accounting prices, i.e. a full social cost–benefit analysis, improves the net present value of the project very substantially. In particular, the high level scheme is only marginally viable in financial terms at the maximum plot charge, but at accounting prices it has a large positive net present value even with a lower plot charge. If this pattern is representative of housing projects in general, it implies that proper cost–benefit analysis might

[1] The interest rate is the rate which will be charged by the central Government on its loan to the City Council, since formally the World Banks lends to the Kenyan Government which then onlends to the city for the project.

lead to the acceptance of many projects which would be rejected on a financial basis.

As a final step in our evaluation of the Dandora project we must test the sensitivity of net present values or payoff periods to alterations in our assumptions about various parameters and to general uncertainty about the figures used in preparing the evaluation. In the first instance we examine the effects of single changes in the values given to specific key variables: these are shown in Table 3·16, which focuses on present values for the high-level scheme with resident plotholders since the alternative schemes behave similarly. The response of the net present value to the parameters examined is linear in most cases so that the effect of different changes can easily be derived from those shown. Two of the variations which stand out in this table are the substantial fall in the net present value caused by a reduction of 0·1 in the accounting ratio for consumption and the large rise induced by widening the differential between the income weights of households and landlords. This is as one would expect, since the social benefits of the project largely rest on the reduction in other consumption expenditures and transfers of income which it brings about. Note that the difference between the two methods of estimating benefits is greatly increased by the change in income weights.

One or two of the changes may seem rather puzzling. In particular lower savings rates and a higher private profit rate both increase present values. The explanation of the former is that a lower saving rate for households implies a greater reduction of expenditure at accounting prices due to the part of household rent payments which go either to the Government as plot charges or to meet the landlords' running expenses. Similarly the higher private profit rate increases the landlords' expenses by raising the cost of capital, thus reducing landlords' net income and the associated expenditure. The net present value of the project would be considerably lower if the general level of rents for this type of housing in the city were lower than assumed. For if it were lower, the rent for the project's housing would also be lower, thus reducing landlords' supernormal profits which generate a net social benefit because of landlords' high marginal savings rate (SB_2) and also tenants' consumer surplus as calculated using method B (SB_4^B). Nonetheless, rents would have to fall to implausibly low levels ($p_a=p_b=$Shs.40 p.m.) before the net present values become negative, so that there is little chance of a decline in the

Table 3·16 *Dandora Project: response of net present values to variations in parameters*

Net present values of high level, resident scheme in £'000

Parameter variations[a]	Method A	Method B
1. Standard parameter values[b]	1,278	2,739
2. Low unskilled labour ARs: v_3=0·6 (0·68), v_4=0·7 (0·75),	1,394	2,855
3. High skilled labour ARs: v_5=0·9 (0·8), v_6=0·85 (0·75),	1,098	2,559
4. High capitalists' extra income ARs: v_7=v_8=v_9=0·7 (0·4, 0·2, 0·5), v_{10}=v_{11}=0·8 (0·7, 0·7)	1,109	2,570
5. Low consumption AR: v_c=0·7 (0·8)	744	2,262
6. Low savings AR: v_s=0·2 (0·3)	1,063	2,467
7. High income weight differential: w_4=0·5 (0·3), w_p=0·0 (0·05)	1,835	4,936
8. Low marginal savings rates: s_p=0·1 (0·2), s_h=0·0 (0·1)	1,575	3,036
9. High private profit rate, 20% (15%)	1,529	2,990
10. No materials loan	1,796	3,257
11. Low rent ceiling and high rent differential: p_a=Shs.70 (80) p.m, p_d=Shs.20 (10) p.m.	1,124	2,739
12. Low rents: p_a=Shs.54 (80) p.m, p_b=Shs.84 (110) p.m.	458	1,751
13. Low initial housing stock: q=60,000 (80,000)	1,278	2,589
14. Low Nairobi growth rate, 4% (7%)	1,278	2,936
15. Low elasticity of rents: ϵ=1 (2)	1,278	2,394

Notes: (a) Only the parameter(s) specified for each set of figures are taken as different from their standard values. The latter are given in brackets next to the special value.

(b) See Tables 3·1 and 3·12.

overall rent level making the project socially unprofitable. The project's net present value under method A would also be reduced if the differential between rents in the project and the general market level of rents were larger than that assumed. Thus rent control applied specifically to the housing in the project would reduce its net social benefit. Finally it is worth noting that the method B benefits are not particularly sensitive to the parameters in the last three lines of the table—q, g, ϵ —so that we need not worry about the considerable uncertainty in the estimation of their appropriate values.

The second test on these results was to examine the effect of the general uncertainty relating to the accuracy and reliability of the estimates upon which our evaluations are based. It was assumed that each of the significant variables—primary factor accounting ratios, consumption and savings accounting ratios, savings rates, total public and private capital and running costs, rent levels—is in fact normally distributed with a mean equal to its standard value and an assumed standard deviation. The standard deviations used were generally a little over 10% of the mean value, but this depended on the degree of uncertainty about the variable concerned. Then a Monte Carlo simulation was run by choosing values for each of the variables from their distributions with a random number generator and using these values to calculate the net present value, payoff period, breakeven rent and other variables for the project. Repeated many times this gave estimates of the standard deviation of the project outcomes and also of the probability that the net present value might, by chance, be negative.

The results of these simulations for the high- and low-level projects with resident plotholders are given in Table 3·17. As well as giving means and standard deviations the table focuses on the worst outcomes obtained in the simulations. Only for the high-level scheme with method A did the project ever have a negative net present value in these trials; even this occurred only twice in 500 trials. Thus the possibility that uncertainty about our estimates for parameters might lead to negative present values for the project can safely be regarded as negligible. As well as showing the worst outcome the payoff period figures show the best (minimum) payoff period as well as the worst in order to indicate the range of possible values. If we assume that the actual benefits outcome will be close to the B estimates, then the probability of a payoff period longer than 20 years is very small and the mean should be less than 14 years for both schemes.

Table 3-17   Dandora Project: Monte Carlo results

Monte Carlo results based on 500 trials

	High level		Low level	
	A	B	A	B
1. *Net present values* (£'000)				
Mean	1,295	2,755	1,603	3,063
Standard deviation	494	642	461	617
Minimum NPV	−154	676	237	1,067
2. *Breakeven plot charges* (Sh. per month)				
Mean	20·1	0·1	1·8	0·0
Standard deviation	25·4	1·8	6·9	0·0
Maximum value	133·3	37·0	62·8	0·0
3. *Payoff period* (Years)				
Mean	17·0	13·6	14·8	10·7
Standard deviation	2·8	2·2	2·2	1·4
Minimum	10·7	8·9	9·7	7·7
Maximum	>30	19·9	25·0	16·9

5. CONCLUSION

The specific empirical conclusion of this study has already been made clear in the previous section—namely that the Dandora project as presently formulated is certainly one with a positive net present value. Its present value could be improved by increasing the plot charges levied from plotholders, and the project will give a higher present value if the plots are taken by resident holders rather than landlords and also if the low-level scheme were adopted. The investigation of the consequences of uncertainty about the estimates on which the evaluation is based shows that the probability of a negative present value is very low. In assessing the project and sensitivity of its net present value to various assumptions we found that the major sources of benefit were firstly the reduction in other expenditure as a result of rent payments made for the project housing, and secondly the beneficial income redistribution effects of an increase in the housing supply reducing general rent levels.

The most significant of the general conclusions which may be drawn from the analysis of the social cost of housing and social infrastructure is that expenditure on these items cannot provide a panacea for problems of urban unemployment. Certain types of social infrastructure—notably roads and sewers—will generate a substantial demand for unskilled labour, but at the same time these and the other items require equally large complementary inputs of skilled labour. Thus a public works programme intended as a means of increasing employment opportunities as well as providing needed social infrastructure will not be successful unless the requisite supply of skilled personnel is ensured. This would be difficult at the present time in Kenya, and the position would seem to be the same in many other African countries. In addition, it must be borne in mind that the foreign exchange cost of these types of expenditure is not negligible, though again roads and sewers are best in this respect. This does not mean that public works are a poor method of tackling the employment problem, but rather it suggests that there may be better alternatives which should receive priority if finance is limited. Insofar as foreign aid is made available specifically for the construction of infrastructure or housing, then this will more than cover the foreign exchange and skilled labour costs of such investments. Further, the constraint on construction activity due to the limited supply of skilled labour need only be a short-term problem if appropriate action is taken to encourage on-the-job and other forms of training.

A more specific conclusion is that the accounting ratios for housebuilding and infrastructure are generally low by comparison with other components of investment and urban consumption. In particular cement has an especially low accounting ratio which indicates the peculiar features of the industry. Since the major alternative building material—timber—has a much higher accounting ratio, it is clear that market prices reflect very poorly the relative social costs of using these materials. There is thus a strong case for government intervention to lower the price of cement in Kenya. Such a price reduction could be substantial—perhaps Shs.80 per tonne—while still allowing the cement producers a good margin on their domestic sales.

Finally we must recognize the limitations of the kind of project evaluation carried out here. It is fundamentally based on partial equilibrium assumptions concerning the economic system within which the project is operating. The adoption of this kind of *ceteris paribus* approach may rest on the belief that only those variables which are analysed will be significantly affected or on the practical difficulties of adopting a full general equilibrium approach. In the present context the latter must be our justification since it is quite probable that a project such as the Dandora site and service scheme may have wide repercussions. In particular one might expect it to affect significantly the amount and composition of private building in the city and also the level of migration into the city. Only by using a general equilibrium model for the whole Nairobi housing market is it possible to assess the full effects of a project or Government policy. A model of this kind is examined in the full study. It shows that in some cases the net present value of a project in the full model may diverge very significantly—both in magnitude and in sign—from that obtained by a cost–benefit study which makes extensive use of *ceteris paribus* assumptions. However, for the concrete block houses which form the basis of the Dandora scheme the divergence is relatively small and does not require us to modify the conclusions of this chapter.

LIST OF REFERENCES

Currie, L., 1971; 'The Exchange Constraint on Development—A Partial Solution to the Problem', *Economic Journal,* Vol. 81, December 1971, pp. 886–903.

Housing Research and Development Unit, 1971a; *Mathare Valley,* University of Nairobi, 1971.

Housing Research and Development Unit, 1971b; *Site and Services Schemes: Analysis and Report,* University of Nairobi, 1971.

Hughes, G. A., 1975; *Housing Policy in Less Developed Countries: A Case Study of Kenya,* forthcoming, 1975.

I.L.O., 1972; *Employment, Incomes and Equality,* I.L.O., Geneva, 1972.

Lancaster, K., 1971; *Consumer Demand,* Columbia University Press; New York, 1971.

Newbery, D. M. G., 'Estimating the Social Value of Private Investment in Kenya', Chapter 6 of this volume.

Richards, J., 1970; 'The Landbuying Movement in Mathare Valley', N.C.C., 1970, unpublished MS.

Scott, M.FG., 1976; M.FG. Scott, J.D. MacArthur and D. M. G. Newbery, *Project Appraisal in Practice—The Little–Mirrlees Method Applied in Kenya;* Heinemann, London, 1976.

Spence, R., 1970; *A Study of the Use of Soil-Cement in Building,* National Council for Scientific Research; Lusaka, Zambia, 1970.

Wells, E. J., and Rado, E. R., 1968; 'Constraints and Costs in the Kenya Building Industry', I.D.S., University of Nairobi, November 1968 (mimeo.).

CHAPTER FOUR

The Social Efficiency of the Timber Industries in Ghana*

J. M. Page

1. INTRODUCTION

When the Gold Coast Colony achieved independence as Ghana in 1957 the Government initiated trade and industrial policies designed to transform the economy from a producer of primary commodities into a modern industrial state. During the same period efforts were also made to increase the number and share of industrial firms owned by Ghanaian citizens and to decrease the economic influence of foreign international and expatriate-owned companies in the industrial sector.[1] Within the general framework of industrial policy, it was planned to increase Ghanaian ownership of logging and wood-processing firms, and to extend the range of processed wood exports manufactured within Ghana. This study evaluates the success of a number of policy instruments employed to achieve these goals by analysing their impact on the performance of firms when evaluated at accounting prices.

Apart from published data, the study is based on a sample survey conducted by the author of 28 firms in logging, 40 in sawmilling, 5 in plywood and 11 in furniture.[2] Henceforth, these industries are referred to collectively as 'the timber industries'.

Section 2 places the timber industries within the context of the Ghanaian economy and briefly discusses the structure of the four sub-industries examined. In Section 3, the trade and industrial policy instruments used during the 1960s are described and their implications for investment incentives are analysed. Section 4 presents the accounting prices used in the analysis of firm level data

*This study is based on field research conducted in Ghana in 1972–73 for the U.S. Agency for International Development. Neither the Agency nor the U.S. Government is responsible for the findings presented which are wholly the responsibility of the author. I wish to thank Professor I. M. D. Little and Mr M. FG. Scott for helpful comments and discussion of these issues.

[1] An extensive survey and analysis of the trade policies pursued by the government of Ghana during the Post-Independence period may be found in J. Clark Leith, 1974.

[2] For further details of the sample, see the Appendix.

and summarizes the methodology employed in comparing the performance of investments. Section 5 uses original data gathered from the sample survey to analyse the efficiency of investments operating during the 1970–71 financial year. In Section 6 regression analysis is employed to test the significance of relationships between variables influenced by trade and industrial policy and the economic efficiency of the firms evaluated. Some conclusions are in Section 7.

2. THE TIMBER INDUSTRIES IN THE ECONOMY OF GHANA

Timber has been exported from Ghana since Elizabethan times, and has been a major export commodity throughout the twentieth century. Processing of logs into sawn timber and wood products for both export and import substitution began in 1903 with the construction of a sawmill to provide timbers to the gold mining

Table 4·1   Volume and value of log and sawn timber exports, 1950–69

Year	Logs		Sawn timber	
	Volume	*Value*	*Volume*	*Value*
1950	10·39	3·52	..	..
1951	9·13	6·36	..	..
1952	7·53	6·48	..	..
1953	10·39	6·48	..	..
1954	12·62	7·28	..	..
1955	16·90	8·88	..	..
1956	19·61	10·20	..	..
1957	24·55	10·80	..	..
1958	27·03	12·44	..	..
1959	35·60	15·94	..	..
1960	35·90	19·64	8·34	12·18
1961	21·48	18·10	8·70	14·88
1962	20·34	11·58	9·32	15·90
1963	23·65	14·44	8·34	17·33
1964	24·26	16·16	8·90	13·34
1965	19·72	13·26	8·11	11·43
1966	16·82	10·88	7·24	9·98
1967	17·86	12·83	6·69	9·66
1968	20·10	16·26	7·60	12·30
1969	24·60	24·12	7·73	14·96

Notes: Volumes in cu. ft. millions
Values in millions of Cedis (₵). For exchange rates with the U.S. dollar, see Table 4·6.

Sources: Economic Surveys, 1960, 1961, 1965, 1969.

industry, and has expanded to include plywood manufacturing and the manufacture of furniture and furniture pieces.[1]

The volume and value of timber industries' output and exports from 1950 to 1970 is presented in Table 4·1. The data closely reflect the pattern of investment and resource depletion in the forest products sector. The major growth of investment and output took place during the late colonial period, when unexploited forests were made accessible by the expansion of transportation facilities, and when government policies were favourable to foreign investment and international trade. In the 1960s, forests outside controlled reserves were rapidly depleted and the pace of investment slackened. Thus, between 1960 and 1970 the value of timber industries' output and exports remained virtually constant. Since 1950, timber industries' exports have represented more than 10% of total exports. The sectoral structure of Gross Domestic Product reveals that forestry and wood processing are an important, but clearly not a dominant, sector of the Ghanaian economy. Between 1960 and 1970 they represented approximately 5% of GDP. Within the manufacturing sector, sawmilling, plywood and furniture manufacturing declined in relative importance from 40·4% of total manufacturing output in 1958 to 12·7% in 1969, as the structure of industrial production shifted away from traditional commodity-based exports towards import substitutes.

Firms in Ghana's timber industries are classified by size, degree of vertical integration and nationality of ownership in Table 4·2. They are dominated by five very large-scale vertically integrated companies which together produced 42% of log output, 47% of lumber and 64% of plywood in 1970. Three of the five major firms are subsidiaries of foreign international companies which engage in timber exploitation, processing and marketing in other producing countries and in Europe.[2] Resident expatriates—defined as non-Ghanaian citizens permanently residing in Ghana—were an important element in the early development of the wood processing

---

[1] For a brief survey of the history of timber industries in Ghana and for additional discussion of the structure of the industry see J. M. Page, 1974.

[2] In late 1972 the Government of Ghana promulgated a decree expropriating majority holdings in the three major foreign international timber companies. The terms of the settlement under the decree remain unclear, but the foreign-owned firms appear to have retained technical and managerial control over their enterprises. For the purposes of this study, which is based on financial data from the accounting year 1970–71, the foreign companies are considered as wholly foreign-owned and controlled.

Table 4·2 Number (and share of output) of size and ownership classes of firms

	Very large scale			Large scale			Medium scale			Small scale		
	Foreign	Expat.	Ghanaian	Foreign	Expat.	Ghanaian	Foreign	Expat.	Ghanaian	Foreign	Expat.	Ghanaian
Logging												
Vertical Integ.	3 (29·0)	1 (8·5)	1 (4·8)	1 (1·5)	2 (2·1)	4 (5·7)	—	2 (1·9)	2 (1·0)	—	3 (1·0)	9 (3·7)
Non-Vert. Integ.	—	—	—	—	—	1 (1·4)	—	1 (1·7)	6 (5·2)	—	—	334 (32·8)
Sawmills												
Vertical Integ.	2 (27·6)	1 (11·9)	1 (7·2)	1 (1·9)	2 (4·1)	4 (5·2)	—	2 (1·3)	2 (2·2)	—	2 (1·4)	8 (3·2)
Non-Vert. Integ.	—	—	—	—	3 (8·7)	2 (3·8)	—	6 (9·0)	3 (2·2)	—	12 (5·0)	11 (5·3)
Plywood												
Vertical Integ.	3 (72·6)	—	—	—	—	2 (25·9)	—	—	—	—	—	—
Non-Vert. Integ.	—	—	—	—	—	—	1 (1·5)	—	—	—	—	—
Furniture	—	—	—	1 (15·3)	1 (10·2)	2 (22·9)	—	2 (10·2)	5 (25·9)	—	2 (3·4)	11 (12·0)

Notes: Very large scale: Employing more than 250 workers.
Large scale: Employing 100–250 workers.
Medium scale: Employing 50–100 workers.
Small scale: Employing less than 50 workers.
Numbers of firms: (Percentage share of total output).
Source: Forestry Division unpublished data.

industries. Their continued importance in the forest products sector is indicated by the large proportion of processed timber output produced by firms under expatriate ownership. Although the major share of processed wood output and exports originates from firms under foreign and expatriate ownership, the bulk of log production is controlled by Ghanaian-owned enterprises. Between 1960 and 1970 the number of Ghanaian firms producing logs on their own forest concessions increased from 10 to 110 and the total number of registered Ghanaian timber producers increased from approximately 100 to more than 300. Ghanaian logging firms range in size from very small enterprises employing less than five workers with annual output valued at less than ₡ 15,000 to firms employing between 25 and 50 workers with output valued at ₡ 100 to 150 thousand.

Managers in Ghana's timber industries are drawn from expatriates and Ghanaian citizens in approximately equal proportions. Managerial experience and efficiency, however, vary widely from firm to firm. Table 4·3 provides an indication of the composition of the management staffs of firms surveyed in 1972. Foreign and expatriate firms have higher proportions of their managerial staffs drawn from expatriates than do Ghanaian firms of similar size and type of output. The proportion of expatriate managers also increases with firm size, although the high incidence of single proprietorships found among medium- and small-scale expatriate-owned firms causes those categories to exhibit the highest ratios of expatriate managers to total managers. Table 4·4 represents an attempt to use data from the sample survey to analyse the relative experience of firms. As a proxy for a direct measure of managerial experience the age of the firm in 1970–71 was employed. This measure may be misleading if the ownership of firms altered without a corresponding change in the composition of the managerial staff, or if experienced managers were drawn into a new firm from other enterprises, but in most cases it provides a reliable estimate of the approximate average level of experience of management.

The general pattern of experience in the timber and wood-processing industries follows their historical pattern of development. Very large-scale and large-scale foreign- and expatriate-owned firms were the pioneers in the industry and exhibit the longest periods under single management. Non-Ghanaian-owned firms in general show higher levels of managerial experience than Ghanaian enterprises, and logging firms show longer periods of

Table 4·3 Ratio of expatriate managers to total managers by ownership and size of plant

	Foreign firms				Expatriate firms				Ghanaian firms			
	Very large	Large	Medium	Small	Very large	Large	Medium	Small	Very large	Large	Medium	Small
Vertically integrated loggers	0·433	0·500	..	..	0·412	..	0·333	0·500	0·125	0·000	0·000	0·000
Non-vertically integrated loggers	..	..	..	..	..	..	..	..	..	..	..	0·000
Vertically integrated sawmills	0·438	0·666	..	..	0·474	0·500	0·666	1·000	0·333	0·333	0·333	0·000
Non-vertically integrated sawmills	..	..	..	..	..	0·643	0·800	0·733	..	0·500	0·000	0·000
Vertically integrated plymills	0·456	..	..	..	..	..	..	..	0·400	..	..	..
Non-vertically integrated plymills	..	..	..	..	..	..	..	..	..	..	..	..
Furniture mfg. firms	..	1·000	..	..	..	0·500	1·000	..	0·000	..	0·000	0·000

Source: Sample survey.

Table 4·4 *Average Age of establishment by size and type of firm*

Years

	Foreign firms				Expatriate firms				Ghanaian firms			
	Very large	Large	Medium	Small	Very large	Large	Medium	Small	Very large	Large	Medium	Small
Vertically integrated loggers	24	16	..	..	21	..	17	7·7	15	7	3·3	6·0
Non-vertically integrated loggers	..	..	..	..	..	..	..	..	..	..	..	5·5
Vertically integrated sawmills	24	2	..	..	11	3·0	17	8·5	11	3	2·5	3·0
Non-vertically integrated sawmills	..	..	..	..	..	9·7	9·7	7·0	..	1	2	3·0
Vertically integrated plymills	3·0	..	..	..	..	..	..	..	..	3·0	..	..
Non-vertically integrated plymills	..	..	..	..	..	..	..	..	..	..	..	..
Furniture mfg. firms	..	11	..	..	..	15	..	..	..	..	6·5	..

Source: Sample survey of timber and wood processing firms.

managerial experience than timber processing operations. Medium- and small-scale Ghanaian firms show particularly short relative levels of managerial experience. Average ages of firms in these categories range from 3 to 6 years, reflecting the impact of recent attempts to increase the number of Ghanaian-owned enterprises.

During the course of the sample survey, efforts were made to observe the standards of financial management, prior education or training of managers, and general levels of organization and supervision, of all firms contained in the final sample. These three characteristics were evaluated for each firm, and a composite index of managerial efficiency was constructed. Firms exhibited widely varying standards of financial management. Among a minority of companies—generally those of large and very large scale—sophisticated cost accounting systems were employed and regularly consulted by the senior management staff. The majority of firms in the processing industries possessed more rudimentary accounting systems consisting of cash-flow ledgers for a number of different cost items, with annual summaries prepared for the purpose of establishing tax liability. Managers of these firms exhibited less detailed knowledge of production costs, but the firm's accounting system remained a management tool consulted on a regular basis. Among many firms—particularly those in the logging industry—accounting practices were poor and frequently non-existent. Of the sixty firms initially selected from the population of logging contractors, forty-five indicated that they kept no regular accounts. Frequently the proprietors of logging companies exhibited little understanding of depreciation and capital replacement, and very imprecise recollection of approximate annual expenditures.[1]

The nature and extent of the management staff's prior training and experience appeared to be quite closely linked to their understanding of the possibility of increasing productivity through organizational or technical innovations. Managers were grouped into three classes: those with prior formal training and experience; those with either formal training or industry experience before entering their present post; and those with no previous training or industry experience.

A final measure of managerial efficiency was taken from the

---

[1] It is possible that a number of firms interviewed had better awareness of costs than they were willing to admit, due to the fear of revealing tax liability. However, in most cases where entrepreneurs desired to evade answering questions for tax reasons they professed ignorance of revenues rather than costs.

organization and supervision of the firm's plant. Particularly in logging and sawmilling, careful layout of the production process and energetic supervision of labour avoided production bottlenecks, duplication of effort and idleness of workers. Firms were put into three categories according to the apparent levels of organization and supervision observed during the interview process. Those falling into the most efficient category for each characteristic received a total score of 3·0; those falling into the least efficient class for each item were awarded a score of 9·0. A summary of the average managerial score for firms in the sample is presented in Table 4·5.

The index of managerial efficiency varied considerably among firms and classes of firms. Companies under foreign ownership ranked high in terms of their management score compared with Ghanaian and expatriate-owned enterprises, and size of firm appeared to be positively correlated with managerial efficiency. Regressions of the management score on firm size and ownership were attempted for both logging and sawmilling firms.[1] The regressions explained between 40% and 50% of the variation in managerial quality as measured by the index, and indicated a strong correlation between the quality index and firm size. The role of ownership was more obscure. Intercepts for Ghanaian and expatriate firms tended to be above those for foreign international companies, indicating that the quality of expatriate and Ghanaian-managed firms was lower, but the differences were not significant at conventional levels. In part this may reflect collinearity between the labour force variable (size of firm) and the ownership dummies; Ghanaian firms are concentrated in the smaller size categories while foreign-owned firms are wholly concentrated in the two largest size groups.

The broad spectrum of firm sizes in the logging and sawmilling industries raises the issue of the nature and extent of scale economies

---

[1] Results of the regressions were:

Logging: $SCORE = 6·185 + 0·516EXPAT + 1·529\ GHA\ -0·006LAB‡\ \bar{R}^2 = 0·540$, 28 observations. $(5·218)(0·431)\qquad (1·326)\qquad (-2·938)$

Sawmilling: $SCORE = 5·625 + 1·514EXPAT + 1·256GHA\ -0·005LAB‡\ \bar{R}^2 = 0·395$, 40 observations. $(4·723)(1·360)\qquad (1·038)\qquad (-3·021)$

Notes: LAB: number of employees
EXPAT: 1 for expatriate-owned firms
GHA: 1 for Ghanaian-owned firms
Management score increases for less efficient firms
t values in parentheses
‡significant at the 0·01 level

Table 4·5 *Average index of managerial efficiency*

	Foreign firms				Expatriate firms				Ghanaian firms			
	Very large	Large	Medium	Small	Very large	Large	Medium	Small	Very large	Large	Medium	Small
Vertically integrated firms	3	3	..	..	3	5·0	6·0	7·3	5·0	5·0	6·8	8·0
Logging firms	..	..	..	..	..	..	6·8	7·3	..	..	..	8·9
Sawmills	..	..	..	..	..	4·8	6·8	..	..	6·0	7·0	7·3
Furniture mfg. firms	..	4	..	..	..	4·5	4·0	..	..	5·0	5·8	8·0

Source: Author's survey of timber and wood processing firms.
Notes: Possible values range from 3·0 best practice firms to 9·0 worst practice firms.

in log and lumber production. Data from the sample survey were adapted to econometric estimates of scale coefficients using the Cobb–Douglas production function.[1] The estimated production functions performed reasonably well, with corrected R^2 ranging between 0·45 and 0·72 and F statistics significant at conventional levels. The Cobb–Douglas function strongly supported the hypothesis of increasing returns to scale in logging with estimated scale coefficients significantly greater than zero in all cases. However, there did not appear to be evidence to warrant departure from the assumption of constant returns to scale in sawmilling.

3. DEVELOPMENT POLICY AND POLICY INSTRUMENTS

Ghana's ambitious development programme was led by extensive Government investment in industry and infrastructure. Between 1958–59 and 1965 Government capital expenditure increased at an annual rate of 15%, moving from 22% to 31% of gross domestic capital formation. The investment programme coupled with rising current expenditure contributed to a shift in Ghana's budgetary and balance of payments positions from surpluses immediately following independence to major deficits in the mid-1960s. The ensuing foreign exchange crisis resulted in the proliferation of tariff and quantitative controls on foreign trade which had major impacts on exporting industries.

The initial response to the rapidly deteriorating balance of payments was to increase the number and magnitude of tariffs on 'non-essential' imports. During 1961 and 1962 a substantial number of ordinary consumer goods and consumer durables were added to the tariff schedule, and rates on existing items were increased. The tariff structure which resulted from these changes exhibited a pyramidal pattern, with low duties on capital and producers' goods intended for basic industries, and progressively increasing rates on inputs into consumer goods production, consumer durables, ordinary consumer goods and luxury items. On the export side, the taxes on commodities begun during the colonial period remained largely unaltered after independence.

The distortions introduced by taxes on trade may be summarized in terms of the effective exchange rate faced by importers and

---

[1] Further details of the econometric work and engineering estimates of economies of scale in logging production may be found in J. M. Page, 1974, unpublished thesis.

exporters. The effective exchange rate represents the rate at which purchasers on the local market offer, or exporters receive, local currency per unit of foreign currency. Effective exchange rates for imports and exports between 1955 and 1970 appear in Table 4·6. The effective exchange rate for imports increased fairly steadily from 1960 to 1970, and comparison of the rates for importers and import competing industries with those for exporting industries reveals a widening gap between the Cedi prices of foreign exchange faced by importing and exporting firms.

The principal instruments employed to close Ghana's trade deficit were not taxes on trade, however, but quantitative restrictions on international transactions. Foreign exchange control regulations affected exporting firms in two major areas. First, transactions on capital account were required to pass through the central bank for approval, and queuing systems were instituted for both personal and corporate remittances. Frequent delays in granting remittances of profits and dividends created incentives for exporting firms to evade the exchange control regime by means of illegal understatement of foreign exchange receipts. Second, the controls over the quantity and composition of virtually all goods imported into Ghana between 1962 and 1970 became a primary determinant of the structure of industrial investment and production. In many industries (including timber), ability to obtain an import licence became a prerequisite for operation at or near full capacity, and small or prohibitive quotas on consumer items provided considerable stimulus for import competing industries. Maintenance of the restrictive trade regime biased the pattern of incentives within the economy away from export production toward investment in import-substitution.[1]

The Government penchant for direct intervention and controls extended also into the market for investable funds. Government policies in the 1960s served to suppress the real rate of interest for both loans and deposits. Faced with competing demands for a limited pool of investable funds and no effective price rationing mechanism, the Government responded by creating a number of financial institutions designed to allocate loans among 'desirable' recipients. The institutions of particular importance to the timber industries were the

---

[1] Leith, 1974, has computed effective rates of protection to value added for a number of Ghanaian industries in 1970. Rates of effective protection on import competing industries range from negative value added at world prices down to 14%. Effective protection rates on exportables range from −3 to −14%.

Table 4·6 *Effective Exchange Rates (EER) for imports and exports, 1955–70*
Percentage *Duty* and *EER* in *Cedis per U.S. dollar*

Year	Imports (total)			Exports								Official exchange rate
	Nominal duty rate	Other taxes	EER	Cocoa Duty	Cocoa EER	Logs Duty	Logs EER	Sawn timber Duty	Sawn timber EER	Total exports Duty	Total exports EER	
1955	17·07	—	0·836	44·74	0·395	1·67	0·631		0·702	21·26	0·491	0·714
1956	17·14	—	0·837	13·22	0·620	1·99	0·680		0·700	8·55	0·653	0·714
1957	17·46	—	0·839	33·79	0·473	1·72	0·678		0·702	19·61	0·524	0·714
1958	17·61	—	0·840	49·55	0·360	1·93	0·680		0·707	30·86	0·494	0·714
1959	15·39	—	0·824	37·07	0·450	2·26	0·631		0·693	24·00	0·543	0·714
1960	17·03	—	0·836	19·68	0·574	2·94	0·679		0·693	12·36	0·626	0·714
1961	21·45	—	0·868	39·70	0·431	4·64	0·681	1·64	0·702	25·68	0·531	0·714
1962	25·92	—	0·899	4·04	0·685	4·75		1·75	0·701	3·07	0·692	0·714
1963	26·73	1·86	0·919	22·73	0·552	5·02		2·02	0·699	15·80	0·601	0·714
1964	27·90	2·24	0·930	−3·02	0·736	4·70		1·70	0·701	−1·46	0·725	0·714
1965	26·45	21·50	1·057	54·25	0·327	4·63		1·63	0·702	51·26	0·348	0·714
1966	30·83	9·54	1·009	40·59	0·424	4·95		1·95	0·700	35·78	0·459	0·714
1967(a)	28·93	9·44	1·000	27·95	0·515	4·60		1·60	0·702	17·94	0·586	0·714
(b)	25·89	9·29	1·390	27·95	0·735	4·47	0·974	1·47	0·999	17·94	0·832	1·020
1968	20·10	15·48	1·394	40·66	0·606	3·96	0·979	0·96	1·010	25·93	0·776	1·020
1969	17·07	15·39	1·352	46·87	0·542	3·18	0·988	0·18	1·018	30·95	0·705	1·020
1970	13·06	12·10	1·278	57·73	0·431	3·26	0·982	0·26	1·017	37·25	0·640	1·020

Sources: Logs and sawn timber: *Quarterly Digest of Statistics*, External Trade Statistics.
Others: 1955–69, Leith, *op. cit.*, 1970, *Quarterly Digest of Statistics*, External Trade Statistics.

Notes: (a) Before devaluation of the Cedi.
(b) After devaluation of the Cedi.

National Development Bank and the Ghana Timber Cooperatives Union. The National Development Bank was intended for the general promotion of manufacturing and to assist in the Ghanaianization of industry. Loans were provided at rates of interest below the commercial bank rates of 5·5–10·0% for periods from three to twenty-five years. The Ghana Timber Cooperatives Union served as the loan window for the Ghana Timber Marketing Board. Its primary function was to provide medium-term credit and loans of capital equipment to Ghanaian-owned logging firms. Loan recipients were to repay over a period of six years at rates of interest which apparently did not exceed 6%.[1] Between 1963 and 1967, when the last public accounting for the Timber Cooperatives Union was made, 6·5 million Cedis in cash and equipment were distributed to 302 timber

*Table 4·7 Number of firms in the sample survey
using particular sources of finance for capital purchases (multiple responses)*

Type of firm	Hire purchase	Equity finance	Commercial bank loan	Government Development loan	Timber mkt'g board loan	Total responses
Foreign firms						
a) Logging and processing	—	5	2	2	—	9
b) Furniture manufacturing	—	1	1	—	—	2
Expatriate firms						
a) Logging and processing	—	5	3	—	1	9
b) Sawmilling only	1	19	10	1	—	31
c) Furniture manufacturing	—	2	2	1	—	5
Ghanaian firms						
a) Logging only	3	10	1	—	9	23
b) Logging and processing	1	8	5	2	4	20
c) Sawmilling	—	5	2	2	2	11
d) Furniture manufacturing	—	8	5	4	1	18

Source: Sample survey.
Notes: Jointly owned firms included under dominant nationality of ownership.

[1] Actual loan rates for the GTCU were not made public. During the course of the sample survey an attempt was made to estimate the rates of interest paid on loans obtained from the Union. Responses ranged from zero to 6% p.a.

producers. Because of the ambiguity of the repayment terms for loans, and the limited administrative machinery possessed by the Union, the loans scheme became *de facto* a grants programme, providing much of the capital for Ghanaian firms at zero cost.

Table 4·7 presents responses from the sample survey to questions regarding the source of capital funds. Of particular interest is the high degree of segmentation in the capital market. Access to the various sources of capital varied considerably among firms. Foreign and expatriate owned firms had limited access to the subsidized segments of the capital market provided by Government loans. Ghanaian firms adopted a wider variety of sources of finance than non-Ghanaian firms, and Ghanaian-owned logging firms in particular had substantial recourse to Timber Cooperatives Union loans. The high degree of capital market segmentation was reflected in substantial variation in the relative price of capital. If the opportunity cost of capital to a firm financed wholly by equity is taken as a base, indices of capital costs from other sources ranged from 20% above the norm to 84% below. Loans from the National Development Bank and the Timber Cooperatives Union had indices of 0·500 and 0·200 respectively, implying a substantial subsidy to capital investment from these sources of finance.

Large variations in the relative cost of capital should produce some variation in the choice of productive techniques. In Table 4·8 Capital–Labour ratios (adjusted for capacity utilization) are presented for firms of varying size and ownership. The most striking aspect of the table is the large variation in factor intensities among groups of firms in the same industry. In the logging industry firm size is significantly and negatively correlated with capital intensity.[1] Smaller firms choose more capital-intensive techniques of production, depreciate their machinery over a shorter period of time and use their capital equipment less intensively than other firms. Each of these phenomena is a rational response to the large implicit subsidies offered to capital by Government loans to small producers.

---

[1] When the logarithm of the capital–labour ratio is regressed on firm size it yields

$$\log. \text{SK/LMH} = -0·921 \quad -0·171 \text{ LAB} \qquad \bar{R}^2 \quad 0·195$$
$$(3·416) \qquad (2·746) \qquad \qquad F \quad 7·532$$

obs: 28 (*t* values in parentheses)

SK: Capital services assuming constant and equal rates of return and depreciation.
LMH: Man-hours of labour in unskilled labour equivalents (wage weighted).
LAB: Labour force.

Table 4·8 Capital–labour ratios by size of firm and type of output

	More than 100 employees			50–100 employees			Less than 50 employees		
	Foreign	Expatriate	Ghanaian	Foreign	Expatriate	Ghanaian	Foreign	Expatriate	Ghanaian
Logging									
VI	0·171	..	0·113*	..	..	0·194	..	0·165	..
NVI	..	..	..	..	..	..	..	..	0·288
Sawmills									
VI	0·112	0·105	..	..	0·108†	..	..	..	0·114
NVI	..	0·104	..	..	0·088	..	..	0·107	0·119
Furniture									
IS		0·081‡			0·069‡			0·124‡	
Export					0·111				

Source: Sample survey.

Notes: All cells contain three or more entries. See footnote 1 on p.102 for explanation of the capital–labour ratios.
*Jointly owned firms allocated to category of majority ownership.
VI: Vertically integrated.
NVI: Non-vertically integrated
IS: Import substitution.
†Expatriate and Ghanaian combined.
‡Foreign, Expatriate and Ghanaian combined.

In sawmilling the variation in capital intensity is not significantly related to either firm size or ownership. In the light of the figures in Table 4·7, this is not wholly surprising. There is less variation in the access of various categories of sawmilling firms to all segments of the capital market, and the ability of firms to obtain loans at low rates of interest does not appear to be strongly correlated with either firm size or ownership.

Apart from the incentives to producers provided through the capital market, the Government employed several policy instruments specific to the timber industries to further the goals of Ghanaianization and increasing the volume and range of wood products processed for export. The Ghana Timber Marketing Board was empowered to fix producer prices for logs and sawn timber, to vet international contracts and to exercise control over and promote the development of the wood processing industries. The Board never assumed the role of a marketing agency, and confined its activities to the vetting of contracts. Its implementation of policies to increase wood processing was inconsistent and erratic. Loans financed by the Marketing Board were provided to a limited number of processing firms, and for a brief period in 1972 the Board experimented with the use of an export quota on logs. The Timber Marketing Board functioned primarily as an export tax collection agency and as a source of funds for the Ghana Timber Cooperatives Union.

Of more fundamental importance to the present structure of the forest products industries was the application of forest concessions policy. Most forest lands in Ghana are communally owned and held in trust by the central Government. Prior to independence, concession agreements were undertaken between timber contractors and local tribal authorities and validated by the courts. The colonial Government exercised little control of or supervision over the allocation of timber lands. In 1962 the Government removed all control over timber lands from the tribal and judicial authorities, and centralized decisions regarding forest concessions in the Ministry of Lands and Mineral Resources. Two themes were of major importance to the centrally directed concessions policy. First, the central Government sought to expand the proportion of log output produced by Ghanaian firms by allocating new concession lands primarily to Ghanaian citizens, by reallocating some timber lands from foreign to Ghanaian companies, and by systematically excluding most resident expatriates engaged in wood processing from

Table 4·9 *Number, area and average size of timber concessions issued, 1900–70*

	Number of Concessions			Area (square miles)			Average area of concession (sq. miles per concession)		
	Total	Ghanaian	Non-Ghanaian	Total	Ghanaian	Non-Ghanaian	Total	Ghanaian	Non-Ghanaian
1900–60	29	10	19	7,683	1,152	6,531	264·9	115·2	343·7
1961–65	59	57	2	2,442	2,045	397	41·4	35·9	198·5
1966–70	43	43	0	698	698	0	16·2	16·2	0
Totals	131	110	21	10,823	3,895	6,928	82·6	35·4	329·9

Source: Office of the Chief Conservator of Forests, unpublished data.

vertically integrating into log production. Second, the Government sought to increase the total number of firms operating in the logging industry, and to encourage the development of small-scale enterprises by limiting the area of forest granted to any single producer.

Both the shift in the nationality of concessionaires and the decline in the average size of concession in the period following 1961 were marked (see Table 4·9). Concessions were granted in a highly arbitrary fashion without adequate screening of applicants, and a substantial area of forest lands was granted to timber contractors without the ability to harvest their concessions. Leases were not subject to competitive bidding by prospective lessees, and secondary markets in timber lands were prohibited. Thus acquisition of a concession entitled the lessee to resource based or locational rents, subject only to payment of a small fixed royalty and direct taxes, but prohibited him from capitalizing the rents if he was unable to exploit the concession. The thrust of the concessions policy, coupled with the Ghana Timber Cooperatives Union loans programme, was to create a large number of small-scale Ghanaian-owned logging firms operating on timber concessions of limited size. Concessions were also used to provide an incentive for firms to engage in wood processing. Attempts were made several times during the period from 1960 to 1972 to compel firms to invest in sawmilling capacity as a prerequisite to obtaining or extending timber holdings. The policy was not consistently applied, however, and only five firms in the sample survey noted that concessions policy had provided a major incentive to invest in wood processing facilities.

4. EVALUATING THE EFFICIENCY OF OPERATING INVESTMENTS

In this section criteria are developed for evaluating the social returns to existing investments when data are limited to observations during a single period. The criteria employ the techniques of estimating accounting prices developed by Little and Mirrlees, 1974. Estimates of accounting prices for goods and factors of production are presented at the end of the section.

The most general method for evaluating the costs and benefits arising from an investment decision is based on the present discounted value of the net cash flow measured in accounting units. If past streams of project inputs and output are not fully known, however, the discounted value criterion becomes difficult to apply meaningfully, and an efficiency criterion based in a single period's observations may be substituted for the present value criterion:[1]

$$B_j = P_j' - \sum_i^n a_{ij} P_i' - \sum_s^m f_{sj} P_s' \qquad (4\cdot1)$$

B_j = annual social (accounting) profit per unit of output
where

P_j' = accounting value of one unit of output j
a_{ij} = input of material i per unit of output j
P_i' = accounting price of input i
f_{sj} = input of primary factor s per unit of output j
P_s' = accounting price of factor s.

Investments are judged efficient if the level of unit social profit, B_j, is non-negative. The extent to which the unit social profit criterion is a satisfactory substitute for discounted present value is determined by the profile of the cash flows in inputs and outputs of the project evaluated. If the net stream of social profits is well-behaved (i.e. changes sign from negative to positive only once during the lifetime of the investment), and uniform (i.e. the stream of social profit is of the same magnitude in all years in which it is positive), the two criteria will yield consistent results. Since these conditions are rarely fully met, use of a single period measure is best confined to evaluations of operating investments when application of the present value criterion is made impossible by insufficient data.[2] Some flexibility in the application of the unit social profit criterion is gained by using production coefficients for average output levels and projected full capacity output, as well as the actual coefficients for the year observed.

The interpretation of the unit social profit criterion is straightforward. The first two terms in expression (4·1) give the annual value added at world prices per unit of output generated by the investment. This represents its net addition to national income, evaluated at the opportunity costs established by the given

---

[1] This was developed in a programming context by H. B. Chenery, 1961, pp, 18-51.

[2] For example, if the project is expected to increase its capacity utilization over the lifetime of the investment, the stream of social profits will be well-behaved but not uniform. Thus, if annual unit social profit is computed for an early year of operation, the project may be deemed inefficient, although the discounted present value of the project may be positive.

international terms of trade. The third term represents the opportunity cost of factor inputs evaluated at accounting prices. When the opportunity cost of the factor inputs exceeds the net addition to national income, unit social profits are negative and the resources employed could be more efficiently used in their best alternative.

If compatible projects produce homogeneous output and have similar time patterns associated with their expenditure and income streams, criterion (4·1) may be applied to a cross-sectional sample of firms, and firms may be ranked in descending order of their level of unit social profits. Those projects with negative unit social profits are deemed inefficient. Within industries, the intra-marginal ranking of firms provides an index of relative efficiency. Expressing social profitability per unit of output enables the evaluator to compare the performance of firms of different size. When average and marginal social revenues are constant and equal for all firms—as for example in an export industry selling a standard product at given international prices—differences in the level of unit social profits will arise from variations in the level of average social costs. Firms with relatively high unit social costs will exhibit lower than average unit social profitability.[1] Rankings derived from the unit social profit criterion may be directly related to Little and Mirrlees's suggestion[2] for establishing the appropriate value of the accounting rate of interest. If, following the initial choice of the ARI, too many projects are approved, the accounting rate of interest is increased until the marginal project exhausts the funds available. Increasing the ARI raises unit social costs and should cause some of the firms exhibiting relatively low unit social profits to be reclassified as inefficient. Similarly, increasing the opportunity cost of other factor or commodity inputs should cause marginally efficient firms to show social losses. Where differences in the performance of firms within the same industry are large, ranking by the level of unit social profit provides a measure of which firms are most efficient at minimizing unit social costs, and which are likely to be classified as inefficient if opportunity costs increase.

---

[1] Comparison of unit social profits is advocated only as a criterion for comparing the performance of firms at their chosen levels of output, not as a decision rule for selecting an optimum level of output. Maximizing unit social profits will correspond to maximizing total social profits only if there are constant or increasing returns to scale.

[2] Little and Mirrlees, 1974.

However, relative rankings are not unambiguous. The ordering of firms may shift in response to a change in relative commodity or factor prices, and, unless all firms have quite similar input–output coefficients, alterations in accounting prices will affect unit social costs differently for each firm. If differences in unit social profitability are small, firms may change position in the order. In the present study the analysis is concentrated on the relative performance of firms within industries. Because the input–output coefficients of these firms are generally similar, and because differences in relative efficiency are quite large, the problem of shifts in the rank ordering is of limited empirical significance.

Accounting prices for commodity inputs are presented in Table 4·10. The methods used to estimate the accounting ratios for commodities and factors of production were similar to those discussed by Scott.[1] Accounting ratios for factors of production are presented in Table 4·11. Skilled labour was assumed to be drawn from alternative employment elsewhere in the economy; its accounting ratio is an average of the accounting ratios for individual industries identified in Table 4·10, weighted by each industry's share in total employment of skilled labour. The accounting ratios for urban and rural unskilled labour (shadow wage rates) were based on the assumptions that workers in the organized sector of the economy were drawn directly or indirectly from the agricultural sector or out of unemployment, and that the value of an agricultural worker's marginal product was adequately reflected by the annual earnings of a fully employed casual labourer. Benefits from extra income accruing to formal sector households were computed on the basis of an assumed elasticity of the marginal utility of income of unity. The sensitivity of the reported values to changes in the elasticity of the marginal valuation of income, to variations in the proportions of workers drawn from agriculture and unemployment and to alternative values of the output foregone in drawing a worker out of agriculture, was tested, and the final values were found to be satisfactorily stable with respect to reasonable variations in the parameters.

The accounting rate of interest was set at 10% on the basis of evidence regarding the foreign and domestic markets for investable funds, and on fragmentary evidence regarding the yields of public and

---

[1]See Chapter 5, and Scott, 1972; or Scott, MacArthur and Newbery, 1976. For details of the assumptions and methods employed to estimate the accounting prices used in this study see Page, 1974, unpublished thesis.

Table 4·10 Accounting ratios for commodities

Forest products tradeables
FPT

1	Lorries and Land-Rovers	0·784
2	Machinery spares	0·856
3	Miscellaneous inputs	0·813
4	Paints	0·715
5	Tools	0·908
6	Tyres and tubes	0·603
7	Traction equipment	0·965
8	Upholstery fabrics	0·622
9	Vehicle spare parts	0·855
10	Wood working machinery	0·914
11	Cocoa	0·854

Forest products non-tradeables
FPN

1	Equipment repairs	0·811
2	Overheads and office expenses	0·724
3	Non-traded logs	0·965
4	Harbour charges	0·772
5	Rail transport (timber only)	0·814
6	Upholstery fabrics (local)	1·005*
7	Paints (local)	0·652*

* Marginal social cost of production

Tradeable goods
T

1	Bottles	0·669
2	Cement	0·610
3	Chemicals	0·676
4	Clothing	0·678
5	Coffee	0·844
6	Construction machinery	0·957
7	Consumer durables	0·661
8	Diesel oil	0·657
9	Fish (tinned and smoked)	0·852
10	Hops	0·670
11	Iron and steel	0·818
12	Lubricants	0·726
13	Oils (edible)	0·730
14	Machinery (industrial)	0·856
15	Machinery (office)	0·762
16	Maize	0·820
17	Malt	0·671
18	Meat	0·919
19	Medicines	0·877
20	Metal products	0·664
21	Milk	0·856
22	Miscellaneous tradeables	0·728
23	Paper products	0·759
24	Packing materials	0·836
25	Petrol	0·609
26	Rice	0·739
27	Sugar	0·798
28	Textiles	0·571
29	Tobacco	0·588
30	Vehicles	0·772
31	Wheat flour	0·657

Non-tradeable goods
N

1	Baking	0·729
2	Beer brewing	0·546
3	Bread	0·726
4	Building and construction	0·738
5	Cigarettes	0·428
6	Cinema	0·755
7	Electricity	0·833
8	Entertainment	0·699
9	Fuel and light	0·748
10	Harbour charges	0·730
11	Housing	0·716
12	Insurance	0·966
13	Meat processing	0·804
14	Non-traded agriculture	0·776
15	Passenger transport	0·766
16	Petroleum refining	0·717
17	Posts and telecommunications	0·822
18	Prepared meals	0·728
19	Rail transport	0·258
20	Retail distribution	0·722
21	Road transport	0·767
22	Wholesale distribution	0·677
23	Miscellaneous office services	0·772

private sector investments. Annual capital consumption for firms in the sample was found by establishing the annuity yielding a present value equal to the initial purchased value of the capital item (in 1970–71 prices) when discounted at 10% per annum over the estimated economic lifetime of the input. Accounting prices for

Table 4·11   Accounting ratios and prices for factors of production

---

A.

Accounting ratio for labour inputs

Expatriate manager	0·759
Skilled labour	0·802
Urban unskilled labour	0·700
Rural unskilled labour	0·659

B.

Accounting ratios and prices for capital inputs

ARI	10%

Extra capitalists' incomes

All manufacturing	0·385
Foreign timber	0·486
Expatriate timber	0·543
Large and medium Ghanaian	0·352
Small Ghanaian	0·211

Accounting price for private investment

All manufacturing	0·916
Foreign timber	0·015
Expatriate timber	0·914
Large and medium Ghanaian	0·949
Small Ghanaian	0·983

C.

Accounting prices for miscellaneous inputs

Forest lands	₵ 3·00 per sq. mile

---

private investment and the value of capitalists' extra incomes were found using models similar to those developed by Newbery.[1] In general it was assumed that capital funds provided by Ghanaian and resident expatriate investors were diverted from alternative employment within the economy. The high share of capital provided by central Government loans, either directly or through the commercial banking system, caused a substantial proportion of 'private investment' in the forest products industries to be indirectly provided by the central Government and raised the accounting price for private investment above 0·90.

Although agricultural land is apparently in excess supply in Ghana at present, a number of experts have argued that cocoa-producing land is not. Because the forest areas represented potentially productive cocoa land, an accounting rent for forest lands was

---

[1] See Chapter 6.

computed on the assumption that its opportunity cost was represented by alternative employment in cocoa production.

5. RESULTS OF THE ANALYSIS

Data were gathered from 63 firms broadly representative of the structure of Ghana's timber industries for the financial year 1970–71.[1] Vertically integrated firms were subdivided into component plants according to type of output produced, and a separate level of unit social profits was computed for each activity. Figure 4·1(a) portrays unit social profits by industry for the 84 individual plants contained in the sample survey.

The results provide some interesting contrasts in the relative performance of firms. Overall, the extent of inefficiency of firms in the sample is rather modest. Approximately 14% of the logging firms are classified as inefficient on the basis of their actual 1970–71 levels of output. However, the sample of logging firms employed in the study contained only a small proportion of non-vertically integrated Ghanaian enterprises. Fifty per cent of the firms in this subset show zero or negative unit social profits, and, if this trend is reflected by the population, the proportion of total output produced by inefficient logging firms may be as high as 16%.[2] Approximately 20% of Ghana's sawmills, producing 14% of total output, are inefficient at 1970–71 production levels. Unit social profits range from 0·745 to −1·55 accounting Cedis per cubic foot of sawn timber. Inefficient firms are drawn from all ownership and size categories. All of the plants evaluated in plywood were efficient on the basis of their sample year production levels. The results for furniture show the highest proportion of inefficient firms. Forty-five per cent of the firms in the sample, producing 36% of sample output, had negative unit social profits in 1970–71. All of the inefficient firms were drawn from the subset of enterprises producing for import substitution.

Levels of capacity utilization may vary substantially from year to year, producing corresponding variability in the observed level of

---

[1] The Appendix to this chapter provides a brief discussion of the sample characteristics.

[2] The non-random nature of the sample of small logging firms makes any attempt at statistical inference dubious. It is likely that the firms represented in the sample are among the most efficient small-scale firms, and that 50% may be an under-estimate of the overall extent of inefficiency in the population.

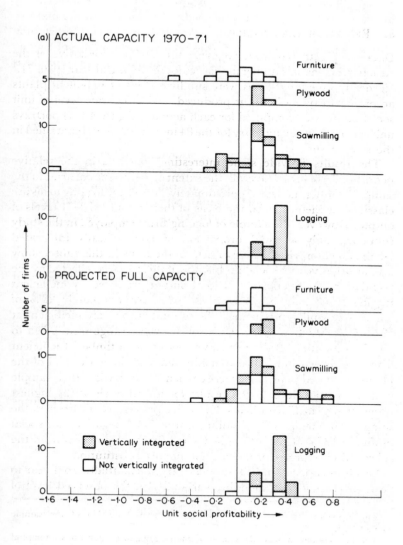

Figure 4·1   *Distribution of Firms by Unit Social Profitability*

social profits. For this reason Figure 4·1(b) shows estimates of unit social profits for the same sample of firms at projected full capacity output.[1] The improvement in the performance of non-vertically integrated logging firms at projected full capacity is quite marked, and only one firm in the logging sample is inefficient. Substantial differences remain, however, in the relative performance of logging firms. The highest quartile of the distribution of unit social profits is about 2·5 times as great as the lowest quartile. In sawmilling the effects of increased capacity utilization appear to have a greater impact on non-vertically integrated firms. The persistence of inefficiency among some vertically integrated plants at projected full capacity may arise from the incentives for logging firms to conduct processing operations as a means of holding and extending timber concessions. Such plants are frequently built at minimum scale to avoid major investment costs and are run by the firm for 'cosmetic' purposes. Of the furniture firms in the sample, 26%, producing 33% of sample output, remain inefficient at projected full capacity output.

The bias against exports arising from Ghana's restrictive trade regime should be reflected in divergences between the private and social profitability. Movements in the effective exchange rate and the effective protective rate in Ghana since independence suggest that exporting firms should exhibit higher levels of social than private profitability. Data from the sample survey support this hypothesis. Table 4·12 shows the distribution of private and social profitability in each of the four industries surveyed. The bias against manufactured exports is quite striking. Rates of return at market prices for sawn timber and plywood are low; most firms earn rates of return after tax of less than 10%. At accounting prices the pattern of profitability alters markedly, for more than 80% of the output is produced by firms with single period rates of return exceeding 25%.

In furniture, the pattern of private and social profitability is reversed. Import substituting firms which benefited from progressive increases in tariff and quota protection of the domestic market show higher levels of private than social profitability. Even so, a substantial minority show negative profits at market prices despite relatively high levels of protection. These firms have low levels of capacity

---

[1] Full capacity was estimated from the survey by asking managers to establish the level of output and associated input levels at which the firm would operate if inputs were available at fixed cost and there were no constraint on the ability of the firm to sell its output.

Table 4·12 Firms classified by single period rates of return at market and accounting prices

Rates of return, per cent per annum, of:

	0 or less		0 to 5		5 to 10		10 to 15		15 to 25		Over 25	
	No. of firms	% output	No. of firms	% output	No. of firms	% output	No. of firms	% output	No. of firms	% output	No. of firms	% output
Market prices												
Logging	—	—	7	4·0	4	12·3	1	0·4	4	34·2	12	49·1
Sawmills	10	13·8	14	59·9	5	5·0	5	7·9	6	13·4	—	—
Plywood	—	—	—	—	3	53·5	1	19·3	—	—	1	27·2
Furniture	3	26·0	—	—	1	4·5	2	16·3	3	26·6	2	26·6
Accounting prices												
Logging	—	—	2	0·3	3	0·3	—	—	2	0·5	21	98·9
Sawmills	5	8·7	2	3·1	2	2·0	1	0·3	2	1·7	28	84·2
Plywood	—	—	—	—	1	—	—	—	1	13·4	4	86·6
Furniture	2	23·7	2	7·9	1	5·1	3	20·5	2	26·6	1	16·2

Source: Sample survey

115

Using Shadow Prices

utilization, are faced with declining market shares and have presumably failed to adjust to a situation in which average revenues fail to cover average variable costs.

Only in logging is the pattern of high social profits supported by a generally high level of private profitability. When firms are evaluated at market prices, more than 50% show rates of return exceeding 15%. However, small-scale firms are significantly under-represented in the sample, and have rates of return at the low end of the range, both at market and accounting prices. Judging by those included in the sample, more than 60% of them may be earning less than 10% per annum at market prices. This would help to explain the Government's apparent willingness to provide loans at highly subsidized rates of interest, and to accept high rates of default.

6. EXPLAINING INEFFICIENCY

The substantial variations in economic efficiency observed in three of the industries studied may be explained in part by the effects of Government policy on the performance of individual firms. Table 4·13 summarizes the results of a multiple regression model designed to test some relationships between a number of variables directly influenced by development policy, and relative economic efficiency in the logging, sawmilling and furniture manufacturing industries. The regressions are reasonably successful in explaining variations in the level of social profitability. Corrected R^2 range from 0·689 for logging to 0·327 for sawn timber manufacturing, and all regressions have omnibus F statistics which are significant at or above the 5% level. The results are interpreted separately for each independent variable.

Firm size is measured by the number of workers employed. It may be expected to be of particular relevance in the logging industry, where there is persuasive evidence of economies of scale. Small-scale logging firms should exhibit relatively high unit social costs and low levels of social profitability. The role of size in the logging regression is consistent with the hypothesis. The coefficient for firm size is significant at the 90% level of confidence and is positively related to the level of unit social profits. In sawmilling and furniture, the regressions fail to support the hypothesis of a relation between firm size and social profitability.

Government policies have tended to favour the adoption of capital-intensive techniques, particularly for firms with access to the

116

Table 4·13 *Explaining inefficiency: coefficients of the regressions*

Industry	CONST:	LAB:	SK/LMH:	CAP:	LANDADJ:	MGMT:	VERTD:	YEARS:	ISI:	$\bar{R}^2$	F:	OBS:
Logging	−·1564	·00017*	−·1907†	·4685‡	·1429	−·0138	..	−·0051	..	·689	10·95	28
	(·2488)	(·00011)	(·0974)	(·1559)	(·1221)	(·0150)	..	(·0037)	..			
Sawmilling	·7315†ᵃ	·00037*ᵃ	−·3953	·1339*	..	−·0855‡	−·1339†ᵃ	..	..	·327	4·70	40
	(·2526)	(·00023)	(·4055)	(·1042)	..	(·0259)	(·0636)	..	..			
Furniture	·4125†ᵃ	..	·8476	..	..	−·0079†	..	..	−·1259	·526	4·70	11
	(·1430)	..	(·7357)	..	..	(·0032)	..	..	(·1147)			

Notes: * Significant at 0·10 level.
 † Significant at 0·05 level. (std. errors in parentheses)
 ‡ Significant at 0·01 level. (a) two-tailed test.
Variables: the dependent variable is unit social profits, as in Figure 4·1(a)
 LAB: Number of workers
 SK/LMH: Capital service–labour service ratio
 CAP: Percentage of full capacity utilized
 LANDADJ: Adjustment for variations in concession quality
 MGMT: Management index
 VERTD: Dummy variable 1 for vertically integrated firms
 YEARS: Age of firm
 ISI: Dummy variable 1 for import substitution firms

117

subsidized Ghanaian capital market. Hence, capital-intensive firms when evaluated at accounting prices should experience higher social costs than firms with factor proportions more appropriate to Ghana's factor endowments; and within individual industries higher capital-intensity of production should be associated with relatively inefficient firms. The results of the regressions confirm this hypothesis only for the logging industry, in which the capital–labour ratio is significantly and negatively correlated with unit social profits. This is not altogether surprising, since the greatest differences in factor intensities and in opportunity costs of capital occur in this industry. In sawmilling and furniture, the choice of factor proportions was less heavily influenced by specific industry policies, and the incentives to choose markedly inappropriate techniques were presumably less strong.

Inefficiency is more prevalent at actual levels of output than at projected full capacity. Capacity utilization should therefore be positively correlated with relative efficiency, and firms with higher levels of capacity utilization should exhibit higher unit social profits. In both logging and sawmilling, capacity utilization was positively and significantly correlated with relative performance at the 90% level or better. In furniture, the capacity utilization coefficient was less than its standard error and was dropped from the regression.[1]

Managerial experience varies widely among firms in the industries studied. If learning by doing lowers the average costs of more experienced firms, the age of the firm should be positively correlated with the level of social profitability. Coefficients for managerial experience, however, fail to show a significant relationship between the age of the firm and the level of social profit. Problems concerning the use of age of establishment as a measure of experience have already been discussed. In addition, the variable suffers from important problems of multi-collinearity with other independent variables.

The role of managerial efficiency in the production process has not been fully explored in the literature on industrial organization. Inefficient managers are generally assumed to be technically or 'X' inefficient in the sense that they fail to obtain maximum output from a

---

[1] Capacity utilization in the furniture regressions was strongly collinear with several of the independent variables, including firm size, factor intensity and managerial quality.

given level of inputs.[1] If this is the case, inefficiently managed firms should experience higher levels of unit social costs and exhibit lower levels of unit social profit. In Section 2 managerial efficiency was measured by a composite index based on the financial and organizational management practices observed during the course of the sample survey. If poorly managed firms are less 'X' efficient, the management index should be negatively correlated with unit social profits, since poorly managed firms are identified by high index numbers. The variable for managerial efficiency performs quite well in explaining variations in relative economic efficiency, despite important problems of multi-collinearity. The management index is significantly and negatively related to the dependent variable in all regressions, although technical efficiency is apparently more important in determining the relative performance of manufacturing processes than in timber extraction. This does not appear unreasonable. As the complexity of the production process increases, the dimensions in which managerial inefficiency acts on production costs presumably increase as well.

Government policies have been ambivalent with regard to the vertical integration of logging with processing firms. On the one hand, concessions policy has been occasionally used to encourage firms to increase their processing facilities; on the other hand, the authorities have prohibited resident expatriates from obtaining logging concessions to supply existing sawmills. Vertically integrated processing firms might be expected to exhibit lower unit social costs if savings from inventory control and an assured supply of raw material inputs are realized. In the regression analysis, however, the dummy variable for vertically integrated firms is negatively and significantly correlated to the level of unit social profits. Apparently vertical integration contributes to increased social costs in the sawmilling industry. Several sources of increased costs may be reflected by the variable. First, too high a price may have been imputed to the log inputs employed by vertically integrated firms raising their estimated social costs above actual levels. Second, because vertically integrated firms are also engaged in the more highly profitable export logging trade, some firms may accept inefficient processing plants as a cost of maintaining or extending forest holdings.

---

[1] Important contributions have been made by M. J. Farrell, 1957, and H. Leibenstein, 1966.

The emphasis on promoting Ghanaian-owned enterprises during the 1960s was based on the assumption that foreign ownership was not in Ghana's best interest. The accounting prices for private investment and for extra capitalists' income presented in Section 4 contain estimates of the social cost of repatriation of capital and profits by foreign and expatriate-owned enterprises, and welfare weights attached to the incomes of small Ghanaian entrepreneurs. It is therefore of interest to ask whether ownership of the firm has a detectable influence on the level of social profits when other potential sources of inefficiency are held constant. Dummy variables for expatriate and Ghanaian ownership were introduced into the logging and sawmilling regressions. In both cases the estimated coefficients were less than their standard errors and were dropped from the regression. This is not surprising in view of the very similar accounting prices of private investment and extra capitalists' incomes. The higher opportunity cost of remittances by foreign firms is to some extent offset by the lower opportunity cost of capital funds provided from this source. Ownership is quite strongly related to a number of other variables affecting efficiency, and it is not accurate to assert that Ghanaian and non-Ghanaian firms are similar in all other respects. Ownership alone, however, does not appear significantly to influence relative social profitability.

Furniture is the only industry studied in which a substantial number of firms produce import substitutes for the protected local market. If the structure of protection has resulted in the misallocation of resources, import substituting firms should show detectably lower levels of social profitability. A dummy variable assigned to firms producing wholly for the local market yielded a coefficient of correct sign which was not significant at conventional levels. Thus, although import substituting firms apparently tend to be less efficient, this conclusion cannot be stated with any degree of certainty.

7. Conclusions

During the years following independence Ghana experimented with a number of policies designed to modernize and industrialize the economy through import substitution rather than through the development of manufactured exports. Efforts to maintain the price of foreign exchange below the equilibrium exchange rate, while taxing both imports and exports, strongly favoured production of goods for home consumption rather than for trade. The structure of private incentives in the economy is reflected in the low levels of private returns to capital in the industries studied, particularly among firms engaged in processing timber for export. When market prices are replaced by accounting prices, however, most firms producing for export are found to be efficient. Valuing commodity and factor inputs at accounting prices implicitly involves comparing the firms analysed with the rest of the economy. Industries with positive unit social profits are those into which the Government should be directing resources if it wishes to pursue development policies compatible with comparative advantage. The results of the present study indicate that additional resources directed into timber exploitation and the manufacture of wood products for export would have represented an efficient means of increasing national income.

Despite the relatively good overall performance of the industries studied, within each industry there was substantial variation in the performance of individual firms. Industrial policies applied to the timber industries gave rise to a number of distortions which increased the social costs of production. Industrial policy was guided by two central themes—the desire to increase the number of Ghanaian-owned firms exploiting and processing timber, and the intention to increase the proportion of logs processed into manufactured exports.

Policies designed to alter the structure of ownership without altering other aspects of industrial structure need not have resulted in major alterations in the social returns to investments. However, the policies chosen by the Ghana Government to implement 'Ghanaianization' had important implications for firm size, the choice of techniques and, perhaps, managerial efficiency. The decision to increase the number of Ghanaian-owned logging firms by creating a large number of small-scale enterprises was incompatible with efficient exploitation of the resource. Significant economies of scale in logging production implied that firms below minimum efficient scale faced relatively high market and social costs. Yet concession policies fragmented forest reserves into individual parcels too small to support firms of optimum economic size, creating a class of firms producing as much as 15% of total output which were of dubious commercial and social viability. The effects of this concessions policy were exacerbated by Government subsidies to some timber producers. Confronted with a large number of firms earning little or no return to capital at market prices, the Government provided capital funds and equipment at negative real rates of interest and tolerated high rates of default. Subsidies provided in this manner encouraged increased levels of capital intensity, under-utilization of capacity, and may have contributed to reductions in managerial efficiency.[1] All three variables are significantly correlated with poor economic performance. Against these considerations some benefits undoubtedly did accrue which are more difficult to quantify. The spread of Ghanaian ownership provided some amount of political gain to a new nation in the process of political as well as economic development, and there was presumably some benefit derived from the training of Ghanaian entrepreneurs in management skills as a result of the growth of small firms. These benefits, however, were incurred at a rather high cost in terms of the efficient use of resources.

In the timber processing industries, Ghanaianization was pursued with less vigour and perhaps therefore with greater success. Economies of scale are apparently not an important factor in the production costs of sawmilling and furniture. For this reason, Ghanaian-owned firms, which tend to be concentrated in the smaller size categories, do not appear to incur higher costs of production than foreign and expatriate-owned firms. The policy of prohibiting vertical integration by expatriate-owned firms also appears to have had no detectable effect on economic efficiency. Because access to the subsidized elements of the Ghanaian capital market appears to have been more random in the timber processing industries, the negative effects of inappropriate choices of factor proportions and low capacity utilization are spread more evenly over all ownership and, size categories.

Efforts to increase local processing of timber exports consisted of a number of haphazardly applied fiscal incentives, coupled with attempts at direct Government intervention. Investments in timber processing made during the 1960s exhibit widely different levels of social profitability. Plywood and furniture manufacturing for export appear to offer substantial opportunities for additional investments yielding acceptable social returns. Furniture firms producing for import substitution, on the other hand, exhibit a high incidence of inefficiency. Excess capacity in domestic furniture manufacturing,

---

[1] W. M. Corden, 1970, has presented a model in which managerial efficiency is made a function of effort. Subsidies to management encourage entrepreneurs to take more leisure and thereby reduce managerial efficiency.

coupled with low social rates of return on existing investments, make it appear unlikely that future investments in this sector will yield acceptable social returns.

In the sawmilling industry, the pattern of social profitability is uneven. On the one hand, most firms show positive unit social profits either at actual or projected full capacity. On the other hand, a number of recent investments by Ghanaian-owned logging firms appear to be inefficient at all projected levels of output. Although the evidence is inconclusive, it is possible that the poor performance of these latter firms is the result of concessions policies designed to encourage investments in timber processing.

APPENDIX: SAMPLE CHARACTERISTICS

The sample covered 28 of 329 logging operations. Firms contained in the sample produced 54% of total logging output and held 59% of registered concessions in 1971. Analysis of the industry and the sample by size of firm and ownership indicates that the sample is quite strongly biased towards large-scale firms which are vertically integrated with processing activities. Firms engaged only in logging are most under-represented in the sample; sample firms in this category produced less than 2% of the output of all firms in their class in 1971. The logging sample is also biased somewhat toward foreign-owned firms. In large measure this bias reflects the availability of consistent accounting data.

The sample of sawmills shows greater coverage and is more representative of the general structure of the industry than the logging sample. The sample contains 40 of the 62 sawmills currently operating in Ghana. Firms included in the sample produced 84% of the gross value of industry output in 1970, and 85% of the volume of output in 1971. Coverage within the sample is broadly representative of the structure of sawn timber producers in Ghana, although there is some bias towards large-scale vertically integrated firms, largely at the expense of small-scale firms.

The plymill sample represents virtually the whole population. The single firm excluded from the sample was a small-scale veneer producing firm which was closed during the reference year.

Coverage in the sample of furniture manufacturing is less complete than for sawmilling and plywood. Eleven of 26 firms were included, and sample firms produced 64% of industry output in 1970. All firms exporting furniture pieces were included in the sample. Import substituting firms were less well represented; the sample contained import substituting firms producing 58% of the output of all import substituting firms in 1970. The structure of the sample is biased towards large-scale firms and exporting firms and against medium and small-scale firms engaged in import substitution. Small-scale firms are least well represented.

The analysis of relative efficiency can provide an insight into the way in which the structure of the sample may bias inferences concerning the pattern of efficiency in the industries under study. In logging the bias towards large-scale firms should cause the sample results to exhibit a higher general level of efficiency than for the industry as a whole. Firm size is significantly correlated with performance itself, and it is correlated with two other important variables, capital-intensity and capacity utilization, in such a manner as to raise the probability that small-scale firms will be relatively less efficient than large and medium-scale enterprises. Most of the excluded firms in the logging industry would have low levels of managerial efficiency, if the firms included in the subset of small Ghanaian-owned firms are representative. This should bias the estimation of the overall level of efficiency upwards, although the impact should not be as significant for the management variable as for firm size. Ownership does not appear to be a significant explanatory variable for differences in the efficiency of logging firms; consequently the bias in the sample towards foreign and expatriate ownership should not greatly affect the conclusions drawn.

The structure of the sawmill sample is broadly representative of the population of sawmilling firms. The slight sample bias towards large-scale enterprises may mean that there is a higher incidence of relatively less efficient firms in the sample than in the industry as a whole. Similarly, the higher incidence of vertically integrated firms in the sample than in the population should tend to raise the apparent level of inefficiency. Working in the opposite direction, however, is the role of the management variable. Returns included in the final sample were determined in large measure by the availability of comprehensive and consistent accounting data. Since this is one of the arguments of the index of managerial efficiency, most firms in the sample should rank higher in terms of their management variable than excluded firms. The lower levels of managerial expertise displayed by excluded firms should tend to lower the estimates of social profitability for the industry relative to the sample. The sample also contains all of the sawmills engaged in multiple shift working and probably exhibits a higher overall level of capacity utilization than the industry. Capacity utilization is significantly and positively related to the indices of efficiency, implying that sample firms may be drawn from the more efficient subset of all sawmills. Finally the bias towards expatriate and foreign ownership may produce a tendency for firms in the sample to be relatively less efficient than those in the population. On balance it is difficult to determine in which direction these countervailing forces draw the sample. It is doubtful, however, that the inferences drawn from the sample of firms would be overturned by application of the analysis of efficiency to the population.

The bias in the furniture sample towards large-scale firms may imply that sample firms are relatively less efficient than all firms in Ghana's furniture industry. In general, though, the structure of the sample is sufficiently similar to that for the industry to support the conclusions drawn from the regressions.

LIST OF REFERENCES

Chenery, H. B., 'Comparative Advantage and Development Policy', *American Economic Review*, March 1961.

Corden, W. M., 'The Efficiency Effects of Trade and Protection', in I. A. McDougall and R. H. Snape (eds.), *Studies in International Economics*, Amsterdam, North-Holland, 1970.

Farrell, M. J., 'The Measurement of Productive Efficiency', *Journal of the Royal Statistical Society* (Series A), 120, 1957.

Leith, J. Clark, forthcoming study for the National Bureau of Economic Research, Amsterdam, North-Holland, 1974.

Liebenstein, H., 'Allocative Efficiency vs. X-Efficiency', *American Economic Review*, 56, 1966.

Little, I. M. D., and Mirrlees, J. A., *Project Appraisal and Planning for Developing Countries*, Heinemann, London, 1974.

Page, J. M., 'Timber Exports and Ghanaian Economic Development', in S. R. Pearson and J. Cownie (eds.), *Commodity Exports and African Economic Development,* Lexington, Mass., D. C. Heath, Lexington Books, 1974.

Page, J. M., *Development Policy and Economic Efficiency in Some Ghanaian Export Industries,* Nuffield College, Oxford, unpublished D. Phil. dissertation, 1974.

Scott, M.FG., *Estimates of Accounting Prices for Mauritius,* Nuffield College, Oxford, mimeo., April 1972.

Scott, M. FG., MacArthur, J. D., and Newbery, D. M. G., *Project Appraisal in Practice: The Little–Mirrlees Method Applied in Kenya,* Heinemann, London, 1976.

CHAPTER FIVE

Shadow Wages of 'Surplus' Labour in Mauritius

M. FG. Scott

1. INTRODUCTION

Mauritius is a beautiful island situated in the Indian Ocean about 500 miles off the East Coast of Madagascar and a little north of the Tropic of Capricorn. It covers only some 720 square miles, and nearly all the agricultural land is planted to sugar cane. Sugar represents over 90% of its exports, and workers on sugar estates and small-holdings account for over a third of all those at work. The inhabitants of the island numbered 310,000 in 1861, just before the first malaria epidemic of 1866–67. This almost halted the expansion of population, which grew to only 419,000 by 1944, with an average expected life at birth of about 33 years. Malaria was eradicated shortly afterwards, and the growth of population accelerated to 3·1% a year in the decade ending in 1962, with an expected life of close to 60 years. By 1970 the population had reached some 815,000, and the growth rate had been brought down to about 2% a year. The doubling of population since the war has led to an acute unemployment problem, of which more below.

The island was uninhabited when it was discovered by the Portuguese in the 16th century. The Dutch attempted to colonize it, but gave up, after about 70 years, in 1710. Shortly afterwards it was colonized by the French, bringing in African slaves to work the sugar estates. In 1810 it was seized by the British. Slavery was abolished in 1833, and this led to the introduction of Indian labourers. At the end of 1967, 52% of the inhabitants were Hindus, 16% Moslems, 3% Sino-Mauritians and the remaining 29% were of African, mixed or European descent. The island became independent in 1968.

The estimates of shadow wages described here were made following a four-week visit to Mauritius by the author in January 1972. They formed part of a set of accounting prices which were made in connection with the Harbour Master Plan prepared by Sir Alexander Gibb and Partners in conjunction with Freeman Fox and

Associates. The economic aspects of the plan were examined by a team led by Mr I. G. Heggie[1], and including Mr J. Ebden and Mr S. Wanhill. The author acknowledges the help received both from them and from many officials working for the Mauritius Government and in the public sector generally, as well as by others in the private sector and outside the island[2]. The estimates are, however, the author's responsibility, and do not commit any of those mentioned.

The Little–Mirrlees method, which was used to estimate the accounting prices, is peculiarly well suited to Mauritius, since so much of its output is exported, and so much of its expenditure is on imports. Furthermore, at least up to January 1972, direct import controls were unimportant, and import taxes were *ad valorem* rather than specific, so that the accounting prices of imported goods could be quite easily estimated. The accounting price of sugar, the main export, was more difficult, since it was sold in different markets at widely differing prices, whose future was hard to predict. The marginal price of sugar taken in the Plan[3] was used as the basis for the estimate. This price is of crucial importance to the economy of Mauritius, but it does not appreciably affect most of the other accounting ratios (i.e. the ratios of accounting prices to market prices) which were calculated. It does, however, for reasons discussed below, have an important indirect effect on shadow wage rates via its effects on the Government's budgetary position.

Apart from traded goods, estimates of accounting ratios for various non-traded goods and services, for skilled labour and for extra income accruing to companies were made, as well as an estimate of the accounting rate of interest (ARI). The estimates are not described here. Instead, we concentrate attention on the estimates of shadow wages, as these were made in a way which was novel at the time, and which may be of general interest.[4] It must be remembered, however,

---

[1] Author of Chapter 8.

[2] I should like to mention: in the public sector, the Bank of Mauritius, the Central Statistical Office, the Ministry of Commerce and Industry, the Customs & Excise, the Development Bank of Mauritius, the Development Works Corporation, the Economic Planning Unit, the Ministry of Finance, the Ministry of Labour, the Government Sack Factory, the Ministry of Town & Country Planning, the University of Mauritius and the Ministry of Works; in the private sector, the Chamber of Agriculture, the Chamber of Commerce & Industry, the Sugar Syndicate, and a number of private firms; outside the island, Professors James Meade and Ross Parish, the Overseas Development Administration of H.M.G., and the World Bank.

[3] Government of Mauritius, June 1971, p.121. (Referred to as 'Plan' in what follows).

[4] The method has been incorporated in Little and Mirrlees, 1974, p.238 *et seq.*

that the estimates of accounting prices were interdependent, and had to be made simultaneously. They took the author only about two months of full-time work (including the month spent in Mauritius). This shows that, at least in as favourable circumstances as those of Mauritius, it is not very costly to produce a rather comprehensive set of estimates of accounting prices. On the other hand, the estimates could undoubtedly be improved by those with more time and better local knowledge.

In what follows we first give estimates of unemployment and wage rates in Mauritius in January 1972, the date to which our estimates refer. We then explain our general formula for the shadow wage of a worker recruited from the ranks of the unemployed, and our estimate of the cost of his (or her) extra effort. The net cost of employing a previously unemployed man depended on his family circumstances, and we consider several typical cases and then strike an average, which is 40% of the actual wage for men and 50% for women. The assumptions underlying these best guesses are certainly open to question, but, after discussing the main ones, we conclude that it is unlikely that the Government of Mauritius would want to take a figure outside the range 25 to 55% for men, or 35 to 65% for women. An Appendix shows how our estimates allow for multiplier effects on employment, although our estimate of the multiplier is small (1·14).

2. UNEMPLOYMENT

According to the Plan, p.250, unemployment in 1969 was about 45,000, or nearly 20% of the active population. After 1969, the number of registered unemployed increased from an average of some 14,000 to a figure towards the end of 1971 of some 31,000. There was no one-to-one correspondence between changes in registered unemployed and changes in total numbers unemployed. However, it seemed likely that the total also rose, and we estimated it at 60,000, including those for whom relief work was provided, at the end of 1971. This total was subdivided as follows:

	Thousands
Relief workers	14
Outdoor relief	10
Other	36
	60

Relief workers were those workers who would otherwise have been unemployed, or only partly employed, and who were employed by the Government for four or five days a week. Their pay at the beginning of 1972 was Rs. 5·04 per day.[1] The work they did was apparently of very little value, and some allege that they were at times paid for doing no work at all. The system was being superseded by the *'Travail pour Tous'* Programme (T-P-T) in 1971–72, which provided full-time employment on socially productive work.

According to the Plan, p.249, 'ad-hoc payments, known as "outdoor relief", have for many years been made on a modest scale to people without other sources of income. There are on average 30,000 such persons receiving outdoor relief at any one time, 70% of them through being unable to work on account of sickness'. The system of outdoor relief had not changed substantially since 1960 when the Titmuss Report was written. According to this Report, p.80, 'To obtain assistance, many of the unemployed claimed relief on account of sickness'. In the above estimates we somewhat arbitrarily assumed that about half of those unable to work through sickness were not really sick, and we therefore included them amongst the unemployed.

3. WAGES FOR UNSKILLED WORKERS[2]

We estimated that the average male unskilled worker, when he found regular employment, and possibly after a few months at a lower rate, would earn about Rs. 7 per working day in early 1972. This estimate was based on statistics of wages, earnings and normal hours of work of typical occupations in selected industries in October 1970, and of average earnings of daily paid workers in industries with little or no female employees in March 1971, as provided by the Ministry of Labour. The earnings and rates were adjusted upwards by 12% to allow for increases made up to January 1972. For female unskilled workers, average earnings were estimated to be Rs. 3 per day.[3]

4. GENERAL FORMULA FOR THE SHADOW WAGE

In describing the method used, we take the case of an unskilled

---

[1]The exchange rate was Rs. 13·33 = £1 sterling.
[2]Our estimates referred to workers in commerce, transportation, construction, services and manufacturing, but not in agriculture.
[3]Ministry of Commerce and Industry, January 1972.

worker employed on a public sector project whose wages were, therefore, paid by the Mauritius Government. This simplifies the exposition, though the conclusions are the same whether we are estimating shadow wages for public or private sector projects. The method was essentially the same as that subsequently used to estimate shadow wages in Kenya,[1] although in Mauritius the calculation was simpler. We start by distinguishing four components of the shadow wage of a worker in occupation i drawn into occupation j by the offer of employment at a wage W_j:

(i)   the social cost of employing him had he been employed at the same wage and under the same conditions as in occupation i;

(ii)   the social cost of providing the resources needed to meet the extra expenditure resulting from any excess of W_j over W_i, and from any bidding up of W_j as a result of increased employment in j;

(iii) the social benefit accruing to the worker and to others resulting from any excess of W_j over W_i, from any difference in the conditions of work between i and j, and from any bidding up of W_j as a result of increased employment in j;

(iv) The 'external cost (or benefit)' of employing one more man in occupation j.

The total social cost, or shadow wage, is then

$$W_{ij}^* = \text{(i)} + \text{(ii)} - \text{(iii)} + \text{(iv)}.$$

Each of the four parts distinguished above must be expressed in terms of our numéraire, which is foreign exchange in the hands of the Government. We consider each in turn below.

We took the view that all unskilled workers could be considered as being drawn from the large pool of those unemployed (including relief workers and those on 'outdoor relief'), so (i) was always zero. We neglected the externalities mentioned in (iv). It seems likely that there were net benefits from employment of various kinds, but we were unable to estimate them. Somewhat inadequately, we attempted to offset the resulting error by underestimating two components of the costs, namely, the cost of wage payments which were saved, and the

---

[1]Scott, MacArthur and Newbery, 1976, Chapter 4.

cost of effort (both discussed below). Consequently, we needed estimates only for (ii) and (iii). As a further simplification, we assumed that the employment of extra unskilled workers did not lead to a bidding up of their wages, as seemed plausible given the very high level of unemployment.

The social cost of providing the extra resources, part (ii) above, was reached in three steps. First, we estimated the extra net money payment itself. This was equal to the wage, or (for relief workers or those on outdoor relief) to the wage minus the payments received from the Government whilst unemployed. Second, we subtracted savings out of this extra payment. We assumed, for simplicity's sake, that the marginal propensity to save, s, was the same for everyone, and that money paid out by the Government which flowed into personal savings was socially costless. Insofar as it took the form of permanent extra cash holdings, this was correct, but insofar as it took the form of interest-bearing loans to the Government or private sector, this understated the social cost. However, the error here was probably small. Third, the rest of the money paid out was multiplied by the accounting ratio for marginal consumption expenditures, c, so that the total resource cost in terms of the numéraire, (ii), was:

$$(1-s) \ c \ (\text{wage } less \text{ any Government payments when unemployed}).$$

The social benefit, (iii), may also be considered in three stages. First, there was the extra money received by the worker or his relatives. This was just the wage *less* any Government payments he received when unemployed. Second, there was the cost of the extra effort made by the worker, which had to be subtracted from his money receipts. Third, this net sum had to be expressed in terms of our numéraire. It is convenient to consider this third stage first.

If the Government had taken the view that the worker's increase in income was as valuable as the cost, to the Government, of providing the extra consumption on which it was spent, then (ignoring the extra effort involved) we would have had the value of item (iii) equal to and offsetting the cost of item (ii), and the shadow wage would have been zero. Government expenditure to increase workers' incomes would have been as good as any other kind of Government expenditure. However, other actions taken by the Government implied that it did *not* believe this. Perhaps the two most convincing examples were the following:

First, the ending of the system of relief work and its replacement by the Development Works Corporation and the T-P-T Programme in 1971. As we have seen, relief workers were paid for doing work of very low value. The Development Works Corporation had a different philosophy. Even if the work done was of less value than the wages paid (and this was not easy to prove) it was not of negligible value. The implicit labour subsidy was almost certainly much less than the wage.

Second, the system of outdoor relief. Under this, in January 1972, a single male adult who had no financial resources, and had a medical certificate to show that he was unable to work, was paid rather less than Rs. 17 per month (i.e. less than Rs. 1 per working day) plus half his rent (to a maximum of Rs. 12 a month). This was less than the minimum subsistence income estimated in the Darlow Report (about Rs. 30 a month at January 1972 prices, excluding rent and clothing), the assumption being that the recipient would somehow or other manage to get other help. Even if he did, and if his income reached subsistence level, the Government was apparently unwilling to supplement it beyond that level, and was therefore unlikely to be willing to supplement incomes at even higher levels.

Arguments which told the other way were that family allowances were paid to families whose incomes were less than Rs. 225 per month (about Rs. 10 per working day), and that income tax allowances for a married man with three children amounted to Rs. 9,000 a year, or Rs. 34 per working day. However, one could justify the payment of family allowances to people with higher incomes on the grounds that this preserved the incentive to earn more. Likewise, the exemption of higher paid workers from income tax could be justified on grounds of incentive, and also the need to keep down the administrative costs of tax collection and to make the tax acceptable.

It seems reasonably clear, then, that the Government did not regard marginal increases in workers' incomes, when they were earning as much as the average worker, as being as valuable as other forms of Government expenditure. On the other hand, it clearly did not regard them as valueless either. This was shown by the concern expressed in the Plan for increasing employment, by the probability of *some* implicit wage subsidy for T-P-T workers (though we were unable to calculate how much), and by the regulations for off-peak employment of sugar workers and dock workers. These regulations compelled employers to pay wages to workers in the slack season if those workers had been employed for a certain minimum amount in the busy season. The effect was to reduce the profits of the employers, and so to reduce the tax on those profits received by the Government. Hence the Government was implicitly losing revenue in order to increase the employment and wages of certain groups of workers, who were certainly earning more than minimum subsistence.

Thus it is likely that the Government valued marginal increases in workers' incomes as somewhere between the two limits we have considered: they were worth less than the same amount of foreign exchange, our numéraire, but more than zero.

There was, unfortunately, no agreed method of arriving at a valuation. The Government had certainly not made it explicitly, and we were told that nothing of the kind had been done in the Economic Planning Unit.[1] We could have avoided making it and, instead, have shown the effects of this or that alternative plan for the harbour on the incomes of different groups of people. However, not only would this have become extremely complicated (if, for example, one distinguished between people with many different income levels), but it would also have made it difficult to arrive at positive suggestions for project design, since one needed to be able to reject or accept alternatives in order to narrow down the choices to a manageable number. In principle, no doubt, this process of narrowing down could have been done in consultation with officials or members of the Government, but this was impracticable. Rightly or wrongly we therefore felt it necessary to make assumptions of our own about the way in which different increases in income were valued. We used these assumptions to arrive at our best guesses of shadow wages in Mauritius, and we used these best guesses, in turn, to arrive at our best guesses of accounting ratios for goods and services.

These best guesses, involving as they did an element of arbitrary judgement on our part, were open to question. Indeed, it must be recognized that decisions about shadow wages are, in the last resort, important matters of political judgement.[2] A wide variety of considerations is involved, including, for example, the seriousness of

---

[1] We were, indeed, told that for one project a zero shadow wage had been used, but, for the reasons given, we did not think that this could reasonably be held to reflect Government policy.

[2] The decisions are important only if taken seriously and followed through by the Government. If so, there are important implications, not only for project selection and design but also for fiscal policies used to encourage, for example, export processing industries.

the unemployment situation, the relative desirability of other forms of public expenditure (i.e. other than adding to workers' incomes directly), the political, economic and administrative problems of raising additional tax revenue and the costs of obtaining funds from abroad (or of investing less abroad). We return to some of these matters in Section 7, where we consider a range of estimates. First, however, we describe our best guesses.

There were two principal assumptions: first, that the Government was prepared to supplement incomes up to the level (hereafter referred to as the 'base level'[1]) of Rs. 6·50 per working day per household of three adults and 2·7 children (i.e. the average household); and, second, that the Government regarded increases in income beyond this level as of steadily diminishing value, the rate at which the value diminished being given by an elasticity (n) of marginal value (or utility) with respect to income of 1·5.

The first assumption derived some support from the Outdoor Relief scheme. We have already mentioned the Darlow Report.[2] This was the name given to an official inquiry in 1952 to ascertain the minimum sum upon which families could live. On the basis of this Report, and making adjustments for changes in prices from 1952 to January 1972, we estimated the minimum cost of living for the average household of three adults and 2·7 children at Rs. 150 a month including rent and clothing. Hence the expenditure per working day (assuming 22 working days a month) to cover this was Rs. 6·8. Our figure of Rs. 6·50 for *income* per working day then assumed that dissaving was Rs. 0·30 per working day at this level of income.[3]

Our second assumption of diminishing marginal value or utility was one which had a strong intuitive appeal, and was consistent with, for example, the Government's progressive tax on incomes. However, it must be admitted that the actual value chosen for the elasticity of marginal utility with respect to income, 1·5, cannot easily be defended.[4] We give the results of making different assumptions, and we doubt whether any reasonable assumptions would have made much difference to our conclusions. Nevertheless, it is not easy to be

---

[1]Little and Mirrlees, 1974, p.238.
[2]The First Report of the Outdoor Relief Committee (Darlow Report) quoted in R.M. Titmuss, 1968, p.77.
[3]See footnote 2 on p.141.
[4]See Scott, MacArthur and Newbery, 1976, chapter 3, for references which suggest that 1·5 is towards the lower end of the range of likely values, which has been put at 1 to 3 or 1 to 5.

sure just what a 'reasonable assumption' is in this context, and this is therefore one which could well be challenged.

There are some (weak) reasons for believing that the elasticity is greater than one. If it were one, then an $x\%$ increase in the income of a poor man would increase his utility by the same absolute amount as an $x\%$ increase in the income of a rich man. It seems more plausible to believe that, in this case, the utility of the poor man would increase by more than that of the rich man, which implies an elasticity greater than one. Moreover, if the elasticity were constant, and if one believed that there was an upper limit to the utility achievable through increases in income, then the elasticity would have to be greater than one. It must be admitted, however, that neither of these arguments is very compelling, especially if the elasticity is taken to represent the Government's valuation of income changes, as it is here.

Returning to our first assumption, we need to express the cost of supplementation in terms of our numéraire and to equate it with the benefit, measured in terms of utility. For this purpose we express all incomes and changes in incomes in terms of income per adult equivalent, and we introduce the following symbols. Let $[\Delta Y; Y]$ be an increase in income, measured at actual (not accounting) prices, of ΔY accruing to a family with income level Y. Now define $u[\Delta Y; Y]$ as that increase in income accruing marginally to families at base level income, Y_b, which has the same social value as $[\Delta Y; Y]$. Thus $u[1; Y_b] = 1$.

Now suppose that the Government pays out Rs.1 to a household at the base level of income Y_b. The consumption expenditure of the family, we assume, rises by $(1-s)$, and the cost in terms of the numéraire of this is $(1-s)c$. Consequently, since we have defined the base level of income as being that at which the social benefit of a marginal increment in income is equal to the social cost in terms of the numéraire, we can say that the value of a marginal rupee to a household with a base level of income is $(1-s)c$ in terms of the numéraire.[1] Hence, if a rise in income of ΔY accrues to households with incomes of Y, its value in terms of the numéraire is:

$$u[\Delta Y; Y] \ (1-s)c.$$

---

[1]Some may wonder what has become of the multiplier effects of increases in consumption expenditure. They are, however, implicitly allowed for in the definition of c as is explained in the Appendix.

In order to make further progress, we have to find a way of expressing increases in income, to whomsoever they accrue, in terms of equivalent increases to households at base level; that is, we have to find a way of calculating $u[\Delta Y; Y]$. This brings us back to our second assumption, that the marginal value or utility of income diminishes as incomes rise. We specify a utility function with a constant elasticity of marginal utility, n, and so arrive at the following results[1]:

$$(1) \qquad u[Y - Y_u; Y_u] = \left(\frac{Y_b}{1-n}\right)^n (Y^{1-n} - Y_u^{1-n}).$$

$$(2) \qquad u[1; Y_r] \qquad = \left(\frac{Y_b}{Y_r}\right)^n.$$

(1) shows how to value a *greater than marginal* increment in income which raises the recipient from an income of Y_u to one of Y. (2) shows how to value a *marginal* increment in income accruing to someone whose income is Y_r. These values are all per adult equivalent, so that to get the total benefit to a household we must multiply by the number of equivalent adults in it.[2] Furthermore, in each case, in order to express the result in terms of our numéraire we must multiply u by $(1 - s)c$ for the reason given above. It is clear from (1) and (2) that to evaluate the benefit, item (iii), we need to estimate not merely its total money value, which is the wage minus any Government payments when unemployed, but also its allocation between recipients with different income levels. This is done in Section 6. Before turning to that, we explain our estimate of the cost of effort, which must be subtracted from the money benefit.

5. THE COST OF EFFORT

Since our 'surplus' worker came from the ranks of the unemployed or marginally employed (e.g. relief workers), some extra effort, loss of leisure and cost of getting to and from work were involved. There is little doubt that hard physical work in the climate of Mauritius involved a real cost, and it would surely have been a mistake to have neglected this. Other types of work (e.g. driving a vehicle) must also

---

[1] See Scott, MacArthur and Newbery, 1976, Chapter 3, for a derivation.
[2] See footnote 1, p.141, for explanation of the derivation of adult equivalents.

have involved some cost, though less than hard physical work. Female work, e.g. in an office or factory, might be supposed to have involved less cost, though even here there was an undoubted loss to a home which dispensed with some of the services of a mother or daughter. It seems certain that there was some cost, then, but the problem was to put a value on it. In what follows, we first describe our estimates as originally made in 1972; we then reply to a criticism of them made by Professor Ross Parish.

According to information derived from the Ministry of Labour, the minimum daily wage rate for unskilled labourers in construction in October 1970 was Rs.4·20 per day. This should be increased by 12% to Rs. 4·70 to get the rate in January 1972. The minimum subsistence (i.e. base level income) for an adult male estimated in the Darlow Report was Rs.20 per month, without rent or clothing. Allowing for increases in prices since 1952, we put this at Rs.30 per month in January 1972, and at Rs.36 per month allowing something for rent and clothing, equivalent to Rs.1·60 per working day. We assumed that an unemployed labourer could, somehow or other, from relatives or the Government (through Outdoor Relief), scrape together this sum without actually working, and that he was prepared to accept work at Rs.4·70. We then argued that the cost of the extra effort, etc., involved was unlikely to be more than about Rs.3 per day. Expressing this in terms of income equivalent in value to marginal increases in base level income, it came to about Rs.1·33 per day.[1] We decided to take a figure of Rs.0·7 per day to allow for the likelihood that *some* net benefit accrued to the worker, and also because unskilled labourers on construction work probably incurred more effort than the average surplus worker we were considering. For female workers we took Rs.0·2 per day.

As Professor Parish pointed out to the author, the above reasoning assumes that the worker altogether ignores the benefit received by his family or other relatives who no longer have to pay him the Rs.1·60 per day of base level income. If he placed *some* value on it, the cost of effort, etc., could well be higher. This is a valid point, although difficult to allow for. We might reasonably suppose that the worker would attach less value to the Rs.1·60 the wealthier his relatives.

---

[1]That is, using formula (1) with $n = 1·5$, we have

$$\frac{1.6^{1.5}}{-0.5} \left[4.7^{-0.5} - 1.6^{-0.5} \right] = 1.33.$$

Later (p.143) we estimate that a marginal Rs.1 drawn at random from the incomes of all households included in the I.L.O. Family Budget Inquiry of 1961–62 (which excluded households whose head earned more than Rs.1,000 per month) would be worth Rs.0·26 in terms of our standard of marginal rupees given to base level households.[1] Consequently, we might add Rs.1·60 × 0·26 = Rs.0·4 to our estimate of the cost of effort on this account.

Professor Parish also argued that the wage-rate for casual labour, which one might suppose was freely determined by supply and demand, would give a reasonable measure of the supply price of effort. We had no estimate of this wage, but guessed that it might be about Rs.4 per day. Its value in terms of our standard depends, again, on who gets the benefit. If the casual labourer were drawn from the average household, the value of an extra Rs.4 per day to that household in terms of our standard may be put at Rs.1·1,[2] which is also somewhat higher than our original estimate of Rs.0·7, though not a great deal. The figure would be greater, however, if casual labourers tended to come more from poorer families, as is likely.

Our original estimate of the cost of effort is probably too low, though perhaps not very much too low. We have, however, not made any correction to the figures, partly because the error here may be offset by the neglect of significant externalities attaching to extra employment (see p.131), and partly because it did not seem worthwhile making small corrections to the figures at this stage.

6. SOME TYPICAL CASES

The income changes which occur when a worker finds employment depend on a whole variety of circumstances. Those considered were: the worker's sex, whether he or she was in casual employment beforehand, whether he or she was the head of a household, whether

---

[1] That is, $u[1; \bar{Y}_y] = 0.26$, where $\bar{Y}_y$ is the weighted average income per adult equivalent when the weights are household *incomes* (rather than households). See Table 5·1 (c).

[2] As explained on p.141, we take the average household for this purpose as having an average income for the whole household of Rs.13·1 per working day and 3·80 adult equivalents. Base level income for this size household is Rs.6·5 per working day, and we have

$$3.80 \; u \left[\frac{4}{3.80} \; ; \; \frac{13.1}{3.80} \right] = 1.1.$$

he or she was a relief worker, or in receipt of outdoor relief. These circumstances may be expressed schematically as follows:

	Male				*Female*	
	Casual	*Unemployed*			*Casual*	*Unemployed*
Head	x	x	x	x		
Not head	x	x		x	x	x

Relief worker / Outdoor relief / Other

It will be noted that some categories did not exist; for example, there were no female relief workers, and we assumed that outdoor relief, insofar as it went to members of the labour force, only went to males. We also assumed (as may not have been strictly the case) that no relief workers or recipients of outdoor relief were in casual employment. We did not consider all possible cases, but only those marked with a cross above. It is thought that they included the bulk of potential workers.

6.1 *Unemployed, not head of household*

Where the new worker was not the head of a household,[1] we assumed that he was drawn at random from all households,[1] but excluding those whose head earned more than about Rs.1,200 a month.[2] In order to value the resulting increase in income, we therefore needed to know the distribution of household incomes. Some information on the distribution of household *expenditure* in 1961–62 was available in the Report of the 1961–62 Family Budget Inquiry, p.29. However, in

---

[1]As households were not of equal size but grew (we assumed) as income per household rose, the effect of this assumption was to give a greater weight to poorer households than if we had used number of persons, instead of number of households, as weights. This seemed reasonable, partly because smaller households contained a higher proportion of adults, and partly because poorer households were likely to look harder for work.

[2]This upper limit chosen by the Family Budget Inquiry mentioned below was Rs.1,000 per month in 1961–62, which was roughly equivalent to Rs.1,200 per month at January 1972 prices. One would not expect 'surplus' workers to come from better-off households.

order to make it useful for our purpose, we had to add some 'guestimates' of our own. The Inquiry gave a frequency distribution of households by consumption expenditure, the mean expenditure and mean household size (and also the proportions of adults and children), but we had to estimate various other items. In particular, we assumed that household size grew with income, as data from other countries suggests, and we converted households to equivalent adults by using weights derived from the scale of Outdoor Relief Payments.[1] We also estimated households' savings which we added to the Survey figures of consumption to obtain household incomes.[2] Finally, by dividing income per adult equivalent for each income group by our estimate of base level income,[3] we obtained the frequency distribution of relative incomes shown in the first two columns of Table 5·1. The last three columns of that table show the value of marginal additions to incomes of different groups of households in terms of our standard of marginal increments to base level incomes, taking different values for *n*. Two sets of weighted averages of these are given: (b), weighted by households, is appropriate if the income in question is randomly distributed over *households;* (c), weighted by the *income* of households, is appropriate if the income in question is a random addition to household *incomes*. We made use of both of these averages.

In the case of the new worker who was not the head of a household, drawn at random from all households, the appropriate weighted average was (b), or 0·35 with $n = 1·5$. Since we assumed that he would not be a relief worker or in receipt of outdoor relief when unemployed, his household gained the whole wage of Rs.7 per day. To simplify matters, we assumed that he came from a household with an income of Rs.13·1 per day at January 1972 prices, and with 3·80 adult equivalents; that is, from a household with approximately double the base level income of Rs.6·5 per day, and with a *marginal* value of its income in terms of our standard of 0·35. Applying formula (1), the value of the Rs.7 gain in terms of our standard base level income

---

[1]See Titmuss, 1961, p.77. The average household of 3·07 adults and 2·69 children (i.e. under 15 years old) equalled 3·80 adult equivalents, successive adults in the household being given smaller weights.

[2]We assumed that at the base level of income, 5% of income was dissaved, and that 10% of all additions to income were saved. These estimates were based on Indian National Council of Applied Economic Research, June 1962, January 1965, July 1965 and June 1966.

[3]See p.135. We adjusted the estimate of Rs. 150 p.m. to Rs.125 p.m. to express it at the Inquiry's 1961–62 prices.

worked out at Rs.1·8. For a female worker, the value of a Rs.3 gain worked out at Rs.0·9.

Table 5·1   *Marginal Value of Additions to Incomes at Different Income Levels*

Households (%) (1)	Income per adult equiv. divided by base level income (2)	Marginal value of additions to income as proportion of marginal value of additions to base level income assuming		
		n = 1 (3)	n = 1·5 (4)	n = 2 (5)
5·8	1·67 (a)	0·599	0·463	0·359
29·0	1·53	0·654	0·528	0·427
26·1	1·99	0·503	0·356	0·253
15·2	2·53	0·395	0·249	0·156
8·3	2·92	0·343	0·200	0·117
5·8	3·38	0·296	0·161	0·088
3·8	3·95	0·253	0·127	0·064
2·4	4·48	0·223	0·105	0·050
1·5	4·98	0·201	0·090	0·040
0·7	5·44	0·184	0·079	0·034
1·4	6·29	0·159	0·063	0·025
100·0	2·60 (b)	0·483 (b)	0·347 (b)	0·254 (b)
		0·390 (c)	0·256 (c)	0·174 (c)

Notes: Cols. (3) to (5) were derived from col. (2) using formula (2).
(a) The reason why this figure is larger than the next below it is that we estimated that income *per adult equivalent* was greater in the 5·8% of households with the lowest *household* incomes than in the 29·0% with the next lowest because the average size of the households was smaller.
(b) The first line of means were obtained using col.(1) as weights.
(c) The second line of means were obtained using total household incomes as weights.

6.2   *Unemployed, head of household*
For heads of households who were unemployed and neither relief workers nor in receipt of outdoor relief, we had little information to go

on. We assumed that the household was of average size, with 3·07 adults and 2·69 children (i.e. under 15 years of age). If it spent the Darlow Report's minimum subsistence amount, which at January 1972 prices we estimated at Rs.150 per month or Rs.6·80 per working day, this expenditure might have been financed as follows:

	Rs. per working day
Family allowance*	0·50
Casual earnings of other family members†	5·00
Receipts from relatives	1·00
Dissaving‡	0·30
Total expenditure	6·80

*Family allowance was Rs.12 per month (Rs.0·55 per working day) for families not paying income tax with three or more children under 14.
†This might have included old age pensions, which were Rs.25 per month (Rs.1·14 per working day) to those 60 years old or over not paying income tax or earning more than Rs.225 per month.
‡Assumed to be roughly 5% of income. See footnote 2 on p.141.

Assuming that this represented the pre-employment situation, and that the household benefited by Rs.6 when the head of it became employed, and relatives benefited by Rs.1, we estimated the value of this benefit in terms of our standard at Rs.3·9, with $n = 1·5$. We assumed that the rupee per day from relatives came at random from the total *incomes* of all households included in the Survey. Its value was then about 0·26 of the value of our standard base level income.

For heads of households who were relief workers, or in receipt of outdoor relief, before becoming employed, we made similar assumptions, but allowed for the loss of Rs.5·04 per working day by the former and Rs.1·5 per working day by the latter. The benefits in terms of our standard worked out at Rs.0·9 and Rs.3·2 per working day respectively.

6.3 Casual workers

Given the high level of unemployment in Mauritius, it seemed reasonable to assume that if a casual worker were given regular employment his place would be taken by someone who had been unemployed, so that the former's shadow wage would be just the same as someone who was drawn directly from the ranks of the unemployed. We made this simplifying assumption, while recognizing that it ignored the (probably slight) effect on wage rates for casual labour. These would tend to be bid up, so that total casual employment would tend to fall. The resulting loss of output was neglected in our procedure, but there was an offsetting benefit in the transfer of income from employers of casual workers to the workers themselves which was also neglected.

This simplifying assumption just described only held strictly where the household circumstances of the casual worker who was given regular employment were the same as those of the unemployed person replacing him. We thought it unlikely that relief workers or those receiving outdoor relief would accept casual employment, and we assumed that all the rest of the unemployed were not heads of households.[1] Consequently, we only needed to consider the case of a casual worker who was a household head being replaced by someone who was not. In this case we assumed that the income of the household was Rs.9·5 per working day before regular employment (i.e. Rs.0·5 family allowance, the rest casual earnings), that this rose to Rs.12·5 after the head found regular employment, and that an extra Rs.4·0 of casual earnings accrued to someone drawn at random from all households. The total income gain was then Rs.7·0, and it was worth Rs.2·5 in terms of our standard.

7. CONCLUSION: SHADOW WAGES OF AVERAGE 'SURPLUS' WORKERS

The first three columns of Table 5·2 summarize the preceding discussion. Col. (4) shows the net cost of labour in different categories. Since we required an estimate of the cost of an *average* 'surplus' worker, we needed some average of the figures in col.(4). We started with estimates of the numbers in each category, given in

---

[1] This may seem an extreme assumption, but there is evidence from other countries that most unemployed men are young. For example, Government of India, 1966, found that some two-thirds of the unemployed males were unmarried. See also Turnham and Jaeger, 1971. We were told that the position was similar in Mauritius. Since we assumed that *all* relief workers and recipients of outdoor relief were heads of families, it seemed right to assume that none of the remaining male unemployed were. This simplified calculations and led to offsetting errors.

Table 5·2 Elements in the Shadow Wage Calculation

	Net payment (1)	Income gain in terms of standard base level income (2)	Cost of effort in terms of standard* base level income (3)	Net cost (1) − (2) + (3) (4)	Number of cases (thousands) (5)	(5) × (2) (6)	(5) × [(2) − (3)] (7)
						Rupees per working day (unless otherwise stated)	
Male workers							
1. Not head of household	7·0	1·8	0·7	5·9	14	25·2	15·4
2. Head of household, no grant	7·0	3·9	0·7	3·8	0	0·0	0·0
3. Ditto, relief worker	2·0	0·9	0·7	1·8	14	12·6	2·8
4. Ditto, outdoor relief	5·5	3·2	0·7	3·0	10	32·0	25·0
5. Ditto, casual replaced by not head of household	7·0	2·5	0·7	5·2	14	35·0	25·2
Average net cost†	··	··	··	3·9	4·1	4·3	4·4
Female workers							
6. Not head of household	3·0	0·9	0·2	2·3	··	··	··

Source: see text.

* The *utility* cost of effort is assumed to be the same for all categories of male workers because all, broadly speaking, make the same transition from unemployment to average unskilled employment.

† Col. (4) is an unweighted average. The rest are weighted averages of col. (4) using cols. (5), (6) or (7) as weights.

145

col.(5). Of the 60,000 unemployed mentioned on p.129, 14,000 were relief workers and 10,000 were in receipt of outdoor relief. We estimated that there were 8,000 unemployed women, and split the remaining 28,000 men arbitrarily in half between categories 1 and 5. We assumed, for the reason given in the preceding footnote, that there were no heads of households in category 2. Weighting by these numbers gave an average net cost of Rs.4·1 per working day. To allow for the probability that more workers would be recruited from those categories benefiting most from employment, we also calculated the weights shown in cols. (6) and (7). As our best guess, we took Rs.4·25 for the average 'surplus' male worker, and Rs.2·3 for the female.

These figures of net cost had to be multiplied by $(1-s)c$ to give shadow wages in terms of our numéraire. However, c, the accounting ratio for workers' marginal consumption expenditure, itself depended upon the shadow wage. We were able to express the marginal cost of consumption in terms of four components: foreign exchange, men's wages, women's wages and taxes. For foreign exchange the accounting ratio was one, and for taxes it was zero. We thus had simultaneous linear equations for men's and women's shadow wages which we solved to give the figures shown in Table 5·3.[1]

What were the different assumptions underlying these different estimates? The estimates of zero shadow wages assumed that the Government ignored the cost of extra effort and regarded a given increase in incomes accruing to families with different income levels

---

[1] Using the same notation as in the Appendix, with the addition of suffixes m and f for male and female wages, we have

$$c = f + w_m l_m + w_f l_f.$$

Also, $w_m = (1-s)c \cdot C_m/W_m,$

$\qquad w_f = (1-s)c \cdot C_f/W_f,$

where C is the average net cost and W is the market wage. These three equations contain three unknowns, c, w_m and w_f, for which they can be solved.
The resource cost element in the shadow wage for men, see p.132, is then $(1-s)c\, W_m$. The net benefit depends on to whom it accrues, but, assuming it all accrues to one worker with income, when unemployed, of Y_u, its social value (ignoring the cost of effort) is $(1-s)c\, u[W_m\;;\;Y_u]$; see p.137. Consequently the shadow wage, W_m^*, is

$$W_m^* = (1-s)c\,(W_m - u[W_m\;;\;Y_u]).$$

A similar equation can be derived for female workers. The figures in Tables 5·2 and 5·3 allow for the cost of effort and for different distributions of the net benefit as described in Section 6.

Table 5·3 Estimates of Shadow Wages for Average 'Surplus' Male and Female Workers

Value of n	Male		Female	
	Rs/day	% of market wage	Rs/day	% of market wage
0	0	0	0	0
1	2·4	35	1·3	43
1·5	2·9	41	1·6	52
2	3·4	48	1·8	60
∞	4·2	59	2·1	71

as being of equal value both to each other and to money in the Government's own hands. The estimate was then zero because we assumed that the average marginal 'surplus' worker came out of the ranks of the unemployed, whether directly or at one remove, so the cost to the Government was exactly offset by an equally valued benefit to the worker. This estimate seemed implausibly low, since the Government pursued various policies which implied that it did *not* regard equal increases in income to families with different income levels as being equally valuable. For example, it levied a progressive income tax, it gave outdoor relief only after a means test had been applied, and the Plan's main aim was to increase employment opportunities, which would tend to benefit the poorer members of society most.

Furthermore, this estimate ignored the fiscal problem. It was precisely because there were costs involved in increasing taxation further (political costs, economic distortion costs and administrative costs) that the Government could not 'afford' to behave as if shadow wages were zero. If it had done so, it would soon have found itself with greatly increased expenditure on wages or wage-subsidies, and so with the necessity of raising further taxation. Hence, although in one sense the opportunity cost of labour was zero, it was only in a very limited sense. On a wider view, the opportunity cost of labour included the cost of raising the extra taxation (or curtailing Government expenditure) to pay for employing it, and this was not zero.

The next three estimates therefore assumed that the Government placed a diminishing value on equal increases in income as the level of income of the recipient rose. The rate at which this value diminished was measured by n, and was faster the greater was n. Our best guess was that n was 1·5, but all three values given in Table 5·3 yielded estimates which were reasonably close together. It seemed rather unlikely, for the reasons given on p.136, that n was less than one, although one could not altogether rule this out.

Besides guessing the value of n, we had to guess at what point on the income scale the Government regarded marginal additions to income as being equally valuable to the cost (to it) of providing them. As discussed in Section 4, we assumed that this point was given by 'subsistence' income as estimated in the Darlow Report (i.e. our base level income), because the Government appeared to wish to supplement incomes up to this level through its Outdoor Relief Scheme. However, the Government could have taken a different view from the one we attributed to it. It might, for example, have taken the view that the unemployment problem was so acute that, at least over the next few years, it would place a higher value on increases in incomes to workers than we assumed. It could also be influenced by the high price of sugar and the favourable outlook for the balance of payments and the budget over the next few years. If it chose a lower shadow wage, strict consistency would, at first sight, require that it should *also* have been willing to supplement incomes to a higher level than 'subsistence'. For example, one can calculate that, if the Government had taken shadow wages for men at about 25% of market wages instead of about 40% (our best guess), then it should have raised the income level for supplementation from Rs.6·5 per day to about Rs. 8 per day. This may not appear to be much of an increase, but, in fact, it would have implied doubling the average outdoor relief payment, which we estimated at Rs.1·5 per day.

The final estimates in Table 5·3 assume that the Government altogether ignored the value of benefits accruing to workers as a result of obtaining employment. This was implausible in view of the objectives of the Plan. However, even so, shadow wages would still have been appreciably less than market wages for two reasons. First, the Government recovered tax on expenditures by workers, so that the cost of financing those expenditures, in terms of our numéraire of foreign exchange, was less than the market wage. Second, insofar as the workers who were employed would otherwise have received payments as relief workers, or by way of outdoor relief, the Government made an additional saving. For these reasons, and because we assumed that a Government which ignored the benefits to workers of extra employment would also ignore the cost in terms of extra effort, the last estimates in the table are not a great deal higher than our best guesses.

To sum up, we thought that the first and last estimates in Table 5·3 were implausible. In view of all the uncertainties, we took as best guesses 40% of market wages for male workers and 50% for female. A figure outside the range of 25% to 55% for men or 35% to 65% for women seemed unlikely. However, in the last resort the choice was and is a matter of political judgement by the Government of Mauritius, weighing up the factors mentioned above.

Two further points may be made by way of conclusion. First, the estimates given here refer to *average* 'surplus' labour and to January 1972. For higher paid workers the ratio of shadow to market wages was higher (e.g. for dock workers earning Rs.18 per day we put the ratio at 50% for the head of a family, and 60% for others). The Plan estimated that full employment would be reached by 1980. Were this to happen, shadow wages would rise and could eventually equal the ratio of 0·80 estimated for fully employed skilled workers. Second, we adopted throughout the standpoint of the Government of Mauritius, so far as we could. Had we adopted the standpoint of an aid donor, for example, we might have made different estimates of both the base level income and *n*. An advantage of the method described here is that it permits one rather easily to make adjustments of this kind and, we hope, focuses attention on the most important magnitudes.

APPENDIX

The Shadow Wage and the Multiplier

This Appendix shows that the formula in the text for the shadow wage takes account of multiplier effects. In order to simplify the exposition, we retain only the parts of the formula which are essential for the argument. Thus, let the fractions of marginal consumption expenditure going directly and indirectly on foreign exchange, surplus labour and taxes be respectively f, l and t, so that

$$f + l + t = 1.$$

Using Shadow Prices

Let the average wage of surplus labour be W,
the shadow wage be W^*
and the accounting ratio for surplus labour be w
so that

$$w = \frac{W^*}{W} .$$

Let the marginal propensity to save be s.

Let an increase in income of ΔY accruing to households with income Y, measured at actual prices, be equivalent in social value to an increment of $u [\Delta Y; Y]$ accruing marginally to households whose incomes are at base level. Then the formula used in the text for the shadow wage may be written (see footnote on p.146):

$$W^* = (1-s) \ (f+wl) \ (W - u[W; \ Y_u]),$$

where Y_u is the income of the average worker's household when the worker himself is unemployed, and c in the text $= f + wl$.

In this formula we have neglected Government grants, the cost of effort and changes in relatives' incomes. However, they do not affect the substance of the argument.

If we now divide through by W, write

$$\frac{u \ [W; \ Y_u]}{W} = u$$

and solve for w, we can rewrite the formula as

$$w = \frac{(1-s) \ f \ (1-u)}{1 - l \ (1-s) \ (1-u)}$$

We now show how the same formula can be derived using multiplier analysis. Consider an initial wage payment of W made to surplus labour. This leads to extra consumption of $(1-s) W$ in the first round. Of any unit increase in consumption, f consists of foreign exchange (or its equivalent), l of further expenditure on surplus labour and t of tax. Consequently, in the second round, incomes increase by $(1-s) Wl$, and consumption by $(1-s)$ times this amount. The total increase in incomes resulting from the initial wage payment of W is thus

150

$$W(1+(1-s)\,l+(1-s)^2 l^2+ \ldots) = \frac{W}{1-(1-s)\,l}$$

and the total increase in consumption is

$$W\,(1-s)\,(1+(1-s)\,l+(1-s)^2\,l^2+ \ldots) = \frac{W\,(1-s)}{1-(1-s)\,l}.$$

The foreign exchange cost of this increase in consumption is then

$$\frac{W\,(1-s)\,f}{1-(1-s)\,l}.$$

In order to find the shadow wage, we must subtract from this cost the social value of the increase in income, which we now proceed to work out.

Consider a marginal payment of one rupee made by the Government to a family at the base level. Following the argument in the text, the Government is assumed to regard the social cost of this as equalling the social benefit. The social cost, in terms of our numéraire of foreign exchange, is the foreign exchange equivalent cost of the total increase in consumption, after allowing for multiplier effects, that is

$$\frac{(1-s)\,f}{1-(1-s)\,l}.$$

The increase in incomes which it produces consists of two parts. There is, first, an increase of one rupee in incomes of families at base level. Second, there is the indirect increase in incomes of surplus workers' families resulting from the working of the multiplier. The total increase in incomes is therefore

$$1+\frac{l(1-s)}{1-(1-s)\,l}.$$

In order to express both parts in terms which are socially equivalent to marginal increases in incomes to families at base level, we must multiply the second part by u. Hence, the increase in incomes in these terms is

$$1+\frac{u\,l\,(1-s)}{1-(1-s)\,l}.$$

151

Using Shadow Prices

It follows that the social value (and cost) of a marginal unit increase in incomes to families at base level, expressed in terms of our numéraire, is

$$\left[\frac{(1-s)\ f}{1-(1-s)\ l}\right] \div \left[1+\frac{u\ l\ (1-s)}{1-(1-s)\ l}\right] = \frac{(1-s)\ f}{1-(1-s)\ l+u\ l\ (1-s)}.$$

Now the total increase in incomes resulting from the initial wage payment of W, expressed in terms equivalent to marginal increases in incomes to families at base level, is

$$\frac{W\ u}{1-(1-s)\ l}.$$

The social value of this, in terms of the numéraire, is thus

$$\frac{Wu\ (1-s)\ f}{(1-(1-s)\ l)\ (1-(1-s)\ l+ul\ (1-s))}.$$

The shadow wage is thus the cost of the total increase in consumption minus the value of the total increase in incomes, that is

$$W^* = \frac{W\ (1-s)\ f}{1-(1-s)\ l} - \frac{Wu(1-s)\ f}{(1-(1-s)\ l)\ (1-(1-s)\ l+ul(1-s))}.$$

Dividing through by W and simplifying the right-hand side we get precisely the same formula which we had before for w.

We estimated that $s=0.1$ and $l(=l_m+l_f)=0.14$. Hence the multiplier,

$$\frac{1}{1-(1-s)\ l} = \frac{1}{1-0.9\times0.14} = 1.14.$$

It must be stressed that this is a long-run multiplier, and assumes that the only spare resource is surplus labour. Output of tradeables does not increase, the increased demand being met by increased imports or reduced exports. Output of non-tradeables does increase but, in so far as this requires more tradeables, they are imported, or come from reduced exports. Insofar as it requires more skilled labour or land, these are diverted from other uses and so, ultimately, the demand for them is met from foreign sources.

152

LIST OF REFERENCES

A. *Government of Mauritius, Official Publications:*
Central Statistical Office, *Survey of Employment and Earnings in Large Establishments,* 25 March 1971.
First and Second Reports of the Outdoor Relief Committee (Darlow Report), 1952, 1953.
Four-Year Plan for Social and Economic Development 1971-75, Vol.1, General Analysis and Policies, June 1971.
Ministry of Commerce and Industry, *Investors' Guide,* January 1972.

B. *Other:*
Government of India, Cabinet Secretariat, *National Sample Survey 16th Round, July 1960–June 1961, No. 103,* Delhi, 1966.
Indian National Council of Applied Economic Research, *Urban Income and Saving,* New Delhi, June 1962.
Ditto, *All–India Rural Household Survey 1962: New Insights into the Propensity to Save in India,* New Delhi, January 1965.
Ditto, *Saving in India 1950–1 to 1961–2,* New Delhi, July 1965.
Ditto, *Saving in India During the Plan Periods,* New Delhi, June 1966.
International Labour Office, *Report to the Government of Mauritius on the 1961–62 Family Budget Inquiry and the New Consumer Price Index,* Geneva, 1963.
Little, I.M.D., and Mirrlees, J. A., *Project Appraisal and Planning for Developing Countries,* London, 1974.
Scott, M. FG., MacArthur, J. D., and Newbery, D. M. G., *Project Appraisal in Practice: the Little-Mirrlees Method Applied in Kenya,* London, 1976.
Titmuss, R. M., *Social Policies and Population Growth in Mauritius,* London, 1961, (also published as Sessional Paper No. 6 of 1960 for the Government of Mauritius).
Turnham, D., and Jaeger, I., *The Employment Problem in Less Developed Countries,* Paris, 1971.

CHAPTER SIX

The Social Value of Private Investment in Kenya

D. M. G. Newbery

1. INTRODUCTION

Kenya, like many developing countries, has a high proportion of production and investment in the private sector. Social cost–benefit analysis (SCBA) was developed in the first instance to evaluate public sector projects, and this natural focus has meant in most cases that the existence of the private sector was, if not ignored, at least not emphasized. Thus, in the first edition of the Little–Mirrlees *Manual* (Little and Mirrlees, 1968) the Appendix for Professional Economists which succinctly summarizes the theory of industrial SCBA begins by assuming that all production is public, and only spends two pages (pp. 264–66) discussing the additional complications raised by the existence of the private sector. The U.N.I.D.O. *Guidelines* (U.N.I.D.O., 1972) develops a method for the valuation of investment on the assumption that the project is in the public sector and devotes a short section (§14·7, pp. 181–84) to the modifications needed if the project is in the private sector. The conclusion of the section is that given the difficulty of estimating the various parameters in the formulae with any accuracy one . may as well assume that public and private investment are equally socially valuable, which permits the use of a single shadow price for investment (p. 184).

It is clear, however, that in a mixed economy the valuation of

Acknowledgements
Field work for the study was undertaken in Kenya during March–April 1973 and supported by the Nuffield College Research Project on Cost–Benefit Analysis for Developing Countries, itself supported by grants from the Leverhulme Foundation and O.D.A. I have derived enormous benefit from the discussions with Maurice Scott and other members of the Nuffield Project, and I have relied heavily on data collected by other research workers often for quite different purposes. I am particularly indebted to Nicholas Snowden, Barry Wasow and the Chief Statistician, S. Heyer, but other debts will be evident from the references. The interpretation of the evidence is, however, entirely my responsibility.

private investment, of profits, and the social rate of return on private projects will all be important. If public projects purchase inputs from the private sector or sell output to that sector it will in general affect the level of profits in the private sector, and the valuation of these profits will thus enter into the accounting price of the input or output. This is particularly noticeable in Hughes' evaluation of low cost housing in Chapter 3 of this volume, since a significant proportion of the price of housing is the profit element paid to landlords. The shadow wage of urban workers will in turn be significantly affected by the cost of housing, since 27% of marginal urban expenditure by Nairobi lower-income workers is on rent. (Scott, MacArthur and Newbery, 1976,—hereafter SMN—Chapter 8.) Even if there is no change in private profits when the public sector buys a privately produced good, it will still be paying interest and depreciation on the privately owned capital, whose social and private costs may differ and therefore need to be calculated.

In addition the Government may need to decide whether to licence a private sector project, to encourage it with tax concessions or loans or to enter into partnership. In such cases it should estimate the social cost of allowing or encouraging private funds to be used in these various ways. More generally the banking sector will permit a partial transfer of funds between the sectors, the direction and extent of which should presumably be guided by the social valuation of the transfer. Finally, the planning office is likely to be interested in the rate of profit in the private sector (calculated at accounting prices) as an indicator of the appropriate level for the accounting rate of interest (ARI). Inevitably, then, SCBA will need to look at the valuation of private investment.

We have seen that planners will need to value private profits, private investment, private finance and indirect capital inputs such as interest and depreciation. These are closely inter-related, and the relation between them is discussed in Sections 4 and 5 below. It is convenient to calculate as the basic private sector accounting price the accounting ratio for private investment (ARPI),[1] but for exposition it is often easier to discuss the effects of a transfer of £1 to the private company as the first step in a chain which will lead to such socially valuable consequences as investment and tax payments. In the following sections we shall concentrate on the valuation of this transfer.

---

[1] See footnote 1, p.156.

1.1 *Why the valuation of private profits is particularly difficult*

Suppose some action leads to an increase in the profit received by a particular private enterprise (perhaps an increase in demand for its output at a price above marginal cost). The planner wishes to calculate the net social cost of this extra profit on a basis consistent with the remaining accounting ratios[1] (AR's). The theoretical solution to the problem is clear if we accept the utilitarian framework of Little and Mirrlees, which starts with a specification of the objective sensitive only to the level and distribution of consumption.[1] We ask what is the difference between the evolution of the economy when the firm receives this extra profit, and when it does not? Part of the extra profit will be distributed to the owners of the firm and consumed, the rest will be retained to finance increased investment, which in turn will increase employment, and allow profits to grow through time as the process of reinvestment continues. If we compare the evolution of the economy with and without the initial profit, we will observe the paths of profits and employment diverging as the cumulative process of accumulation out of the initial profit continues. The difference between the two paths consists of a stream of costs and benefits, and the social cost of the initial profit is the present value of the costs less the benefits. The costs in any year will be the cost at accounting prices of the extra resources used—the consumption of the dividend recipients, the investment goods purchased and installed, the labour employed and the material inputs purchased for processing in the new plant. The benefits will be the value at accounting prices of the goods produced by the new plant. If we have costed the labour employed at the shadow wage rate then the employment benefits will have been netted out of the input costs, otherwise the benefits from consumption would have to be added to the value of the extra output. Benefits and costs are then discounted at the accounting rate of interest (ARI).

The problem of shadow pricing profits is that the net present discounted value of the stream of costs and benefits flowing from the initial profit will depend quite sensitively on the time pattern of profits

---

[1] The accounting ratio is the ratio of the accounting price to the market price, and the most convenient way of describing accounting prices. A glossary of abbreviations is given at the end of the chapter.

[2] Specifically, the objective is to maximize the present value of the total utility of consumption of individuals imputed by the planner (Little and Mirrlees, 1974, §14.51). Alternative objectives will in general give equally clear but different solutions.

and reinvestment generated. These future profits are peculiarly difficult to predict, and the question is whether the prediction will give a net present value which lies within an operationally narrow confidence interval. Other accounting prices do not face such serious difficulties, as we can see by contrasting the valuation of profits with estimating the shadow wage rate (SWR). The method of estimating the latter is set out in Chapter 14 of *Project Appraisal and Planning* and illustrated empirically for Kenya in SMN Chapter 4: one has to calculate the extra cost to the country at accounting prices (APs) of employing one extra man, less the benefit of any resulting increases in consumption. The first part of the calculation requires a set of relevant APs and a quantified description of the impact on the economy of employing the man (output falls where he was employed, wages or the probability of being employed in various neighbouring occupations change, different consumption goods are consumed in different places, etc.). The second part requires an estimate of the value of current consumption in terms of foregone investment, which could yield future consumption, and thus will depend on the expected future evolution of the economy. Neither part of the calculation can be quantified with great precision, but taken as a whole the various uncertainties tend to cancel out so that the confidence range for the SWR is quite narrow. Moreover, at least for industrial projects, quite a large range of alternative values for the SWR will make very little difference to the ranking of projects, since the wage costs are usually a small part of total costs (Little, Scitovsky and Scott, 1970, p.45). In contrast, it appears that for private profits the range of plausible values will be quite large, and, more importantly, almost equally plausible values may suggest quite different rankings of projects.

The reason for this uncertainty about the accounting ratio for profits is that it is difficult to predict how the company will allocate its profits between investment and distribution. What features of corporate investment decisions make them peculiarly difficult to predict? One of the most powerful methods of constructing economic theories is to assume that the agent whose behaviour we wish to predict or explain is maximizing *objectives* subject to some *constraints*, which will enable a relationship to be deduced between what we want to predict and a set of observations.[1] Our difficulty is (i) that there is little consensus as to what are plausible objectives for firms or

---

[1] The technique is most succintly described in Samuelson's Nobel Speech, (Samuelson, 1972, p.2).

capitalists (profits, growth, size, optimal intertemporal consumption of the owners, or what?); (ii) that it is difficult to describe or formalize the constraints facing firms (or believed by the firms to confront them), particularly those limiting access to finance, constraining the structure of finance (gearing, liquidity), limiting price rises (which generate profits for finance), and restricting entry into new markets (which would affect the rate of expansion); and, finally, (iii) that it is frequently difficult to observe the relevant data (the *marginal* as opposed to the average rate of profit, *expected* as opposed to experienced outcomes, the elasticity of demand as opposed to the price, etc.).

Some examples will help to clarify the theoretical problem. Suppose that the firm has reasonable freedom of access to the capital market, which is reasonably competitive. On the face of it this is a favourable set of assumptions for a neoclassical prediction. Consider an increase in current profit. If this is viewed as temporary it will not affect any investment plans in the first instance, since these will have been chosen in the light of the cost of finance and the market opportunities, neither of which has yet changed. On the other hand if the extra profits are thought likely to continue then expectations and hence plans will be revised with presumably increased investment by the firm. In either case part of the extra profits will be saved, part consumed or, more precisely, the pattern of consumption and savings through time will be affected. Now the Government is presumably far from indifferent between capitalist consumption (which has very low value in increasing social welfare) and savings (which permits investment that generates valuable tax receipts and employment), and is therefore very interested in the magnitude and time profile of savings. The firm, with access to the capital market, is, however, on its optimal savings plan and is indifferent between small changes in savings or consumption, so that there is no compelling reason for it to adopt any one particular plan of saving out of the extra profits. The situation is very similar to the permanent income theory of consumption which makes it difficult to predict the immediate change in consumption for a given change in income.[1]

---

[1] There are circumstances under which it will not matter what savings plan is adopted—if taxes on consumption and those generated by investment are equal, and if the firm discounts the future at the same rate as the Government. But it is not clear either that such tax structures are approximated in practice, or that they should be. (The problem of the optimal corporation tax is fraught with the same theoretical difficulties as the valuation of these profits.)

Even if we could predict the change in savings the problem is not over. If the firm's savings increase in a competitive financial market, the rate of interest will fall, leading to increased investment and perhaps increased consumption elsewhere. The problem here is that the new equilibrium with a lower rate of interest is one with a higher *stock* of capital, whereas what is observed is changes in the *flow* of investment. Theories, such as those described in Harberger, 1972, Chapter 4, MacDougall in his classic investigation of the costs and benefits of foreign private investment (MacDougall, 1960), or the full equilibrium two-period analysis of Sandmo and Drèze (1971), which calculate the impact of extra saving on the capital market in terms of the interest elasticity of demand for *investment,* are inadvertently focusing on the adjustment costs and lags which prevent the instantaneous adjustment of capital *stock,* and as such are likely to give very imprecise or unreliable predictions of the total impact—the history of attempts to fit satisfactory investment functions teaches us that tight estimates of the underlying lag structure are all but impossible.

If we are prepared to abandon the assumption of a competitive capital market some of these difficulties can be avoided, but new ones are created. Of course, capital markets in most underdeveloped countries are highly imperfect, and in any case the whole nature of transactions in the market, characterized as they are by incomplete and asymmetric information, moral hazard and the absence of all but a few insurance markets, leads one to doubt whether there could be an adequate approximation to perfect competition. Kenya is unique in newly independent African countries in having a stock exchange, but its scope is narrow and its share prices probably reflect exchange control and the closely controlled credit market rather than the return to investment at the margin. Interest rates are pegged, there are restrictions on the availability of bank credit and access to the market is limited with a few exceptions to large (by Kenyan standards) reasonably efficient enterprises.

The most obvious consequence of capital market imperfections, which are not peculiar to LDCs, is the need felt by established enterprises to finance long term investment by retained profits. It would obviously simplify our problem considerably if we could assume that on average firms would expect to retain a fairly constant fraction of after tax profits, and similarly to invest a constant fraction. This would be rational behaviour for a firm under quite plausible assumptions. The ability of a firm to raise equity from time to time will be greater if potential shareholders can be assured of a stable relationship between profits or assets and dividends (taking one year with another). If the shareholders could predict with certainty the future profits of the company it would be unnecessary to adopt a stable dividend policy, but in the absence of this certainty, and given the moral hazard tempting a management prepared to exploit its less well informed shareholders, a strong convention of financial behaviour is likely to emerge. Many of the recent theories of the firm concentrate on the likelihood that the firm will evolve rules of thumb rather than continuously optimize, either because of the difficulty of handling internal organizational problem and information flows—a limited capacity to handle complicated data and decisions—or because of the need to communicate with external agents, such as stock holders or other competitors (see Cyert and March, 1963, or Cyert and George, 1969). For purposes of prediction these rules of thumb are much easier to observe and discover than the alternative of discovering the objectives and constraints.

However, the absence of a market in which rates of return can be arbitraged and savings channelled to the most profitable investment implies that the investment market will be fragmented, with no guarantee that the same rules of behaviour will be adopted by all companies. This in turn implies that different companies (or groups, characterized by common features such as size, location and type of ownership, product market, etc.) will have different accounting prices for profits. One will no longer be able to talk of 'the' ARPI, except with the same degree of approximation as 'the' standard conversion factor or 'the' shadow exchange rate. Worse, whilst conversion factors may have quite a narrow spread (see SMN, Table 10.1 for the range of values of ARs for Kenya) if the structure of protection is reasonably uniform, there is no similar simple assumption that will make behavioural rules closely similar between differently placed firms.

Finally, no matter what the nature of the capital market, there is one problem which is almost bound to arise. A large part of the benefits of private investment will be generated in the future as profits are reinvested. The present value of a stream of social benefits growing as a result of reinvesting profits will depend on the difference between the ARI and the rate of growth. In the simplest case let T be initial social benefits, r the pre-tax rate of profit, which remains constant with the rate of reinvestment out of pre-tax profits, s. The present value of the social benefits generated will then be

$$V = \frac{T}{R - sr},$$

where R is the ARI. The problem is that neither R, s nor r will be known with great precision, and that it is quite likely for sr (the rate of growth of the firm's assets) to be a substantial fraction of R, making the present value very sensitive to small errors in the estimates of r, s and R.[1] This problem is an aspect of the more fundamental difficulty of choosing between private and public capital formation as the best method of development. At a rather simple level of analysis, the argument in favour of private capitalist development is that it is relatively efficient at discovering and exploiting profitable investments, and that it has a high rate of saving in the early fast-growing phases of industrialization (both Keynes and Marx would probably assent to this), whilst the argument in favour of state enterprise is that it ought to be able to save a higher proportion of profits, since it can dispense with superfluous capitalist consumption. Crudely, then, the choice would turn on the relative rates of reinvestment, [2] which might be very close (higher state savings offset by lower rates of profit). Of course, the problem is not just to choose the type of ownership with the higher rate of reinvestment, but to choose a set of fiscal and monetary instruments which yields the highest rate of social profit. Only if, with all these policies, one unit of private investment is sacrificed at the margin for each unit of public investment will the choice be quite so simple.[3] However, in our case

---

[1] Indeed, if $R < sr$, the formula says that the private sector will generate more than infinite benefits if all the parameters remain unchanged through time. If this is not thought to be true, then the value for the ARI R will have to be changed, or the assumption about reinvestment altered. The alternative of changing R is discussed in Section 2.1, below.

[2] More generally, we are interested in the amount of surplus generated, since the Government may choose to distribute part of the surplus as current consumption benefits, rather than maximizing the rate of growth. The argument is essentially unchanged as in both cases a rate of tax on profits can be set to pay for any current distribution.

[3] Quite apart from all the other dimensions of choice, private enterprise may be better at innovation broadly defined (von Weizsäcker, 1973, Schumpeter, 1954), but will incur monopolistic waste of varying kinds. It may lead to a more flexible but less controllable economy. It may lead to paying higher net of tax wages to some categories than seems socially equitable. In contrast with extensive state enterprise, it may lead to a more diffused power structure which is felt to be less threatening to individual freedom (Popper, 1962, Ch. 9).

where the prime aim is to *value* private profits (and not so much to select policies to maximize total social profit) the relative rates of reinvestment are an important component of the relative values of private and public profits (which, since the latter is taken as numéraire, is equivalent to valuing private profits).

Of course, in some countries the issue may be quite clear cut. It may be that the private sector has been very unsuccessful at reinvesting, or that its investment yields little social benefit, or both—such seems to have been the case in Pakistan (Khan, 1972). In such a case the social cost of private investment (ARPI) is high, at least given the fiscal and monetary policies in force, and the estimate of $R - sr$ can be made with a lower *proportional* error, probably resulting in a more precise estimate of the social value of private profit. Even here, though, had the Government pursued rational policies the social value of private profits may have been far higher, and correspondingly difficult to measure precisely.

2. THE PROPOSED METHOD OF VALUING PROFITS[1]

The previous section concluded that there was unlikely to be a *general,* operational (i.e. quantifiable) method of calculating the accounting prices of private investment and profits, but that the calculations would probably have to be for rather specific categories of investment, and would depend a lot on the institutional environment and particular circumstances of each country. With this in mind it was decided to attempt the calculations for Kenya—a country with a sizeable and dynamic private sector, a Government favourably inclined to private (and foreign) investment and one familiar to the author and for which a comprehensive set of ARs already existed (SMN, Part I). The object was not to calculate private sector ARs in great detail, but rather to identify the quantifiably significant parameters, to see what kind of data were reasonably accessible, how reliable they were and, generally, to explore the possibilities of making useful estimates.

The author visited Nairobi for four weeks in March–April 1973. The main task was to see how far the available published statistics and research material could be used in the calculations. In such a

---

[1] Chapter 11 of Little and Mirrlees, 1974, deals with the general principles involved in calculating the ARPI, and should be consulted. The present model explicitly includes the institutional features of the Kenyan economy.

limited time it was impracticable to attempt to augment this statistical data by any systematic field work and it seemed more sensible when visiting businessmen to concentrate on those aspects of the environment in which they operated, which it would be difficult to identify from numerical data—mainly what criteria they used in deciding to invest, what considerations and constraints were important and how the fiscal system encouraged or discouraged investment, repatriation of profits (where foreign owned), and so on. These interviews confirmed the view that private investment in Kenya is heterogeneous, that the objectives and behaviour of different groups are different and that it may be a bad assumption that firms are approximately in long-run steady growth equilibrium. All this confirms the importance of making distinctions between different kinds of investment and collecting appropriate data. Unfortunately, the available data are mostly not broken down into the appropriate categories, so the calculations that follow should be treated as illustrative, or as an average of the different categories. The rather impressionistic evidence for different ARs is given at the end.

We want to build a simple model of a firm which will enable us to ask what consequences follow when it receives an increase in profits. The simplest consistent model of a firm which invests and grows is one which is in steady growth, saving a constant fraction of its profits, earning a steady rate of return, maintaining a constant ratio of stocks to output and a constant financial structure, with the ratio of equity to debt constant. For such a company we ask, what is the net cost to the Government of a transfer of £1 to pre-tax profits? Some fraction t accrues to the Government as *direct* taxes on profits and dividends, a fraction s is saved as retained profits *and* as net lending by shareholders to this company (or similar companies)[1], and the remaining fraction c is consumed, where

$$c + s + t = 1. \qquad (6.1)$$

The extra savings imply an increase in the equity value of the company and allow it to borrow from the banking system whilst preserving its desired gearing. In most cases this means that the company borrows a fraction b of gross investment at short term directly or indirectly from the banking system which is closely related

---

[1] Note that s is a fraction of *before*-tax profits, and that t will in general depend on the fraction retained. These assumptions are made for notational simplicity, and to be consistent with the earlier model published as Chapter 6 of SMN.

to its short-term assets, particularly stocks. In a highly interesting analysis of Kenya's reserve crisis of 1971, King (1973) provides strong evidence to support two hypotheses—that increases in stock building are matched by equal increases in bank lending, which, unless matched by a decrease in Government borrowing, lead to a fall in foreign exchange reserves. The net effect is thus to transfer funds from the Government to the private sector to finance this fraction b at a rate of interest i. The Government also transfers funds by giving an investment deduction from profits tax on specified categories of fixed investment. Suppose that on an investment of amount k a fraction q is eligible for a deduction of proportion a from tax which would have been payable at rate t_1.[1] The extra funds available for investment as a result of borrowing and reduced tax liability is then $bk + kqa\,t_1$ so that the extra investment k permitted by savings s is

$$k(1-b-qat_1)=s \qquad (6.2)$$

$$\text{or} \quad k=ms$$

$$\text{when} \quad m=\frac{1}{1-b-qat_1}. \qquad (6.2a)$$

If the rate of profit net of depreciation but before tax is r, and if we assume for the moment that 'true' depreciation and depreciation for tax purposes coincide,[2] the extra investment will generate a stream of profits rk, of which $(r-ib)k$ is left after interest payments. Of these a fraction s will be saved and ms reinvested, so that in long-run growth equilibrium capital stock will grow at rate g, where

$$g=ms(r-ib). \qquad (6.3)$$

We have now calculated one of the most important parameters, for on the assumption that the company is growing steadily, g will be the rate of growth of both the costs and benefits generated by the initial transfer.

---

[1] Capital expenditure in industry is eligible if it is 'on construction of industrial buildings and the installation therein where the trade consists in the *manufacture* of goods or materials or subjection of goods or materials of local origin to any process; or on new machinery (excluding replacements) installed in an existing building used for that trade; or on new hotel buildings or extensions thereto and on machinery installed therein' (E.A. Income Tax Dept. 1972). The deduction is 20% ($a=0{\cdot}2$) on a profits tax rate of 40% ($t_1=0{\cdot}4$). t_1 is not the same as t, which includes taxes on dividends.

[2] If depreciation allowances exceed true depreciation (which will be true in Kenya for the low rates of inflation experienced up to 1971) the difference can be considered as a further deduction from profits tax liability to be added to the investment deduction.

The capital stock k will produce rk profits at market prices, or rkf_p at accounting prices, where f_p is the ratio of profit at accounting prices (output less inputs including labour but not including net profit and interest) to profit (similarly defined) at market prices. Of this profit $(r-ib)k$ is attributable to shareholders, who will consume $c(r-ib)k$, and the social cost of this use of resources will be $c(r-ib)kf_c$, where f_c is the AR for capitalist consumption. The remaining profits will be retained and generate physical investment gk if the company continues to grow steadily at rate g. The social cost of the resources used in investment is gkf_k, where f_k is the AR for capital goods. The net social benefit, B, produced in one year by k units of capital is then

$$B = rkf_p - ck(r-ib)f_c - gkf_k. \qquad (6.4)$$

Since B grows steadily at g, the net present value of the resulting stream of benefits is $B/(R-g)$, where R is the rate of discount, or accounting rate of interest (ARI).

We now go back to the initial transfer of £1, which in the first year resulted in the use of resources whose social cost was $cf_c + kf_k$, but thereafter generated benefits, growing at rate g, whose value in the first year was B. The net social cost of the £1 transfer, discounting at the ARI R, will be given the symbol λ_p (which is equivalent to primary input P4 in SMN Chapter 6) and termed the accounting ratio for capitalists' (or companies') extra income.

$$\lambda_p = cf_c + kf_k - \frac{B}{R-g}. \qquad (6.5)$$

After substituting for B from equation (6·4) and rearranging this gives

$$\lambda_p = \frac{R(cf_c + kf_k) - rkf_p}{R-g}. \qquad (6.5\,a)$$

In addition to the accounting ratio for private profits, λ_p, there are a number of other accounting ratios which will also be useful for project appraisal. In particular, we will want to be able to calculate the social rate of return on private investment, both to decide whether to allow a proposed private project to go ahead, and to help estimate a suitable ARI. To that end we start by calculating the accounting ratio of private investment (ARPI) which we will give the symbol λ. This will be the cost of £1 spent on capital goods, f_k, less the benefit generated per £1 of investment:

$$\lambda = f_k - \frac{B}{k(R-g)}. \tag{6.6}$$

After some manipulation this gives

$$\lambda = \frac{\lambda_p - cf_c}{k}$$

or

$$\lambda = \frac{Rf_k + c(r-ib)f_c - rf_p}{R-g}. \tag{6.6a}$$

Similarly, since each unit of saving leads to m units of investment, the accounting ratio for private saving is

$$f_s = m\lambda = \frac{m}{k}\left[\lambda_p - cf_c\right].$$

But $k = ms$ from equation (6.2a), so f_s is given by

$$f_s = \frac{\lambda_p - cf_c}{s}. \tag{6.7}$$

This can also be written

$$\lambda_p = sf_s + cf_c ,$$

showing that the social cost of profits is equal to the sum of the social costs of the fractions saved and consumed.

The next step in calculating the social return to private investment is to find the social value of £1 of net private profit before tax. To convert profits at market prices to profits at APs we multiply by the appropriate AR f_p. The *net* social value will be the profit at APs *less* the social cost of the profits attributable to equity. The fraction of profits attributable to equity is $(r - ib)/r$, and their social cost per unit is λ_p. Call the ratio of the social value of net profit to its value at market prices f_n, then this will be

$$f_n = f_p - \left(\frac{r-ib}{r}\right)\lambda_p \tag{6.8}$$

With the help of equations (6.4) and (6.5a) this can be written:

166

$$f_n = \frac{R}{R-g}\left(f_p - \left(\frac{r-ib}{r}\right)(cf_c + kf_k)\right)$$ (6.8a)

$$= \frac{RB}{kr(R-g)}.$$ (6.8b)

The accounting ratio for private saving is also useful in calculating that for private finance, the latter appearing as a credit or benefit for most projects. If the finance for a private sector project under review is provided by capitalists who would otherwise have invested all of it in typical projects, then the AR of finance, f_f, is the same as the cost of private savings, f_s. Suppose the market net return to this project is r then the social rate of return (which we want to compare with the ARI, the return to the marginal public sector project) is the net social profit per unit of net social cost of capital. £1 of capital at market prices yields rf_n net social profit and costs $f_k - f_f/m$, where the second term is the AR of finance per unit of capital invested, which is supplied by the private sector and is thus a credit. Then the social rate of return is

$$r_s = \frac{rf_n}{f_k - f_f/m.}$$ (6.9)

In this case with $f_f = f_s$, $f_s/m = \lambda$, the AR of private capital.

But from equation (6.6)

$$f_k - \lambda = \frac{B}{k(R-g)}$$

and f_n can be substituted from equation (6.8b) to give

$$r_s = R,$$ (6.10)

which confirms the intuitively evident proposition that other things being equal (in this case, the accounting ratios f_n, f_k, so that social profit is correlated with private profit) the Government will not want to replace a more profitable private project by a less profitable one. More precisely, private investment by companies which is switched from similar investment elsewhere in Kenya (same accounting ratios, same return) has a zero net present social value discounted at the ARI—it confers no additional social benefits.

If, on the other hand, the finance for investment would otherwise have been consumed by domestic consumers, its AR is f_c which will in general be larger than f_s, so that r_s will exceed R. Similarly, *new* capital from abroad, whose AR is 1 (since it is convertible foreign exchange)[1] is likely to lead to an even greater social return. (In fact, if m were near 1 it might lead to a negative value for r_s, which is to be interpreted in this case as 'less than costless'.)

2.1 *The accounting rate of interest*

The previous discussion assumed that we already knew the value of the ARI, R, and in a country where the Government is systematically engaged in project appraisal there should be no ambiguity about its value, for it is the return to the least profitable use of the Government's funds. At the time of writing the Kenya Government was not systematically appraising projects, and had not therefore discovered the appropriate ARI. Previous studies of accounting prices in Kenya were therefore forced to make an estimate for R, and most of them have used a value of 10%, which Scott derived after examining such evidence as the cost of external finance, the rate of profit in the private sector and the rate at which the critical minimum income level is expected to rise (SMN, §2.3). The formulae just presented for the accounting ratios λ, λ_p, f_n, f_s and r_s all contain the factor $R/(R-g)$, and rough estimates of g suggest a value near 8%. Thus the manufacturing sector has been growing at 8·2% p.a. in real terms, whilst most companies have been growing at rates between 5% and 10%. It is clear that if R is as low as 10% the factor $R/(R-g)$ will be large, and very sensitive to small errors in the estimates of either R or g. It seems appropriate to ask whether we can suggest a better way of calculating a trial value for the ARI. It should be emphasized that the only real way to check the estimate is for the Government to engage in systematic project selection using the proposed ARI to see if it does in fact ration the available funds, so the values we calculate here can only be viewed as trial values.

---

[1] This is not strictly true, since increases in foreign private debt may reduce the liquidity of the country's foreign exchange reserves. Looked at another way, large scale indebtedness to private foreign companies restricts the set of feasible actions open to the Government, and may increase the cost of some actions (such as borrowing abroad). On the other hand, the willingness of the country to permit inflows of private investment may increase the willingness of investors to lend, thus reducing the costs of borrowing. Either way, it is difficult to quantify the costs or benefits, though it is clear that the costs are perceived to be very high by some governments.

If the Government could operate projects as efficiently as the *average* private sector project, then the rate of return on these projects would be rf_p/f_k. (rf_p is the profit at APs per £1 of capital at market prices, whose AP is f_k.) If the *marginal* public sector project were this profitable, then the ARI would be rf_p/f_k, though this would seem an upper limit. If the Government thought that the best use of its funds was to make a present of them to the private sector (which it can do by lowering taxes, or providing subsidies) this would imply that the social costs of such transfers were negative, or that λ_p is negative. If the Government does *not* believe free gifts are socially profitable, then it must believe that λ_p is greater than zero. If R is greater than g, λ_p will be positive from equation (6.5a) if

$$R > \frac{rkf_p}{cf_c + kf_k}.$$

Call the right-hand side R_o, the minimum rate of discount at which the Government will not make free gifts to the private sector; then this can be rewritten

$$R_o = \frac{rf_p/f_k}{1 + cf_c/(msf_k)} < \frac{rf_p}{f_k} \qquad (6.11)$$

Provided $rf_p > (r - ib)\ (cf_c + msf_k)$, R_o will exceed g, and for the values calculated below this will always be the case. If the Government were able to produce as efficiently as the private sector they would earn rf_p/f_k, and this would be the ARI. The factor $1/(1 + cf_c/msf_k)$ can thus be thought of as the *critical inefficiency factor*, below which the Government should abdicate from productive investment.

3. EMPIRICAL ESTIMATES FOR KENYA

3.1 *Accounting ratios for an average manufacturing firm*
The parameters in the formulae of the previous section can be conveniently divided into two categories. The first set depend on the structure of taxes and tariffs and include not only tax rates and allowances such as t, a, t_1, but also the accounting ratios f_k, f_c and f_p. The remaining parameters are behavioural constants (we hope!) chosen by the firm and requiring rather different data to observe. The accounting ratio for marginal capitalist consumption can be

calculated assuming that capitalists have the same pattern of consumption as middle-income urban consumers and that the social value of their extra consumption is zero. The method of calculation is similar to that reported in SMN, Table 8.1, and gives a value for $f_c = 0.79$, quite close to the value for urban unskilled workers' consumption of 0.82. The AR for capital goods will depend on the type of asset purchased but for average manufacturing capital is 0.90 as shown in Table 6.1.

Table 6.1   Accounting Ratio for Manufacturing Capital

Item	Accounting Ratio	Proportion of capital stock (%)
Building materials (proxy for construction)	0.84	34
Furniture	0.83	4
Machinery	0.95	56
Transport equipment	0.79	6
Average capital stock	0.90	100

Notes: Proportions of capital stock are taken from 1963 *Survey of Capital Assets* at replacement cost for all manufacturing excluding sectors ISIC 300–311, 381–386. Accounting ratios come from SMN, Table 10.1.

This figure will also be used to adjust the figures for depreciation of capital stock.[1]

The accounting ratio for private profits, f_p, can be calculated using the invaluable data reported in Phelps and Wasow's (P – W) paper on effective protection. Table 6.2 presents the relevant figures for a substantial proportion of the private large-scale manufacturing sector (that is, firms with 50 or more employees). The first column gives value added at domestic prices (DVA) and is directly comparable to the figures for Gross Product in the 1968 *Survey of Industrial Production* (Phelps and Wasow used the raw data collected by the

---

[1] Strictly speaking the AR for depreciation will differ as the proportions of different types of capital written off each year will differ from Table 6.1, their lives being different. The difference is negligible.

Statistics Division for this survey). The next two columns give profits and labour costs also at domestic prices, and it appears from the total that profits include interest payments but exclude depreciation, as required. Column (4) gives Phelps and Wasow's estimates of value added at world or accounting prices (WVA). (They calculated the ratio of world to domestic prices for traded goods, and used a standard conversion factor for non-traded goods, which, given the small dispersion in non-traded accounting ratios, should be very satisfactory.) Profits at accounting prices can now be calculated as WVA less the wage bill and depreciation at APs. The accounting ratio for unskilled labour is 0·7, for expatriate labour is crudely estimated at 0·67, and for skilled labour is between 0·66 and 0·85 (SMN, 9·1), so that an accounting ratio of 0·7 for all labour costs is sufficiently accurate. The ratio for depreciation is 0·9, so that profits at APs will be

$$\text{WVA} - 0.7 \ wL - 0.9\text{D},$$

where D can be calculated as $\text{DVA} - rK - wL$. The ratio of this figure to profits at market prices (rK) is the desired value for f_p, shown in column (7). The average value (weighted by profit shares at market prices) is 0·84 but it is clear that there is a wide variation from one sector to another, mainly explained by the great non-uniformity in rates of effective protection. (The standard deviation of f_p is very large at 0·94.)

The calculation can be refined and the sensitivity of the result can be tested in a number of ways. It is clear, looking for example at sectors 311, 314 and 383, that a very small value for profits at market prices may lead to an unreliable estimate for f_p, as the ratio of two, perhaps unreliable, small numbers each determined as residuals. Year to year fluctuations in profits are to be expected and will lead to substantial variations in f_p, whereas we are interested in a time averaged figure. Table 6·3, which also attempts to estimate the average rate of profit by sector, gives in column (8) average profits for each sector. These figures bear the same ratio to DVA as the average of the shares of profits from 1965 to 1971, and also include the difference between reported and an estimate of true depreciation as described in the notes to the table (these are negligible in most cases). If the average profit is used (and the wage costs correspondingly adjusted) the average value of f_p again comes to 0·84, though the individual figures will be different in many cases.

Table 6·2 Profits at Accounting and Market Prices for Private Manufacturing

ISIC Group	Industry	DVA value added £'000* (1)	rK Profit £'000* (2)	wL Labour costs £'000* (3)	WVA £'000* (4)	Change in DVA 1964-71 (%) (5)	Foreign share of DVA (%) (6)	Profits at APs as fraction of market profit t_p (7)
203	Canned fruit and vegetables	200	-18	185	147	19	52	0·67
205	Grain mill products	1,349	537	579	931	45	1	0·59
206	Bakery products	445	83	288	450	132	52	2·08
208	Confectionery	40	-6	41	71	9		··
209	Miscellaneous foods	520	247	219	-97	108	87	-1·21
213	Beer, Malt	3,066	1,528	1,266	2,250	90	39	0·73
220	Tobacco	1,408	577	670	1,390	3	65	1·34
214	Soft drinks	415	70	308	102	118	91	3·00
232	Knitwear	366	106	203	203	83	100	-0·86
234	Textiles	1,067	627	432	110	210		-0·17
233	Cordage, rope and twine	645	139	410	279	6		-1·89
243	Garments	401	80	292	126	30	83	0·61
244	Canvas goods	155	46	95		162	60	1·02
251	Sawn timber	786	164	510	796	119	59	2·06
260	Furniture and fixtures	227	39	171	165	122	85	0·77
271	Paper	39	7	28	10	202		0·13
272	Paper products	112	48	64	65	129		0·99
280	Printing and publishing	1,569	187	1,170	1,381	93		1·66
291	Tanning	173	52	95	-176	193		-0·21
300	Rubber products	77	29	36	30	163		4·90
311	Basic industrial chemicals	1,030	72	739	1,067	14	100	-1·05
313	Paints	175	67	88	9	85		-0·94
312	Vegetable oils	25	7	18	6	74	78	0·68
315	Soap	824	356	337	596	115		4·85
314	Wattle extract	285	17	138	296	152		1·14
316	Pyrethrum	833	649	152	874	13	··	0·67
319	Miscellaneous chemicals	567	329	185	397	87		0·60
332	Glass products	307	89	157	218		100	1·43
334	Cement	1,920	951	628	2,104		100	1·53
339	Concrete products	87	35	42	92		100	1·04
350	Metal products	1,116	390	629	934	63	56	2·15
360	Non-electrical machinery	145	28	102	145	105	75	5·05
383	Motor vehicle bodies	129	10	108	136	320	53	
	Total	20,503	7,542	10,385	15,918			0·84 (SD=0·94)
	Percentages	100	36·8	50·6	77·6			

Notes and sources for Table 6·2

Column (1) was kindly supplied by Wasow and can be compared with the 1968 Survey. Sectors 201 (meat products), 202 (dairy products) and 207 (sugar) were omitted from the available data as being effectively Government owned or regulated industries. Coverage is 64% of total value added of private large-scale manufacturing, which in turn is 79% of the whole (formal) private manufacturing sector.

Column (2) was recovered from Phelps and Wasow via the rate of return and the capital–output ratio. Since the rate of return was calculated from the capital–output ratio the product rK/Y should be equal to the census material, and corresponds closely with published data.

Column (3) is deduced from the 'world price rate of return' of P – W, defined as $WVA/(wL + 0·1K)$, where 0·1 is P – W's assumed return to capital.

Column (4) is deduced from the rates of effective protection in P – W. The ratio of world to domestic price was in turn calculated by Phelps and Wasow; domestic prices were taken from inter-EA trade statistics and unit values of firms' inputs and outputs, world prices from EA export prices, and Japanese import and export prices corrected for transport costs. When all else failed, tariff deflators were used to obtain the ratios.

Column (5) gives the percentage increase in the quantity index of each industry's output over the period 1964–71 derived from Table 106 of the 1972 *Statistical Abstract*.

Column (6) gives the share in domestic value added of large firms mainly or wholly owned by foreigners as reported in ILO (1973), Table 73, which is based on unpublished data from the 1967 *Census of Industrial Production*. Foreign–owned firms are further analysed in Table 6·4.

It might be argued that the average ratio is misleading in that the highly distorted structure of protection will provide incentives to expand output in highly protected and thus socially less profitable sectors, so that the ratio for marginal increases in profits may be much lower than 0·84. We can test this hypothesis by weighting profits at APs by the rates of growth of each industry, which are given in column (5) of Table 6·2. The result comes to 0·83, surprisingly close to the original estimate, and lending no weight to the hypothesis.

Lastly, we argued that the imperfect nature of the capital market and the likely different behavioural patterns of different types of firms made it desirable to attempt to provide separate estimates for each distinguishable type of firm. It is clear from the wide variation between sectors that it will be difficult to distinguish many different groups, whilst it is not obvious that different types of firm will make differing uses of the structure of protection (though they might be differentially successful in negotiating concessionary tariffs).[1] The most we can do (and, fortunately, do most usefully) is to compare foreign-owned companies with the average.

---

[1] Firms may also differ in their ability to evade taxes, which will have a considerable effect on the APs. The effect of tax evasion is discussed in SMN, Ch.6, but ignored here where the emphasis is on the large incorporated sector.

Table 6·3 *Capital, Profits, and Returns for Private Manufacturing*

ISIC Group	K/Y Fixed-capital-output ratio Phelps Wasow (1)	K/Y 1963 Survey (2)	M/Y Stock-output ratio 1968 Survey (3)	D/Y % 1968 Survey (4)	Assumed total C/Y (C=K+M) (5)	Assumed capital £'000 C (6)	Corrected profits rC (7)	Average profits rC (8)	Average rate of profit r (9)
203	2·0		1·2B	12	3·0	600	−18	−18	−3
205	1·96	2·76	0·6B	15	3·0	4,050	567	689	17
206	1·85	:	0·3A		2·3	1,020	82	82	8
208	1·14	:	0·2A	13	1·2	50	−6	−6	−12
209	0·78	1·98	0·4A	10	1·8	940	282	310	33
213	1·79	:			3·0	9,200	1,530	2,232	21
220	0·95	1·1	0·6A		1·0	1,410	580		
214	1·58			4	1·6	660	70	90	14
232	1·90		0·3	18	2·2	800	104		18
234	1·13	1·87	0·5A		2·4	2,560	640	618	12
233	1·40		0·9B	15	2·0	1,290	168	155	26
243	0·46		0·5A	10	1·0	400	100	146	16
244	0·55		0·6A		1·0	160	54		20
251	0·70	4·9	0·9A	11	1·5	1,180	201	189	25
260	0·50	3·5	0·2A	24	2·0	60	68	90	11
271	0·87		0·5A	9	1·5	220	6	70	19
272	0·96	i·3		7	2·0	2,350	48	259	3
280	1·08	1·3	1·2E	12	1·5	350	188	92	19
291	0·86	3·4	0·4A		2·0	140	53	72	18
300	1·36	6·24*	3·5A	12*	1·8	2,580	29	67	6
311	0·64	1·59	0·5A	11	2·5	350	72	380	79
313	1·23		0·1A		2·0		67	17	60
312	2·72	2·3	0·9A		2·5	2,120	7	657	12
314	1·04			11	1·0	290	356	340	18
315	0·19		0·6C		1·0	830	17	107	32
316	0·40	..			1·0	570	649	1,027	15
319	0·49	0·91	0·5D	9	3·0	920	329	42	18
332	2·24		0·6B	15	1·0	5,760	89	423	17
334	2·05	5·66	0·2C	15	3·0	130	951	27	
339	1·39		0·2C	9	1·5	2,790	35	22	
350	0·81	2·70	0·5A	6	2·5	150	390		
360	0·44		0·8A	6	1·0	130	28		
383	0·46	2·01	0·6A	7	1·0		10		
			0·3B						
Averages	1·26	2·65†	0·48†	14†	2·17				18·4% ±11·4% (SD)
Totals £'000						44,510	7,746	8,179	

* Includes petroleum

The Social Value of Private Investment in Kenya

Data sources and notes for Table 6·3

Column (1) gives the capital–output ratios calculated from Phelps and Wasow who in turn used the 1968 (unpublished) survey data.

Column (2) gives the published 1963 *Survey of Capital Assets* estimates for capital–output ratios at replacement cost, excluding residential building.

Column (3) gives the stock–output ratios (input and output stocks) for all firms with 5+ employees at the end of 1967 (on the same basis as the 1967 *Census of Industrial Production*). The letters indicate the stability of the ratio, itself estimated from the *change* in stocks in 1967. A, B, C, D respectively imply a change in M/Y of less than 20%, 20–40%, 40–80%, greater than 80%. This data was kindly made available by the Director of Statistics.

Column (4) gives the published share of depreciation to value added from the 1968 *Survey*.

Column (5) is col. (1) + col. (3), rounded, and adjusted where the evidence of col. (2) or (4) casts doubt on the accuracy of col. (1).

Column (6) = col. (5) × col. (1) of Table 6·2.

Column (7) = col. (2) of Table 6·2 + col. (1) of Table 6·2 × col. (4) — true depreciation at 10% using asset lives from Powell (1972).

Column (8) = average share of profits from 1965–1971 (calculated from Table 108 of the 1972 *Statistical Abstract)* ÷ actual share of profits in 1968 × col. (7).

Column (9) = col. (8)/col. (6).

3.2 *The accounting ratios for foreign private profits*

It is possible to construct a similar table to Table 6·2 for firms 'mainly or wholly owned by foreigners' using the data from the 1967 *Census of Industrial Production* published in ILO (1973), Tables 73 and 76, if it is assumed that effective rates of protection are the same for foreign-owned and locally-owned industries within any 3-digit sector. Table 6·4 summarizes the results for the ILO sample excluding sectors ISIC 370, 381, 390, for which no rates of effective protection are available, and for all industries, assuming that the average rate of effective protection for those industries not in the sample was the same as the average for all the firms in the Phelps-Wasow sample reported in Table 6·2. The foreign-owned share of the private large-scale (50 +employees) industrial sector is 69% and is thus quantitatively very important.

These figures should be treated with even greater caution than those in Table 6·2 since the coverage is less complete, and since the value for f_p is in this case very sensitive to the ratio of WVA to DVA. (If the ratio were the same as for Table 6·2, the value for f_p would be 0·83.) An attempt was made to identify the domestic-owned firms, but the sample was too small to be much use (only 38% of the total domestic sector, itself 43% of large-scale manufacturing). The value of f_p for this small sample (comprising sectors 205, 6, 13, 14, 20, 51,

Table 6·4 Profits for Foreign-Owned Firms

£'000

	Value added DVA (1)	Net profit plus interest (2)	Labour costs wL (3)	Depreciation D (4)	WVA (5)	f_p (6)
Sample	11,942	4,238	6,115	1,589	8,203	0·59
All industries	19,399	8,018	9,118	2,263	13,992	0·70
Percentages (all industries)	100·0	41·3	47·0	11·7	72·1	

Sources and notes:
Col. (1) From ILO, Table 73, col. 1.
Col. (2) = col. (1) minus col. (3) and col. (4).
Col. (3) = ILO, Table 76, col. (5) multiplied by col. (1) of this table.
Col. (4) = ILO, Table 70 (col. (7) ÷ col. (3)) × col. (1).
Col. (5) Sample WVA was calculated from ILO, Table 73, using the rates of effective protection from Table 6:2. All industries not in the sample had the same ratio of WVA to DVA as the average in Table 6:1, i.e. 0·776.

71/2, 315, 50, 60) was 0·74, but since the value for all firms in these sectors is 0·75 the sample is not very illuminating.

We conclude that there is some evidence that foreign firms have concentrated in slightly more heavily protected sectors, which in turn leads to a lower accounting ratio for foreign profits than local profits, though it would be difficult to reject the hypothesis that there was no significant difference between foreign and local firms. The main useful conclusion is that a major determinant of the accounting ratio for profits (and thus ultimately of the opportunity cost of funds) is the degree of protection in that sector. In many cases it will be clear in which sectors a firm is likely to invest (particularly if it is a product-oriented firm) and for these firms a more accurate ratio can be calculated.

3.3 Rates of growth and rates of profit
The most suitable sector to work with is Manufacturing and Repairing, the statistical coverage is good, and recorded profits exclude managerial incomes, unlike many of the other sectors. In addition corporate investment will be more important in this sector, and the previous estimate for the accounting ratio of profits was derived for this sector, again because of data availability.

There are three basic ways in which the average net rate of profit at market prices, r, can be determined. The first uses cross-section data for profits collected in the *Survey of Industrial Production,* and a capital–output ratio also derived from similar surveys. The second uses the time series data from the national accounts, whilst the third involves looking at company balance sheets. The Phelps-Wasow sample forms the obvious basis for the first method.

3.4 Census data for rates of profit
Table 6·3 gives various estimates of the capital–output ratio and profit share for the Phelps–Wasow sample of firms. We need the share of gross profits plus interest, less true depreciation in value added divided by the ratio of replacement cost fixed capital, K, plus stocks, M, to value added, all measured in prices of the same year, or current prices. Column (1) gives K/Y from P–W, which can be compared with the 1963 estimates of K/Y at replacement cost.

In many cases the 1963 figures seemed high, whilst the Phelps–Wasow figures were low, suggesting that these might be referred to *book* value of assets at historic cost.

If we assume that companies have been investing and growing at a constant real rate of growth g, that the rate of inflation in the price of capital goods is p and that capital goods are written down on historic cost at rate d, and that the age of the oldest capital still in use is T years (which will be the shorter of the life expectancy of the capital and the age of the firm) then the ratio of replacement cost at current prices, K, to book value at historic cost, H, will be

$$\frac{K}{H} = \frac{\emptyset(g,T)}{\emptyset(g+p+d,T)} \qquad (6\cdot12)$$

where $\quad \emptyset(x,T) = \int_{-T}^{0} e^{xt}\,dt = \frac{1 - e^{-xT}}{x} \qquad (6\cdot13)$

If companies have grown at the same real rate as the manufacturing sector, about 8% p.a., and hold the same composition of assets as in Table 6·1, if inflation has proceeded at 3% p.a. (if anything an overestimate for capital goods), if assets were written down at income tax rates and if companies are, on average, 10 years old, then this ratio could be as high as 1·6. With zero inflation it would have been 1·4, and it would also be lower for younger companies. On the other hand, companies faced with a threat of nationalization or accused of profiteering have an incentive to revalue assets, as do those wishing to float share issues, so the extent of under-valuation of capital is hard to assess. The figures used in the calculations were those of column (1) except where under-valuation (compared with col. (2) or (4)) seemed acute, in which case a compromise figure was substituted.

The remaining adjustments, described in the notes to Table 6·3, provided an estimate of the average true net profit plus interest, and assuming that depreciation is adequate to maintain capital intact, will, when divided by total capital, give the average real rate of return before tax, as shown in column (9). The average real rate of return for the whole sample is 18·4%. In general it will differ from the (geared up) return to assets attributable to equity. The standard deviation is as large as 11·4% mainly because of sectors 316 and 319, since deviations were weighted by profits.

3.4.1 *Profits in distribution*

The only other sector with comparable statistics is Distribution, though depreciation data is not available. ILO (1973) gives capital and stock data (Table 38, p.139) which allows an estimate of the gross rate of return. A net return of 20% is consistent with these results, especially if the smallest group is omitted.

Table 6·5   Rates of Profit in Distribution

Size of establishment (no. of workers)	Value added per worker (£)	Gross rate of return (%)
0–4	1,417	101
5–9	867	22
10–14	398	10
15–19	781	36
20–29	1,374	21
30–39	992	10
40–49	1,128	24
50–99	1,007	15
100+	1,230	14
All	£1,108	27%

Source: ILO (1973)

3.5 *National accounts method*

Table 6·6 gives the relevant data for Manufacturing and Repairing, which shows that in real terms the rate of growth was 8·2% p.a. over the period 1964–71 (and inflation averaged 3·4% p.a.). The main problem is that we only have gross values for investment, output and profits, whilst we are interested in computing net rates of return. The survey data on depreciation reported by firms suggests that in an average year depreciation might be 11% of value added (higher values would be expected in years of higher investment, as in 1967–68). This figure is presumably closely related to the allowable provisions under the income tax laws, and tends to overstate true depreciation in the Kenyan situation (as mentioned before). An

Table 6·6 Investment, Growth and Output in Manufacturing and Repairing

	1964	1965	1966	1967	1968	1969	1970	1971	Average
GDP at factor cost (£m current prices) Y	34·2	37·4	41·6	45·3	50·1	56·8	65·0	75·1	··
Capital Formation (£m current prices) I	5·8	6·6	8·1	10·0	12·2	9·5	13·0	17·8	··
I/Y %	17	18	19	22	24	17	20	24	20·1 %
End of year *level* of stocks. M (£m)	16·6	18·9	23·7	24·7	25·2	··	··	··	··
$u=M/Y$ %	49	51	57	55	50	··	··	··	52 %
Wage costs/value added %	52·7	50·5	51·1	55·9	55·1	53·0	51·8	··	52·9 %
Depreciation/value added %	··	··	10·9	12·8	13·0	12·7	··	··	12·4 %
GDP at factor cost (1964 prices) (index 1964=100)	100	106·1	111·7	119·8	130·4	142·2	153·6	174·0	··
Change in real GDP % $\Delta Y/Y$	··	6·1	5·28	7·25	8·85	9·05	8·02	13·28	8·2 %
Gross ICOR $I_{-1}/\Delta Y$	··	2·8	3·4	2·6	2·5	2·7	2·1	1·5	2·51

Sources: 1. GDP and capital formation were taken from 1972 Statistical Abstract, Stocks from Statistical Digest, June 1969.
2. Wage costs as a share of value added were taken from the surveys of industrial production data in the Statistical Abstract, and refer to large firms. In 1968 the wage costs share was the same in large and small firms and so this can be taken as a good measure for the whole sector. Wage costs include salaries and non cash benefits.
3. Depreciation also refers to large manufacturing firms, and is given in the Statistical Digest for December 1971.
4. Averages are unweighted averages except for the growth rate (derived from closing and initial values).

alternative and perhaps low figure of 7% will be contrasted. Suppose that the sector is in roughly steady-state growth at rate g, with a gross investment share of s, and depreciation d, so that the net savings ratio is $s - d$. If we assume that the depreciation is sufficient to maintain output *and* profits from installed capital (which requires a very simple view of technical progress) then the fixed capital–output ratio $v = (s - d)/g$, or, including stocks, the total capital–output ratio is $v + u$, where u is the stock–output ratio. If the share of gross profits in value added is π, the net return to total capital will be $r = (\pi - d)/(v + u)$. We can calculate this, with $s = 0 \cdot 201$, $g = 0 \cdot 082$, $\pi = 0 \cdot 471$, $u = 0 \cdot 52$, and d either $0 \cdot 11$ or $0 \cdot 07$, and the results are shown in Table 6·7.

Table 6·7   Steady Growth Rates of Return

	Depreciation/output	
	11%	7%
$v = K/Y$	1·11	1·60
r %	22	19

The gross ICOR could also be adjusted to give very similar results—its value at 2·51 is slightly higher than $s/g = 2 \cdot 45$, so profit rates would be slightly lower.

An alternative method, more sophisticated but not obviously any better, is to assume that technical progress takes place, is embodied in finite lived capital, increases labour productivity but is fully reflected in rising wage rates. This vintage approach has obvious objections when applied to a single sector, especially where wage rates need not rise with rising labour productivity, but labour costs show no obvious decline as a share of value added, and so the model may not be too misleading. Again we assume steady state, with employment growing at rate n, technical progress at rate z, $(g = n + z)$, wages at date t equal to we^{zt}, and capital remaining uniformly productive for T years, then vanishing.

Total employment $\qquad E_t = L \displaystyle\int_{t-T}^{t} e^{nv} \, dv \qquad\qquad (6 \cdot 14)$

Total output
$$Y_t = X \int_{t-T}^{t} e^{gv} \, dv,$$
(6·15)

where X, L are output and employment on machines installed at date $t=0$. The share of wages will be

$$1 - \pi = \frac{w_t E_t}{Y_t} = \frac{w_t L}{X} \cdot \frac{\emptyset(n, T)}{\emptyset(g, T)}$$
(6·16)

where $\emptyset$ is defined in equation (6·13).

Investment I at $t=0$ will be sY_0, and if the capital output ratio is v, $vX = I$. The internal rate of return, r, will be such that present discounted profits equal investment costs:

$$I + uX = \int_{0}^{T} (X - w_v L)e^{-rv} dv + uXe^{-rT}$$
(6·17)

(allowing for the need to hold stocks u per unit output).

$$sY_0 = X[\emptyset(r) - \alpha \emptyset(r-z) - (1 - e^{-rT})u]$$
(6·18)

where $\alpha = (1 - \pi)\emptyset(g)/\emptyset(n)$, and $\emptyset(x) = \emptyset(x, T)$,

i.e.

$$s\emptyset(g) + u(1 - e^{-rT}) = \emptyset(r) - \alpha \emptyset(r-z).$$
(6·19)

If we know T, g, n and z, this can be solved by trial and error quite quickly, using the previous estimates as starting values. Powell (1972) gives estimated lives of capital as 14 years for equipment, 6 years for transport equipment, and 50 for structures. Roughly one-third of new gross investment is in structures, and an average life might thus be between 15 and 20 years. Table 6·8 shows the effect of varying T and z on r. This is reassuringly consistent with the crude estimates and suggests a figure around 20%.

3.6 *Published company accounts*

The Nairobi stock exchange publishes an official Yearbook in which it summarizes the published accounts of the main quoted companies on a consistent basis. The weaknesses of such data are well known, but they throw some light on an important parameter as yet not fully identified—the rate of savings, and, unlike the previous data, their basis is the same as the individual unit in our enquiry, the firm. We

Table 6·8 Return to Vintage Capital

Life, T years	Technical progress z % per annum	return r %
15	4	23
20	4	20
10	4	27
15	3	22
15	2	21

took as a sample the 13 largest companies which remained in existence between 1966 and 1971. Table 6·9 gives the names and closing sizes of the companies in the sample. (The years referred to in the tables and text are the dates of the Yearbook less one in which the figures appeared. They refer to the latest financial year available at December 31st of that year.) Table 6·10 gives the aggregated stocks and flows of this sample of companies, and reveals that net assets grew 56% over the period, fixed assets plus stocks grew 65%, whilst from Table 6·6 the implicit manufacturing GDP deflator rose 22% in this

Table 6·9 List of Companies in Sample

Company	Net Assets at end of 1971 £'000
Baumann & Co	1,800
Block Hotels	1,351
Car and General	1,458
CMC Holdings	2,188
Consolidated Holdings	2,488
E.A. Bag and Cordage	782
E.A. Breweries	10,526
E.A. Portland Cement	1,614
Hughes Ltd.	1,445
Kakuzi Ltd.	1,368
Marshalls	823
Mercat	3,759
Motor Mart & Exchange	3,353
Total	32,955

[1] All references to pounds in this chapter are to Kenyan pounds except in Table 6·13.

Notes to Table 6·10

Notes: 1. Investment and loans are usually at cost, sometimes at market value.

2. Net assets are tangible net assets attributable to Ordinary capital, equal to Total Issued Ordinary Capital plus Reserves and C/F.

3. Other short debt is a residual net figure.

4. Trading profit is before tax and depreciation.

5. *P-D-T-Y* is equal to dividend payments on Preference shares plus Minority interest payments less profits on sale of assets plus formation and capital expenses.

6. Figures have been rounded *after* all calculations and therefore may not add up exactly.

7. Stocks are as at the end of the year, flows are in the year between the two stock figures.

period (consumer prices rose 13%). This suggests a growth rate of about $7^1/_2\%$ in real terms, though given the discrepancies between different series and the shortness of the time period this is subject to an error of about 1% each way. During the period £11·3 million was paid out in dividends, and £1·3 m. was raised in new equity, the balance of £4·1 m. in the increase in equity being scrip issue essentially equivalent to revaluing shares. This scrip issue is best treated as additions to reserves, in which case the annual additions to reserves compounded at 7% interest give values consistent with initial and final total reserves.

The retention or savings rate was 36% (total retention/total net profit) over the period, and if we regard the new equity as savings by the original shareholders (which is plausible, since even if they paid 40% tax at the margin on dividends, this would represent a marginal rate of savings of 19%, whilst with lower tax rates a lower rate of savings would be implied,) then the average rate of savings comes to 43%.

Depreciation averaged 6·9% of fixed assets, which seems low, since .the allowance is 4% on construction, $12^1/_2\%$ on machinery and 25% on transport, all on written down values. For average manufacturing capital in 1963 these allowances would have given depreciation as 12·6% of book value, or 8·8% of replacement cost. The conclusion is that either a larger proportion of fixed assets are structures, or they are nearer replacement cost than book value. Either explanation is plausible—the latter because of the fear of nationalization and the political motive of making returns seem lower. Net assets amount to 91% of fixed assets plus stocks, 114% of fixed assets plus investments and loans. Average (unweighted) net return before tax to fixed assets

Table 6·10 Accounts of Selected Companies Quoted on the Nairobi Stock Exchange

£ million

Stock Exchange Yearbook of: / for Companies closing accounts in:	1967 / 1966	1968 / 1967	1969 / 1968	1970 / 1969	1971 / 1970	1972 / 1971	1971 less 1966 £m.	as %, of 1966
Physical Balances at end of accounting year								
Fixed assets	13·7	14·0	15·7	18·0	20·4	24·5	10·8	79%
Investments and loans	3·6	5·2	5·3	5·7	6·4	6·3	2·7	77%
Stocks	9·5	10·4	10·5	11·0	11·6	13·7	4·2	44%
Total assets	26·7	29·5	31·5	34·7	38·6	44·5	17·8	67%
Financial Balances at end of accounting year								
Net assets attributable to equity	21·0	22·6	25·7	27·0	28·7	33·0	11·9	56%
(Share equity)	(13·9)					(19·3)	(5·4)	
Long debt	2·6	2·3	2·4	2·8	3·4	5·1	2·6	103%
Tax liability	2·3	2·6	2·9	3·2	3·1	4·2	1·9	
Other short debt	0·8	2·1	0·6	1·7	3·3	2·2	1·3	
Total short debt	3·1	4·6	3·5	4·8	6·4	6·4	3·3	105%
Flows during accounting year							Totals	
Trading profit P	5·83	5·80	6·70	7·05	8·35		33·73	
Depreciation D	0·90	0·93	1·13	1·20	1·47		5·63	
Tax T	1·79	1·82	2·03	2·11	2·71		10·46	
Net profit for shareholders Y	3·06	3·09	3·45	3·38	4·62		17·60	
Retentions R	0·74	1·09	1·36	0·93	2·18		6·30	
R/Y (%)	24	35	39	27	47			

Source: Nairobi Stock Exchange Official Yearbooks

plus stocks is 21·3%, to total assets is 18%, and to net assets is 22%. Again, a net return of 20% is consistent with the evidence, perhaps slightly lower if assets are thought to be under-valued (though a corresponding allowance for depreciation is then needed).

Over the period taxes of £10·5 m. were payable on net profits of £28 m., an average rate of 37% (differing from the corporate tax rate of 40% because of interest payments, etc.). Indebtedness to the tax authorities increased by £1·9 m., so taxes paid only amounted to 31% of net profits. This is because taxes are (or were) payable in arrears, and with profits growing at 9·4% p.a. in money terms (as here) this would be accounted for by a two-year lag between receipt and payment. It is evident that unpaid taxes are a valuable source of short-term finance.

The fast growth in loans made by companies reflects the nationalization of subsidiaries in neighbouring countries, or partnerships with these governments.

Since we are interested in the effect of an increase in profits and net assets on physical assets, it is worth remarking that over the period new loans matched new long debt (and their total amounts were fairly close) whilst new net short borrowing was slightly short of increases in stocks.

The evidence provided by King (1973), mentioned above, suggests that increases in stock building is matched by equal increases in bank lending. It might therefore not be too misleading to suppose that increases in net assets are matched by increase in fixed capital, whilst increased stocks are financed by increased short-term credit lent effectively by the Government.

Finally, the average return of net profits after tax to net assets was 14·1%, which, with a savings ratio of 43%, suggests a real rate of growth of 6% p.a. (and, at 3% inflation in manufacturing, a money rate of growth of 9% p.a.), slightly below that for manufacturing output as a whole.

3.6.1 *Other analyses of company data*

P. N. Snowden, in a chapter of a forthcoming book edited by W. T. Newlyn, reports the results of his analysis of the balance sheets of a group of 43 companies operating in Kenya over the period 1963–69. He investigates the relationships between rates of savings, profit, dividends and outside finance over two sub-periods by size-group and ownership, and comes to some tentative but plausible conclusions.

The main difficulty in attempting any sophisticated analysis is that the period is short, and yet within it several important structural changes occurred which themselves could account for much of the considerable variation in behaviour observed, yet which cannot be quantified. In particular, 'business confidence' changed several times—independence came in 1964, extensive Kenyanization policies were introduced in 1967, the East African Community, which was to ensure a wide market for East African firms, experienced difficulties which led to restrictions on Kenyan exports and hence to excess capacity in some Kenyan-based larger companies, and the convertibility of the Kenyan pound varied, particularly after the sterling devaluation of 1967. These factors all make for considerable uncertainty in estimating such sensitive parameters as the marginal rate of saving, and the normal dividend ratio (normal in the sense of long-run average). With these provisos, and ignoring the group of 12 small closely held companies with net assets of less than £100,000, Snowden's findings are summarized in Table 6·11.

The net after tax return of about 13% is not very different from that in the previous sample of 14%, and corresponds to a before tax rate of about 21%. This may overstate the real return as assets may be entered at original cost and not adequately allow for inflation, quite apart from the fact that we are interested in return to physical capital. The rates of growth of net assets appear modest and lower than in the previous sample, though the variance is high. The marginal rates of savings for large firms are subject to considerable uncertainty, but would seem to be below those for medium size companies, perhaps reflecting their increased vulnerability to the collapse of intra East African Community trade. The lower savings rates for foreign companies might reflect growing political uncertainty or limited market growth in each product—international companies are frequently more product-oriented than domestic companies, which have to diversify into different products, rather than different countries.

Snowden has published aggregated profit and loss accounts for 12 companies in size groups 2 and 3 in Snowden (1972). These give more detail on financial structure, and are summarized in Table 6·12. Here rates of return are slightly higher, rates of growth somewhat lower (though the period is different) and savings rates are averages, though they are again lower for larger companies. Net physical asset formation exceeds increases in net assets, suggesting that the return to physical capital is lower than the return to net assets. Net fixed capital

Table 6·11   Company   Savings,   Profits   and   Growth   in   Kenya's Manufacturing Sector 1963–69

Size group Size (net assets £'000) Number in sample	2 101–899 17	3 900 + 14
Net profit after tax/net assets % (Standard deviation)	12·4 (8·2)	12·9 (5·3)
Rate of growth of net assets % p.a. (SD)	7·7 (7·1)	7·2 (7·1)
Marginal propensity to save % MPS (1) MPS (2) MPS (3)	67 (±9) 64 (±9)	37 (±18) 22 (±19) 55 (±12)

Ownership Number (includes small companies)	Local 24	Foreign 19
MPS (4) % 'Normal' marginal savings rate %	72 (±13) 60	52 (±7) 30

Source: Snowden (1973)

Notes: 1. Net profit after tax is after depreciation but before interest and divididends.
2. MPS (1) is the coefficient b in the regression $S = a + bP$ where S is net savings, P is net after tax profit.
3. MPS (2) is the coefficient b in the regression $S = a + bP + cF$ where F is the net change in external finance.
4. MPS (3) is the coefficient b in the regression $S = a + bP + cD_{-1}$. where D_{-1} is dividend payments in the first three years (grouped).
5. MPS (4) is the coefficient b in the regression $S = a + bP + cD_{-1} + dF$.
6. The normal rate of savings is calculated from the equation for MPS (4) as
$$\frac{b + c}{1 + c}$$
7. Figures in brackets are standard deviations (S.D.) in all cases.

formation is somewhat less than net increase in assets, which is below net physical investment, as with the stock exchange sample. The ratio of stocks to gross fixed capital for size group 2 is 37%, very near the figure of 38% for the stock exchange sample, though it is very low at 17% for size group 3.

Table 6·12   *Balance Sheets for an Average Company*

£'000

Size group	2	3
Gross trading profit P	523	4,686
Depreciation D	96	924
Net profit before tax N	427	3,762
Interest R	35	159
Tax payable T	157	1,441
Net profits attributable to shares Y	235	2,162
Average net assets	2,002	14,360
Net return including interest (%)	13·5%	16·2%
Additions to reserves	146	477
as % of profit	62%	22%
Increased tax liability T_L	43	107
Tax paid as % $((T-T_L)/N)$	29%	37%
New shares	15	111
New long borrowing	−49	201
New net short borrowing	41	172
Gross investment in fixed assets K	181	1,596
stocks M	68	267
Net physical investment $K+M-D$	153	939
Increase in net assets A	112	766
Growth in net assets p.a. (%)	5·6%	5·3%

Source: Snowden (1972)

Notes: 1. Figures are sums for the years 1964–70 and can be divided by 6 to give annual averages for a typical firm iin each size group. The original samples for each group were of six companies in 'basic consumption goods'.

2. Y, R and D are observed. T is calculated as $(\frac{0\cdot4}{1-0\cdot4})$ Y; $P \equiv D+R+T+Y$.

3.6.2   *Balance of Payments Data*

We can draw on the published Balance of Payments accounts of both Kenya and the U.K. to attempt to identify retention rates and rates of return for foreign companies (and, particularly, U.K. registered companies). Naturally these figures must be treated with even greater caution than others since the legal requirements of taxation, repatriation, exchange control and the like may provide incentives to firms to disguise some transactions under different (and for our purposes inappropriate) headings. This is less likely to be the case between Kenya and the U.K. as the double tax agreements in force would provide no *tax* incentive for a U.K. registered company not declaring and paying Kenyan tax on its true profits—which it might otherwise avoid by transfer pricing (over-invoicing imports, underpricing exports). Table 6·13 gives the available data from the *Business Monitor M4* for transactions of large U.K. registered companies investing in Kenya. If the book value of direct investments is accumulated forward by adding net outward investment (which, on past data, would slightly underestimate closing net assets) and revaluing net assets by the extent of sterling devaluation in 1967 (since Kenya remained at U.S.$ parity throughout the period) the average return of net earnings to net assets is 12·5%, consistent with the remaining evidence and a net return before tax of 20% (or possibly less, recognizing that net assets may not measure replacement cost accurately). Retentions averaged 32% over this period. It is clear from the figures for net investment that the period was one of some instability, so that average retentions calculated in this way might be a poor guide to the long-run or normal retention ratio.

Table 6·14 presents the available Kenyan data ultimately derived from the East African Community Secretariat, and published in the *Abstract* and ILO (1973). The figures in row 1 for net private foreign investment may be compared with manufacturing investment in Table 6·6 and amounts to 106% of *gross* fixed capital formation in manufacturing between 1964 and 1970, or 22% of total private gross fixed capital formation— by any criteria a sizeable contribution to total investment. The main value of Table 6·14 lies in the retention rates implied, since growth has been too uneven to allow an estimate of rates of return from a comparison of inflow and outflow data. The average ratio from the ILO data (which were collected to answer this particular question) is 57%, from the UNCTAD data (UNCTAD, 1970) 41%, though this last figure understates retentions by including interest payments in the denominator. A crude correction for this would increase the figure to 48% (matching the two overlapping years) though both this figure and the ILO estimate seem quite high compared with Snowden's data and the U.K. Balance of Payments figures. A figure somewhere in the range 30% to 60% is probably as accurate as can be achieved with the available evidence.

3.6.3 *Limitations of the balance sheet approach*
The main limitations of using company balance sheet data are well known. The main omission is data on value added or even sales,

Table 6·13   Private Investment Financial Flows between UK and Kenya (from M4)

£ million sterling

	1965	1966	1967	1968	1969	1970	1971
Gross outward investment	..	..	..	3·3	11·1	6·7	5·8
Disinvestment	..	..	..	1·7	1·0	3·4	3·2
Net outward investment, including unremitted profits	−3·0	−3·0	−1·9	1·6	10·1	3·3	2·6
of which unremitted profits	..	1·6	..	2·2	2·4	3·0	1·6
Depreciation	..	1·3	..	1·8	2·0	2·3	3·0
Book value of direct investment (net assets at year end)	43·2	..	..	..	..	..	..
Net earnings including unremitted profits	4·1	4·8	4·4	5·7	6·8	8·5	8·5
Kenya Balance of Payments data increase in liabilities on long-term capital to private enterprise (sterling):	..	..	3·4	8·2	10·5	16·6	12·0*

Source: Business Monitor M4

*Provisional

Sources and definitions of private investment flows.

The main recent source book is the Business Monitor M4 of the DTI, HMSO—this is the source of all post 1968 figures. Before that a similar coverage was available in the Board of Trade Journal (19 July 1968; 30 June 1967, etc.).

The book value of overseas investment and the rates of return are given in the journal for 26 January 1968.

Definitions.

Gross investment is the total investment of those affiliates in which U.K. companies increased their stake, and underestimates the true gross amount by the degree of netting out within affiliates.

Net outward investment excludes oil companies (as do all other items) but includes unremitted profits. It is equal to the sum of unremitted profits, net acquisition of shares and loan capital and changes in indebtedness to parent company (trade credit is separately available but is a component of indebtedness).

Net outward earnings = net profits of branches, subsidiaries and interest and is equal to total profits plus interest.

Last row: see Note to row 1 of Table 6·14.

Table 6·14   Inflows, Retentions and Outflows on Foreign Investments

£million

	1963	1964	1965	1966	1967	1968	1969	1970
1. Private long-term capital liability	9·8	10·8	8·8	2·1	4·1	10·0	14·9	18·4
2. New capital plus ret. profits (ILO)	..	..	..	..	10·7	12·1	12·9	18·9
3. Retained profits (UNCTAD)	3·5	3·5	3·0	2·8	4·4	5·0*	..	..
4. Retained profits (ILO)	..	..	..	..	4·8	7·8	6·8	9·4
5. Net outflow of profits and interest (UNCTAD)	9·8	8·7	8·7	8·8	9·2	9·6*	..	..
6. Outflow of profits (ILO)	..	..	..	..	9·1	11·8	12·5	17·4
7. Retention/net profits = row 3/5	36%	41%	35%	32%	48%	52%	..	..
8. Retention/net profits = row 4/row 6 (ILO)	..	..	..	..	53%	65%	54%	54%

* Provisional

Notes and Sources:

Row 1 is the net increase in long-term liabilities including retained earnings after tax, and is taken from the BOP Tables (Statistical Abstract) under the item Long Term Capital Movements: credits/liabilities of private enterprises, which is also the source of the last row of Table 6·13.

Rows 2, 4, 6 and 8 are derived from ILO report (Table 37, p.136).

Row 3 was taken from UNCTAD (1970, pp.37–8), as was Row 5 (p.37). It appears reasonably consistent with the ILO figures, which, since they ultimately derive from the EAC Secretariat, is not surprising.

Row 7 is row 3 divided by row 5 and understates retentions since the denominator includes interest payments.

whilst different firms adopt different accounting conventions for valuing assets, stocks and capital. Apart from the difficulty of measuring the retention or distribution ratio created by the large changes in business confidence and the investment climate, the least satisfactory parameter estimate is for the rate of return, r. Although the evidence points with remarkable consistency to a value between 18% and 22%, there are two reasons for thinking this value on the high side. The first is that many of the estimates use net assets as a deflator, or book value of capital. Both inflation and depreciation (in a growing company) will tend to make this an understatement of replacement cost of productive capital (though revaluation, and the holding of financial assets, both of which are common, will offset this tendency). With no data from companies on value added it is not possible to check implied capital–output ratios against the replacement cost data. Fortunately, inflation was modest during the period 1964–71 (consumer prices rose 16%, the import price index for machinery rose 14%, for semi-manufactures 17%, and for all imports 17%) so that correcting or failing to correct for inflation will make little difference (for capital lasting 10 years and growing at 8% the additional correction for 2% inflation would be about 7% of book value).

The second and more intractable problem is that all the estimates for the rate of return are for the average, whereas we want to measure the marginal return. Indeed, the situation is even more complex, for in a monopolistic situation the relationship between the marginal return at market and accounting prices will differ. Moreover, the perception by the company of a lower marginal than average return will lead them to have a lower marginal than average rate of reinvestment.

A less obvious problem is that it is not clear from the balance sheets what happens to the investment deduction granted against liability to corporation tax (and there is no uniform convention to guide us). Over the period 1966 to 1971 for the sample in Table 6·10 gross investment amounted to £16·4m. If 70% of this were eligible for the 20% deduction, the tax saving should amount to £0·92m or 3·3% of net profits. Tax was in fact 37·2% of net profits, which, however, include some non-taxable items like preference dividends.

3.7 *Final values for behavioural parameters*
The fraction of investment in physical assets financed by increases in

net short borrowing, b, can be derived from the ratio of net assets to physical assets. Table 6·15 gives various estimates which suggest a value of $0·2(\pm0·1)$, a value consistent with stocks financed by net short borrowing. Part of this borrowing will be against tax liability at a real rate of interest of -2% ($=$ rate of inflation), the rest at the short rate of interest of about 5% real. The weighted average rate of interest will be roughly zero. The remaining determinant of the 'multiplier' m is the tax allowance on investment, qat_l. Table 6·16 assumes that 70% of new net investment is eligible for the allowance.

Savings, s, and consumption, c, are best derived from the fraction of net after-tax profits paid out as dividends, h, and the tax rates on retained and distributed profits, using the following equations:

$$s = (1-t_i)(1-h+\sigma h(1-t_d)) \qquad (6·20)$$

$$c = (1-t_i)(1-t_d)(1-\sigma)h, \qquad (6·21)$$

where h is the ratio of dividends to net profits after corporation tax, t_l, t_d is the rate of tax on distributed profits and σ is the marginal propensity to save out of taxed dividends. The effective tax rate, t, will then be $1-c-s$. Dividends will pay taxes at the rate appropriate to the recipient: $12^1/_2\%$ for foreigners and possibly 40% for local residents, which, for a married man with two children is the marginal rate on income between £3,121 and £3,720 p.a.

Table 6·16 summarizes the parameter estimates with the exception of the rate of return and the rate of saving, which are discussed below. The figures in brackets give plausible values for the standard deviation of the estimates (though they have not been estimated as such—they reflect strength of belief or confidence in the estimates for an *average* company, not the range of values that individual companies might display).

The rate of growth, g, is largely determined by the marginal rate of return, r, and the marginal rate of savings, s, neither of which can be accurately estimated, though their upper bound is presumably the average figure in each case. The rate of growth might, however, be known with greater precision than either r or s, and it is plausible that the rate of growth is a prior constraint, in the sense that the attempt by a firm to grow faster than some 'normal' rate might depress the *marginal* return rapidly, which would be countered by lowering the marginal rate of reinvestment. Table 6·17 shows rates of growth for

Table 6·15 Induced Borrowing

Source of estimate: Table	10 average values	10 marginal values	12 medium companies	12 large companies
Net assets/physical assets	0·91	0·80	0·73	0·80
Value of borrowing rates, b	0·09	0·20	0·27	0·20

Table 6·16 Parameter Values for Representative Companies

Parameter	Ownership	
	Domestic	Foreign
Accounting ratios for:		
Consumption f_c	0·79 (0·05)	1·0
Capital f_k	0·90 (0·05)	0·90 (0·05)
net profits f_p	0·84 (0·15)	0·80 (0·05)
Corporation tax t_1	0·4	0·4
Taxes on dividends t_l	0·4 (0·2)	0·125
Allowable fraction q	0·7 (0·3)	0·7 (0·3)
Allowance a	0·2	0·2
Borrowing fraction b	0·2 (0·1)	0·1 (0·1)
Interest rate on borrowing i	0·0 (0·05)	0·0 (0·05)
MPS out of aftertax dividends σ	0·1 (0·1)	0·1 (0·1)
Implied 'multiplier' m	1·344	1·185

various combinations of r and h for domestic companies with the implied rate of saving out of net profit, s, together with the ratio of R_0 to r (it was argued in Section 2·1 above that R_0 might provide a lower bound for the ARI, given the rate of return). The figures in bold provide a rough upper bound for rates of growth (9% p.a. in real terms over the long haul is quite a high rate of growth for a representative company) and thus give plausible combinations of values for r and h.

4. ESTIMATES OF THE ACCOUNTING PRICES FOR PRIVATE COMPANIES

The parameter estimates of Tables 6·16 and 6·17 can now be used to calculate values for the formulae derived in Section 2. Table 6·18 gives values for the accounting ratio for companies' extra income, λ_p, (i.e. the cost to the Government of allowing an increase of one unit of before tax profits), the AR of private investment or capital, λ, (from which can be derived the AR of savings, $f_s = m\lambda$) the AR of net social profits to net profit at market prices before tax, f_n and the social rate of return, r_s, assuming funds are switched from consumption. The table gives preferred combinations of h and r from Table 6·17 for domestic companies, and a range of values of h for these given rates of return for foreign companies. The lower bound on the ARI, R_0, is calculated for domestic companies, and values near this are taken for the ARI (except for col. 1, which allows some comparison with earlier estimates which were based on an ARI of 10% presented in SMN Chapter 6.) The most useful parameter would seem to be λ_p, and the line below gives a measure of its sensitivity to proportional changes in the rate of return. It will be seen that over the range of values chosen λ_p is not very sensitive to the rate of return, but this is not always true, and values for $rd\lambda_p/dr$ are themselves highly variable. (If $r = 17^1/_2\%$, but all the other figures for domestic companies in col. (1) are the same, $-rd\lambda_p/dr = 15·4$, and $= 22604·5$ if $r = 20\%$!) The sensitivity of λ_p and f_n to variations in the other parameters are shown in Table 6·19, which gives absolute changes in λ_p and f_n to absolute changes in the parameters for the larger of two representative columns in Table 6·18 (cols. (3) and (6) for domestic companies, cols. (3) and (5) for foreign companies). Again, the sensitivity can vary quite widely with differing parameter values. Nonetheless, the implication of Table 6·19 is intuitively appealing and clear—apart from more accurate estimates of s and r, f_p stands out as the parameter whose present uncertainty and benefit from reducing uncertainty are highest.

Table 6·17 Growth and Profitability for Domestic Companies

Payout ratio h	Implied savings s	$\dfrac{R_0}{r}$	Implied rate of growth $g\%$ if rate of profit r is		
			15%	17½%	20%
0·3	0·43	0·81	**8·57**	10·02	11·46
0·4	0·37	0·76	7·45	**8·71**	9·96
0·5	0·32	0·70	6·33	7·39	**8·46**
0·6	0·26	0·63	5·20	6·08	6·96

Notes: $g = ms(r - ib)$; $b = 0·2$, $i = 0$.

Table 6·18 *Accounting Prices for Private Companies*

	return r:	10%	15%			17½%		20%	
	ARI R:			12½%	12½%	15%		15%	15%
		(1)	(2)	(3)	(4)	(5)	(6)	(7)
Domestic companies									
Dividend ratio	h	0·4	0·3	0·4	0·5	0·4	0·5	0·6
implied savings rate	s	0·37	0·43	0·37	0·32	0·37	0·32	0·26
rate of growth	$g\%$	7·5	8·6	7·5	7·4	8·7	8·5	7·0
Bound for ARI	$R_0\%$	11·4	12·2	11·4	12·2	13·3	14·0	12·6
AR of company income	λ_p	−0·31	0·05	0·12	0·02	0·15	0·08	0·14
	$-rd\lambda_p/dr$	3·4	1·8	1·1	1·2	1·0	1·0	0·6
ARPI	λ	−0·82	−0·05	0·03	−0·24	0·09	−0·12	−0·03
Social profit/net profit	f_n	1·14	0·80	0·72	0·82	0·69	0·76	0·70
Social rate of return	$r_s\%$	55	38	35	46	39	49	45
Foreign companies									
	h	0·5	0·6	0·4	0·6	0·5	0·5	0·7
	s	0·33	0·27	0·38	0·27	0·33	0·33	0·22
	g	5·8	4·8	6·7	5·6	6·7	7·7	5·1
	λ_p	0·28	0·43	0·35	0·39	0·40	0·35	0·44
	$-rd\lambda_p/dr$	0·7	0·2	0·5	0·3	0·3	0·5	0·2
	λ	0·12	0·45	0·36	0·32	0·44	0·30	0·41
	f_n	0·52	0·37	0·45	0·42	0·40	0·45	0·37
	$r_s\%$	139	100	121	130	124	160	131

Note: r_s is calculated from equation (9) with $f_f=f_c$ for domestic companies, $f_f=1$ for foreign companies.

Table 6·19   Sensitivity of Accounting Prices

Parameter 'p'	Change 'Δp'	Domestic		Foreign	
		Δλ_p	Δf_n	Δλ_p	Δf_n
b borrowing	0·1	0·02	0·01	0·05	−0·06
i interest	0·1	−0·02	0·03	−0·03	0·06
f_k AR capital	0·1	0·12	−0·12	0·07	−0·08
f_c AR consumption	0·05	0·02	··	··	··
f_p AR profits	0·15	−0·20	0·35	−0·17	0·20
t_d dividend tax	0·2	−0·10	0·10	··	··
t_t profit tax	0·1	−0·08	0·06	··	··

Table 6·20   Best Estimates of Accounting Prices

Ownership	λ_p	λ	f_s	f_n	r*_i%
Domestic	0·1	0·0	0·0	0·7	35%
Foreign	0·4	0·4	0·5	0·4	120%

*With $f_f = f_c$ for domestic companies, $f_f = 1$ for foreign companies.

Source: Table 6·18

199

5. Conclusion

The method described in Section 2 was used to find the accounting ratio for an average company's extra profit, λ_p, with a reasonable degree of success. The evidence from a wide range of statistical sources was reasonably consistent, and enabled the final value of λ_p to be placed within a surprisingly narrow confidence interval, given the expected sensitivity of the formula for the accounting ratio.

Domestic companies differ from foreign private investment in the source of their funds, the tax rate paid on dividends and possibly in their retention ratios. Foreign firms appeared to invest in sectors attracting a slightly higher rate of effective protection than domestic firms, and so have a slightly lower rate of profits measured at APs, though the difference observed is almost certainly not significant. As a result of all these factors the accounting ratios differ between domestic and foreign firms. It was also possible to suggest revised values for the ARI, which in turn affect the other accounting ratios. A lower estimate for the ARI, R, would seem to be $12^{1}/_{2}\%$, at which value λ_p for an average domestic company is $0 \cdot 1$, and for an average foreign company is $0 \cdot 4$. The range of plausible values for these average estimates is respectively from $-0 \cdot 1$ to $0 \cdot 3$ and from $0 \cdot 2$ to $0 \cdot 6$, though it should be stressed that individual companies, which differ enormously in the extent to which they are protected, in their rates of profit and their rates of growth, will have values for these accounting ratios which may lie far outside this range. If the intention is to calculate the social profitability of private investment in a given sector, or if the source of the private funds can be identified, then the average figure may give a very misleading measure of the AR for the particular case, and the ratios should be recalculated using the appropriate information. If the Kenyan economy is expected to continue at the past high rates of growth, a higher value for the ARI of 15% (in real terms) may be thought more appropriate, in which case the values for λ_p will be slightly higher at $0 \cdot 15$ for an average domestic company, and fractionally above $0 \cdot 4$ for an average foreign company.

The remarkable thing about all these estimates is that the social cost of transferring £1 from the public sector to private profits is very low, because the private sector is very successful at generating social profits. Not only has the rate of profit at market prices been high, but it has been almost as high (for the average company) when measured at accounting prices. The prospect with a more uniform structure of effective protection must therefore be very good. These high rates of profit, and reasonable rates of reinvestment, lead to very high social rates of return. On the most favourable assumption that private investment is at the expense of private consumption the social rate of return is 35% p.a. in real terms for domestic private investment. The return to new private capital inflows is even higher, at 120%, for although the social cost of foreign profits is higher, the Government provides a lower contribution to the finance of foreign investment, and benefits from the inflow of foreign exchange whilst taxing the goods purchased by foreign firms. The base on which the rate of return of 120% is calculated is rather small, so that the confidence interval for the estimate is fairly wide. Nevertheless, if the assumptions of the model are fulfilled in practice, namely that new foreign private investment enjoys no more than average protection, earns the average rate of profit and retains the average proportion of profits, then foreign private investment is highly socially profitable.

LIST OF REFERENCES

Cyert, R. M. and March, J. G., *A Behavioural Theory of the Firm,* Englewood Cliffs, N. J., 1963.

Cyert, R. M. and George, K. D., 'Competition, Growth and Efficiency', *Economic Journal,* Jan. 1969, pp. 23–41.

Harberger, A. C., *Project Evaluation,* London, 1972.

Hughes, G. A., 'Low-cost Housing in Nairobi' (mimeo.), Cambridge, 1973.

I.L.O., *Employment, Incomes and Equality,* ILO, Geneva, 1973.

King, J. R., 'Financial Policy in Kenya: The Background to the Reserve Crisis of 1971', Working Paper 122, IDS, University of Nairobi, 1973.

Khan, A. R., *The Economy of Bangladesh,* London, 1972.

Little, I. M. D. and Mirrlees, J. A., *Manual of Industrial Project Analysis in Developing Countries, Vol. II: Social Cost Benefit Analysis,* OECD Paris, 1968.

Little, I. M. D. and Mirrlees, J. A., *Project Appraisal and Planning for Developing Countries,* Heinemann Educational Books, London, 1974.

Little, I. M. D., Scitovsky, T. and Scott, M. FG., *Industry and Trade in some Developing Countries,* Oxford, 1970.

MacDougall, G. D. A., 'The benefits and cost of private investment from abroad: a theoretical approach', *Ec. Rec.,* 36, 1960, pp. 13–35, reprinted in *BOUIS 22,* 1960, pp.189–211.

Nairobi Stock Exchange Committee—Official Yearbooks, 1966–72.

Phelps, M. G. and Wasow, B., 'Measuring Protection and its effects in Kenya', Working Paper 37, IDS, University of Nairobi, 1972.

Popper, K. R., *The Open Society and its Enemies,* London, 1962 (4th Edn.)

Powell, R. P., 'The stock of fixed capital in Kenya 1964–71', Working Paper 43, IDS, University of Nairobi, 1972.

Sandmo, A. and Drèze, J. H., 'Discount rates for public investment in closed and open economies', *Economica,* Nov. 1971, pp.395–412.

Samuelson, P. A., *The Collected Scientific Papers,* Vol. 3. (Ed. R. C. Merton), M.I.T., Cambridge, Mass., 1972.

Schumpeter, J. A., *Capitalism, Socialism and Democracy,* London, 1954, (4th Edn.).

SMN—Scott, M. FG., MacArthur, J. D. and Newbery, D. M. G., *Project Appraisal in Practice—The Little–Mirrlees Method Applied in Kenya,* Heinemann Educational Books, London, 1976.

Snowden, P. N., 'Preliminary report on a study of company savings in Kenya's manufacturing sector', Discussion Paper 113, IDS, University of Nairobi, 1972.

'Company Savings in Kenya's Manufacturing Sector 1963–69', forthcoming, in W. T. Newlyn (Ed.), *Sources of Development Finance.*

UNCTAD The flow of financial resources: Balance-of-payments effects of private foreign investment: case studies of Jamaica and Kenya, by L. Needlemans, S. Lall, R. Lacey and J. Seagrave, UNCTAD TD/B/C.3/79/Add 2, 1970.

UNIDO *Guidelines for Project Evaluation* by P. Dasgupta, S. Marglin and A. Sen, U.N., New York, 1972.

Weizsäcker, C. C. VON 'Notes on Endogenous Growth of Productivity', Chapter 4 of *Models of Economic Growth,* Ed. J. A. Mirrlees and N. H. Stern, London, 1973.

Government Publications

Republic of Kenya *Development Plan 1970–74* (Second Plan).
                     Census of Industrial Production 1967, Jan. 1972.
                     Statistical Abstract 1969, 1972.

Statistical Digest:
Survey of Industrial Production 1968. June 1970.
Survey of Industrial Production 1969. December 1971.
Stocks in the Economy of Kenya 1964–68. June 1969.
Survey of Capital Assets 1963.

East African Income Tax Department A guide to income tax in East Africa, 1969.

U.K. Official Publications, H.M.S.O., Business Monitor M4, Overseas Transactions, Board of Trade Journal.

SYMBOLS AND EQUATIONS OF FIRST APPEARANCE

		Equation
a	rate of tax deduction	6·2
b	fraction of investment financed by short borrowing	6·2
B	social benefit produced by capital k	6·4
c	fraction of pre-tax profits consumed	6·1
d	depreciation	6·12
$f_c\,f_k$	AR for consumption and capital goods	6·4
f_s	AR for private savings	6·7
f_f	AR for private finance	6·9
f_n	ratio of net social profit to net pre-tax profit at market prices	6·8
f_p	ratio of profits at APs to market prices	6·4
g	real rate of growth of profits, etc.	6·3
h	fraction of after-tax profits distributed	6·20
i	real rate of interest on short-term borrowing	6·3
k	physical investment induced by 1 unit of profits	6·2
m	a 'multiplier'	6·2a
q	fraction of investment eligible for tax deduction	6·2
r	private real rate of net pre-tax profit	6·3
r_s	social rate of return to private investment	6·9
R	accounting rate of interest, ARI	6·5
R_0	lower bound for ARI	6·11
s	fraction of pre-tax profits saved	6·1
t	fraction of pre-tax profits ultimately taxed	6·1
t_d	rate of tax on distributed profits	6·20
t_1	rate of profits tax	6·20

Using Shadow Prices

u	stock–output ratio	6·17
v	capital–output ratio	. .
λ	AR for private investment	6·6
λ_p	AR for companies' extra income (before tax)	6·5
σ	marginal propensity to save out of disposable income	6·20

Other symbols are used sufficiently close to their definition to need no cross reference.

Other abbreviations

AP	Accounting price
AR	Accounting ratio (AP/market price)
ARI	Accounting rate of interest
APPI	AP of private investment
ARPI	AR for private investment
DVA	Value added at domestic or market prices
LDC	Less-developed country
P–W	Phelps and Wasow (1972)
SCBA	Social cost-benefit analysis
SMN	Scott, MacArthur and Newbery (1976)
WVA	Value added at world prices

CHAPTER SEVEN

Appraising Tourist Development in a Small Economy

D. L. Bevan and D. W. Soskice

1. INTRODUCTION

The Seychelles are an isolated group of islands situated in the Indian Ocean about 1,000 miles due east of Mombasa and a similar distance north of Mauritius. The bulk of the population of over 50,000 reside on the island of Mahé, which accounts for 55 of the colony's total land area of 90 square miles. The economy has traditionally revolved around exports of copra and cinnamon and the fishing industry which provides the main animal protein element in the local diet. With a rate of natural population increase of about $2^{1}/_{2}\%$, emigration becoming more difficult and arable land limited to 2,000 acres, there is a clear need to find new ways of generating income. Given the small scale and isolation of the islands, there seem to be relatively restricted opportunities for setting up manufacturing enterprises, particularly those directed at exports. Already in the latter 1960s imports were running at twice the value of exports and the colony was heavily dependent on U.K. budgetary aid. In 1971 an airport was constructed on Mahé and the decision taken to develop a tourist industry.

The authors visited the islands soon after the airport was opened. The dual purpose of the visit was to examine the application of the Little–Mirrlees method to a tourist project (specifically the Reef Hotel, then under construction) and to explore the problems of using the method to assess a project which is large relative to the total size of the economy.

It seems likely that these two considerations are naturally linked. The current and projected growth of tourism in less developed countries is largely concentrated on small economies, such as islands, or on relatively backward and isolated regions of larger economies. In either case the impact, locally at least, is likely to be great. Only rarely would it be possible to assess the decision whether or not to develop a tourist industry as a small project leaving the main economic aggregates more or less unaffected. Such a decision can only properly be viewed in the context of a plan. Given such a plan it is of course possible to value a particular hotel, or hotel bed, or tourist night. In principle this valuation might take the form of calculating the value of the whole plan with and without the hotel in question. In practice this is not done, and cost–benefit analysis typically proceeds by deriving a set of shadow or accounting prices which are then used to value the outputs and inputs of the project in question. It is unfortunately the case that the appropriate derivation of these shadow prices depends on the nature of the plan. This is always true in principle, but acquires particular force in the case of a small economy undertaking a large project. The next section outlines the nature of these difficulties.

2. Project Appraisal and Planning

It is now a commonplace that social cost–benefit analysis differs from private investment appraisal in using shadow or accounting prices reflecting social benefits and costs rather than market prices. The nature of these shadow prices is perhaps less generally understood. In a private appraisal, a twofold forecasting exercise is involved: it is necessary both to predict the consequences of a project and to predict the future level of prices at which these consequences can be valued. Typically the two exercises are quite separate, as the future level of market prices is unlikely to be influenced by the project in question. Even when this is not so, the required modifications are straightforward. In the public case, the latter step is less clear cut, and the various suggested procedures for cost–benefit appraisal take different (extreme) views of the problem.

At one extreme, it may be assumed that the future path of the economy is predetermined; only the project under immediate consideration is in question, and its effects are trivially small in relation to the economy as a whole. Under these assumptions a parallel procedure can be followed to that used in the private case. The consequences of the project are predicted, a forecast made of the path of the economy through time and the former valued in the light of the latter. Typically a prediction is made of future market prices, and these are then corrected for known or expected distortions to provide the shadow prices. The drawback with this version of cost–benefit analysis is the assumption that the Government, or Department, should wish to optimize as regards the current project, but that otherwise it simply follows arbitrary rules of thumb. If, as seems more plausible, the attempt to optimize is not so confined, then the future path of the economy becomes variable and dependent on present and future project choices; the process is circular.

At the other extreme, it may be assumed that the Government acts in a co-ordinated way, applying the same criteria to all the phenomena under its control. Given the objective function, and some stylized representation of the structure of the economy, an optimal plan can be derived, and, simultaneously, a set of paths for the shadow prices of major inputs and outputs. Cost–benefit analysis then consists simply of using these shadow prices to assess the worth of a particular project, again on the assumption that its impact on major aggregates is trivially small. The drawback with this approach, apart from its greater inherent difficulty, is the artificial assumption of a unified, cohesive and efficient government. Project evaluators are frequently charged with choosing the 'best' set of projects against a background of decentralized departments pursuing fragmented and even contradictory objectives. To the extent that this situation arises simply because of ineradicable inefficiency elsewhere in government (e.g. the persistent use of arbitrary rules of thumb), the solution is, in principle, relatively simple. The behaviour of non-optimizing departments is inserted as an additional set of constraints on the choices available to the optimizing part of the Government. The problem is more complex, but still well defined. To the extent that the difficulty arises from contradictory views as to what is desirable, this is no longer so, as there is now more than one objective function within the Government. Even if self-righteous project planners attempted a solution along the lines above, there would always be the possibility of attempts by other departments to neutralize their choices, and a game-theoretic situation would arise.

The bulk of practical cost–benefit analysis is carried out on the lines of the first extreme. The Little–Mirrlees procedure is one of the relatively few to provide a framework for the more appropriate second type. However, since government plans are typically neither cohesive nor optimal, the application of Little–Mirrlees may involve using formulae derived in an optimum context in conjunction with forecast figures which are not. Ideally this discrepancy should be narrowed, either by improving the planning process, or, where this is not practically possible, by deriving shadow prices from models which contain a fuller specification of constraints. The intention of this paper is to look at this problem, in a very preliminary way, in the particular context of tourist development.

3. Project Appraisal and Tourist Development

The development of a tourist industry necessarily involves a set of interdependent projects, and this in two senses. In the first place the creation of 'tourist nights' (or any other convenient unit of output) requires a variety of ancillary activities over and above the construction and operation of a hotel. These ancillary activities will typically include the provision of major services (power, water, transport) which exhibit economies of scale. In the second place, hotels will exert an influence on each other via their impact on the domestic labour market, food prices and possibly the demand for tourist services, particularly if some of these (e.g. beaches) are in fixed supply.

This high degree of interdependence means that the tourist industry must be viewed as a system, and makes it extremely difficult to identify a 'project'. The impact of adding one more hotel will include consequential design changes elsewhere in the system and the nature of these changes will depend on the shape of the system. One could, of course, still proceed by assuming that whatever broad plan the Government has formulated will be rigidly followed with the sole exception of the next item; that all future decisions have been preempted and that the present choice can take these as data. In the present interdependent case this fiction is more than usually unacceptable. The standard solution to the problem of interdependent projects is to treat the whole set as a single project. When, as in the Seychelles, the tourist industry is intended to become the dominant sector in the economy, this is tantamount to setting up an optimum plan for the whole economy. Even for a relatively simple island economy with a comparatively limited number of productive relationships, this prescription is clearly beyond the present state of the art, not to mention the purses, of most developing countries.

The solution to this dilemma would seem to lie in the sort of compromise that is currently followed by one or two large system operators. A rather stylized model of the system is optimized, giving a set of paths through time of the relevant magnitudes. This information about the future shape of the system is then used in the detailed assessment of the projects under consideration, using the full set of data, rather than the stylized set. If the result of this assessment conflicts with the implied choices in the stylized model, then evidently the latter is a poor approximation, and must be rebuilt. If the result is consistent then it is at least a reasonable gamble to accept the detailed assessments. It should be noticed that these detailed appraisals are still necessary with this method, not only to validate the model, but also because detailed questions like project design will slip through its coarse mesh. For example, it might provide broad estimates of the rate at which hotel beds should be created, while giving no information on the best size, location or class of hotel.

4. OPTIMAL PLANS AND THE LITTLE–MIRRLEES PROCEDURE

A crucial difficulty in optimal planning is the intertemporal one. If we can find a way of attaching a value to those parts of current output which act as a bridge between the present and future states of the economy, in terms of those parts which are wholly committed to the present, we are left with the much simpler problem of optimizing the economy at each point in time. If the Government has complete control (i.e. is restricted only by technological constraints) the intertemporal problem boils down to attaching weights to consumption in different periods. A unit of investment is valued by considering the weighted value of the consumption stream to which it gives rise; at the optimum this weighted value must equal that of a unit of consumption in the period of the investment. As a result, consumption and investment are equally valuable at the margin; and the rate of decline of the consumption weights through time provides a natural 'consumption rate of of interest'.

The Little–Mirrlees procedure is derived in the context of an optimum plan, but makes the more realistic assumption that there are additional constraints on the Government's freedom of action. In particular, constraints on the Government's ability to manipulate the proportion of output going to consumption prevent it from equating the marginal value of investment to that of consumption. In this situation the intertemporal problem becomes more difficult; it requires revaluation of the various components of output in terms of a common numéraire. The Little–Mirrlees procedure takes free foreign exchange currently in the hands of the Government as the numéraire. The negative of the rate of change of the accounting price attached to foreign exchange is then dubbed the Accounting Rate of Interest

(ARI), and provides the required link between different periods. (An alternative but equivalent procedure is to choose current consumption as the numéraire, giving a consumption rate of interest, and requiring that investment be revalued in terms of consumption.) If the path of the accounting price of foreign exchange is known, the remainder of the Little–Mirrlees procedure becomes relatively straightforward. The remaining accounting prices can be calculated from an examination of the detailed constraints in the economy and the path of the ARI.

The primary problem thus boils down to estimating a plausible path for the ARI. In many studies using the technique it is simply assumed that the ARI is steady at some plausible level such as 10% p.a., or equivalently that the accounting price of foreign exchange falls at a constant proportional rate (of 10% p.a.). For relatively large and stable economies which appear to be growing steadily, and in which the severity of the consumption constraints appears unlikely to be much relaxed in the near future, this sort of approach seems quite reasonable as well as remarkably difficult to avoid. For economies undergoing rapid and irregular change any such assumption is dangerously arbitrary; and if they are small, at least, it may be feasible to tackle the problem more explicitly.

In the rest of this paper we discuss one such attempt at an explicit derivation of the ARI. Though the model is now mathematically complete, its formulation has been a lengthy process, and we have unfortunately not yet had time to test it empirically, so no numerical results are available. The present intention is rather to discuss the problems inherent in the exercise, to demonstrate its feasibility and, not least, to lay open for discussion the particular assumptions we have made.

5. GENERAL REMARKS ON THE MODEL

Optimal models are inherently difficult and it is a nice question as to how much realism can be afforded. Non-linear relationships cause considerable problems, but clearly 'real' relationships are often of this type. One method is to build a model containing non-linearities and then make extensive use of approximations in solving it. A drawback here is that these approximations will usually be by series expansion and it may be difficult to ensure sufficiently rapid convergence. Another technique relies on the fact that it is always possible to make a linear approximation to a curve at any point on the curve. The model can then be framed in terms of these linear approximations and solved. The major difficulty with this approach is that in advance of solution it is not known which approximation is appropriate. It will thus be necessary to check that the solution values when inserted into the 'real' relationships tally with the chosen approximations, and a reiterative procedure may be required. Nevertheless, it is broadly the latter approach which we here adopt.

A related difficulty is that optimum models frequently solve to give paths which approach limits asymptotically. One would certainly expect an upper limit to the total of hotels constructed, for example; and that being the case, one would expect, in practice, to achieve the saturation level in finite time. The reason for this 'practical' expectation is bound up, *inter alia*, with indivisibility, which is difficult to model. We have constructed the present model in such a way as to ensure that hotel construction does stop in finite time.

6. THE OBJECTIVE FUNCTION

For reasons discussed below, it seemed desirable to have two consumption goods in the economy, one of them ('food') which could be domestically produced as well as imported, the other ('consumer manufactures') which must necessarily be imported. To keep matters manageable, we take social welfare to be additive in utility; and utility to be of the additive constant elasticity form in these two goods. For this part of the welfare function, we have:

$$W = \int_0^\infty N \ (g_0 c^b + g_1 m_5{}^b) \ e^{-rt} dt \ ; \ b, \ g_0, \ g_1 < 0;$$

where c, m_5 are the per capita quantities of the two goods respectively, N the population and r the rate of pure time preference.

Tourism is often viewed with mixed feelings as a route to development; it can be argued that it is accompanied by 'public bads' of pollution and disruption of the domestic social structure. If this is so, a Government would presumably be prepared to accept a rather lower level of consumption generated by other means. It is by no means clear how to incorporate this idea simply into the welfare function. The disutility per head involved is presumably a function of the number of tourists, but is it also a function of the size of the domestic population? If the domestic population is large, there are more individuals to be adversely affected by a given number of tourists; but the adverse effect per domestic individual may be dissipated as the ratio of tourists to domestic population is lower. This latter situation might arise in the social disruption case, since there it is presumably the proportionate impact that matters; if an average local individual's social and other contacts are very predominantly with others of the domestic population, disruption will be minimized. Alternatively individual disutility of the pollution type (for example, through the overcrowding of beaches and beauty spots) might be increasing in both tourists and the domestic population. Hence there is a spectrum of possible formulations. At one extreme, disutility might increase with the size of the domestic population as well as the scale of the tourist industry; at the other, it might fall with the size of the domestic population while rising with the scale of the industry. We have compromised by including two very simple types, one from the middle of the spectrum (disutility independent of the size of the local population), and one from the former extreme. The objective function finally chosen is then:

$$V = \int_{0}^{\infty} [N\{g_0 c^b + g_1 m_5{}^b - g_2 h\} - g_3 h] e^{-rt} dt \qquad (7\cdot 1)$$

where $g_2, g_3 \geq 0$; and h is the number of tourist nights per unit time.

This formulation ensures that there will be a saturation level for the tourist industry; and that if and when food is imported (i.e. the price ratio between c and m_5 fixed at the world c.i.f. ratio), the proportions of the two goods consumed will be in constant ratio—they have unitary income elasticity. This latter restriction is made, evidently, for tractability alone. The reason why constant proportions hold only when food is imported is that we make the plausible assumption that for isolated economies high transport costs open up a sizeable gap between the world export and import prices. The economy may then initially be in a situation where the domestic food price is between these two. This enables us to examine the realistic case in which tourist development has the additional adverse consequence of causing increases in the relative price of domestic staples, such as (in the Seychelles) fish.

7. CONSTRAINTS

7.1 *Agriculture*
The other requirement for the model to generate a rise in the relative price of food, at least in the early stages of tourist development, is that

there should be diminishing returns in domestic agriculture. Since we require diminishing marginal productivity for this purpose, a linear function will not serve, and we are forced to take this particular bull by the horns and write in a concave function from the start; hence this is the only constraint which we do not linearize.

Diminishing returns in agriculture imply the existence of rents. Since agricultural land is typically in private ownership, a proper treatment would require the incorporation of appropriate behavioural equations both to trace the course of agricultural production and to value the consequential flow of private profit. To accomplish this without unduly complicating the model poses a delicate problem of formulation. We have not yet solved this, and to our regret the present model presupposes state ownership of land, or equivalently, a 100% tax on agricultural profits coupled possibly with optimal payroll taxes or subsidies.

Developing countries are often characterized as having a surplus pool of underemployed labour in subsistence agriculture. We found little evidence of this in the Seychelles, even that little typically involving families who also derived wage income from working on plantations; and recent experience suggests the latter as the source of residual labour in the colony. We thus incorporate a plantation sector producing an export cash crop under constant returns to scale. This last requires that we assume not only constant returns in production, but also that the economy be a small supplier in world market terms. The latter seems plausible enough, but the former is clearly one of those assumptions so oddly termed heroic.

Summarizing the agricultural constraints, we then have:

Food sector (shadow price p_3)

$$f(n_3) + m_3 = cN + d_0 h. \tag{7.2}$$

Plantation sector (shadow price p_4)

$$a_4 n_4 = x_4, \tag{7.3}$$

where n_3, n_4 are the numbers of workers in the two sectors; N is the population; c *per capita* food consumption by the domestic population; h the number of tourist nights; x_4 export earnings in the plantation sector; $f(n_3)$ is a concave function relating the output of domestic food to the labour force; m_3 is imports of food; and d_0, a_4 are constants.

(7.2) simply states that the sum of domestic production and

imports of food must equal the sum of domestic consumption and that of tourists.

(7·3) states that the foreign exchange earnings of the plantation sector are proportional to the labour force employed.

All the variables in these and the other equations are functions of time, but to prevent the text from becoming cluttered, we have omitted the subscript indicating this.

7.2 Hotels: Construction and Operation

We assume that the gross export earnings of hotels (x_2) are proportional to the number of tourist nights, i.e.

$$a_2 h = x_2 \quad \text{(shadow price } p_2) \tag{7·4}$$

(7·4) assumes that the Seychelles is a perfect competitor in the provision of hotel services. It seems more likely that imperfect competition is the rule and hence a downward sloping demand curve would be more appropriate. It is not at all clear how to model this, however. In the early days of development, a new location such as the Seychelles may have a social cachet which it later loses; the erosion of this advantage might be a function of scale or of time. Conversely, a new location may have to underprice initially to become established. In our view the likely saturation level due to the small scale of the Seychelles, reinforced by the selected form of the objective function, will be low enough to make the proportionality assumption fairly realistic. (This stability might of course mask a progressive switch in the type of tourist, from those seeking solitude and out-of-the-way places, to those who desire a rather full range of facilities.)

A more serious problem is that (7·4) obscures one important choice facing the Seychelles, namely, whether to go for the relatively cheap high volume end of the market, or concentrate on a rather restricted number of luxury hotels; or some combination of the two. For an all-or-nothing choice it would be perfectly possible to run the model with values appropriate to the mass case and then repeat with values for the luxury case. But since some mixture may well be preferable, it is better to estimate a_2 (and other parameters discussed below) as a reasonable weighted average, and leave these questions of design to the stage of detailed appraisal.

As regards construction, we again assume proportionality, giving

$$a_1 n_1 = \dot{h} \tag{7·5}$$

with shadow price p_1, where n_1 is the labour force in the construction industry, h the rate of construction and a_1 a constant. It is evident that it is hotels which are constructed, rather than tourist nights, but as long as occupancy rates are constant (which should be ensured by sensible planning at least in the medium and longer run) this raises no problems.

We also assume that while construction proceeds, there are two types of foreign exchange impact, one proportional to the rate of construction (covering imported materials and skilled supervisory labour), the other a constant. This latter is designed to cover the element of fixed foreign exchange cost involved in maintaining contractors capable of undertaking the relatively large-scale works required. In conjunction with the form of the welfare function, this makes it desirable, other things being equal, to press on with construction relatively quickly rather than spinning it out over very long horizons; in short it ensures a finite construction period (or set of separated periods). As discussed above, this seems a desirable characteristic for the model to possess. We discuss these foreign exchange considerations in more detail below.

7.3 *Labour Supply and Population*

Both in terms of the model here presented, and in terms of common intuition, it is difficult to conceive of a satisfactory long-term future for the Seychelles unless the growth of population is eventually halted. Currently the population is growing at about $2^1/_2$% p.a., the people are predominantly Roman Catholic and there is little in the way of family planning. Optimal models can either be extended over infinite time or restricted to a finite period. If the population grows steadily 'for ever', the structure of the present model means that indefinitely large numbers of workers would have to be absorbed by the plantation sector, and in these circumstances it would be impossible to justify the assumption of constant returns in that sector as a (relatively) local approximation. The two solutions available are either to build in the assumption that population growth eventually ceases, or to stop the model at some prescribed date. The difficulty with the latter course is that it is necessary to predetermine the desired shape of the economy at the terminal date—and this really depends on what happens afterwards. We have chosen the former course, both because it is easier to handle and because it is then possible to examine the consequences of achieving a stationary population earlier or later.

Ideally one would like to build in a demographically realistic population profile; for example, by using a polynomial function. In practice this would greatly increase the difficulty of solving the model. We have here taken the extreme and demographically bizarre step of allowing the population to grow at a constant proportional rate until some given date and then abruptly becoming stationary. It would, however, be straightforward to adapt the model to a sequence of phases, with the population growing steadily in each of them at successively lower rates. Provided these rates satisfied certain conditions, the only effect of this modification would be to increase somewhat the necessary volume of computation.

We assume that the Government maintains full employment, so the labour supply constraint is simply

$$d_1 N = n_1 + d_2 h + n_3 + n_4 \qquad \text{with shadow price } W \qquad (7\cdot6)$$

where N, n_1, n_3, n_4 have the senses previously ascribed; and d_2 is the (fixed) number of hotel and ancillary workers required to service a tourist night. The proportionality of d_2 seems to be reasonably well supported by available evidence, except in the very early stages where learning is taking place. d_1 is a constant which relates the available labour force to the population; we here conceive of it as making allowance for government administrative workers as well as the economically inactive.

7.4 *Balance of Payments*

Currently the Seychelles receives budgetary aid to match its (relatively) massive current payments deficit and can freely obtain capital aid from the U.K. for any projects promising a rather low financial return. If this situation were to obtain indefinitely it should be possible to arrive at a full optimum solution rather than a savings-constrained one of the usual Little–Mirrlees type. However, moves are afoot to obtain independence in the near future, and however generous U.K. aid to an independent Seychelles might be, this particular constellation of circumstances seems likely to be atypical of the economy's future as well as that of small economies in general. We have therefore chosen to incorporate a more normal balance of payments constraint into the model, namely:

$$x_2 + x_4 = k_0 + k_1\dot{h} + k_2 h + m_3 + m_5 N \quad \text{with shadow price } \lambda. \quad (7\cdot7)$$

x_2, x_4, $\dot{h}$, h, m_3, m_5 and N have already been defined; k_0, k_1 and k_2 require rather fuller discussion. In one interpretation we could take k_0 and k_1 simply as the foreign exchange costs of the construction industry as already discussed; k_2 then represents the tourist import requirements of goods other than food, per tourist night. In that case (7·7) implies an absence of both foreign investment and of aid. An alternative interpretation is to think of the ks as composites resulting from aid and foreign investment as well as these costs. For example, we might assume that some fraction of construction cost is met by foreign finance; k_1 is then the import costs of construction, net of this flow of foreign finance, while k_2 is a sum of tourist import requirements and interest payments. (Notice that if the proportion of construction costs met from abroad is constant—either by Government decision, or according to the policies of the lenders—then it will be at least roughly true that interest payments will be proportional to the resulting scale of the tourist industry.) Similarly, k_0 might be a net figure reduced by a flow of grant aid calculated to assist the economy during the construction phase.

This device enables us to make some allowance for borrowing, but there is nothing in the model to represent lending to foreigners. Given the structure of the model, this is a serious omission, since the ARI eventually declines to a rather low level. In effect the available domestic investment opportunities become progressively less attractive and at some point it would be rational to switch to portfolio investment abroad. If this were politically feasible, the international interest rate would set a lower limit to the ARI. We hope to embody this possibility in a later version of the model.

8. First Order Conditions and the Nature of the Model

To complete the model one final term is necessary, to allow for the insulation of domestic food production from world prices in the early part of the programme. Thus we have

$$m_3 \geq 0 \quad \text{with shadow price } \psi \text{ (if } m_3 > 0, \ \psi = 0; \ m_3 = 0, \ \psi \geq 0). \quad (7\cdot8)$$

Setting up a Lagrangean in (7·1) to 7·8) with the accompanying shadow prices, and differentiating, we get the first order conditions.

217

(n_1) $p_1 a_1 = W$ (7·9)

(n_3) $p_3 f'(n_3) = W$ (7·10)

(n_4) $p_4 a_4 = W$ (7·11)

(x_2) $p_2 = \lambda$ (7·12)

(m_3) $p_3 = \lambda - \psi$ (7·13)

(x_4) $p_4 = \lambda$ (7·14)

(c) $b g_0 c^{b-1} e^{-rt} = p_3$ (7·15)

(m_5) $b g_1 m_5^{b-1} e^{-rt} = \lambda$ (7·16)

(h) $-\{g_2 N + g_3\} e^{-rt} + \dot{p}_1 + a_2 p_2 - d_0 p_3 + \dot{\lambda} k_1 - \lambda k_2 = W d_2$ (7·17)

The object of the exercise is to use (7·1)–(7·17) to obtain an explicit path for λ, the numéraire. To do this it is useful to see that the path of the economy divides naturally into a sequence of phases. Assuming that the domestic food price is initially below the world import price, there will be a period, say from time zero to time T_0, during which the domestic price rises to the world level. There will also be a period, say from 0 to T_1, during which hotels will be constructed. (Depending on the parameter values, there may indeed be more than one.) Finally there will be a period, say from 0 to T_2, during which population grows. After T_2 it is stationary. What is less clear is the order in time of T_0, T_1, T_2. Of the six possible sequences, only two can be ruled out; those in which T_0 occurs last (and in finite time). In other words, if the domestic food price is to reach the world import level at all, it must do so while either population is still growing, and/or while hotels are still being built.

Given the severely limited scope for expanding domestic agriculture and the current lack of any population policy, the most plausible sequence seems to be T_0, T_1, T_2, and it is on this that we have concentrated. (The derivation of the solution will be very similar for any feasible sequence, so there should be no additional difficulty in examining alternatives, if the solution values should indicate that the chosen sequence is wrong for a given set of parameter values.)

The sequence T_0, T_1, T_2 implies four phases for the path of the economy through time. Phase I is characterized by a rising price of food, a growing population and the construction of hotels. In Phase II the only difference is that the food price is stationary at the world import level. In Phase III the construction of hotels has stopped and only population is changing, while in Phase IV the economy enters a stationary state.

It is possible that this relatively simple picture will be complicated by further bouts of hotel construction. If the population goes on growing for a very long time, there may be a series of alternating Phases II and III in between the single Phases I and IV. For present purposes we intend to choose T_2 sufficiently early to prevent this happening, but it would be a relatively simple matter to extend the model in this direction.

Finally, to check whether it is desirable to introduce a tourist industry at all, the model can be computed with h restricted to zero. The path of the economy then involves a slower rise in the price of food, either to some level still below the world price (when population ceases to grow) or to the world price followed by a further period involving only population growth.

In any period of Phase III type, the structure of the model (full employment guaranteed by (7·6)) ensures that surplus labour is accommodated by expanding the plantation sector.

Our reason for specifying two consumer goods should now be apparent. If there was only one, we should either be unable to model the inflationary Phase I (if the good were already imported) or be forced to assume zero imports initially (there would simply be nothing to spend export earnings on).

It is now possible to proceed by solving each phase separately and then tying these solutions together. In other words we can choose arbitrary values for T_0, h_{T0}, T_1, h_{T1}; given these (unspecified) values we can then compute the optimum path in each phase, and hence a value for the objective function in each phase (V_1 for Phase I, etc.) in terms of these arbitrary values. The final step is to choose the optimum T_0, h_{T0} and so on; the necessary conditions for this can be obtained by differentiating the sum of the V_i and equating to zero.

We are ultimately interested in the path of λ during the hotel building phases (I and II). Equations for this are obtained automatically in the solution process described above, again as functions of the arbitrary values. Inserting the optimum values then gives an explicit optimum path for λ and hence the ARI.

The remaining paths obtained from the model, such as that of h, are of interest mainly in providing checks at the stage of detailed assessment.

At the present time we have obtained explicit formulations for these paths and for the objective function in terms of arbitrary T_0, h_{T0}, T_1, h_{T1}; we have not yet attempted the final step of deriving optimum values for these for any set of parameter values. Since the solutions are extremely lengthy, lack of space limits us to a very cursory description. We also take the phases in reverse order: that is to say, in order of increasing complexity.

9. SOLUTION

9.1 *Phase IV*

Phase IV is extremely straightforward; all variables have become stationary. The value of the objective function is therefore simply:

$$V_4 = (N_{T2}[g_0\bar{c}^{-b} + g_1 m_5^{-b} - g_2 h_{T1}] - g_3 h_{T1})\frac{e^{-rT_2}}{r},$$

where N_{T2} is the eventual stationary level of the population, h_{T1} is the saturation level of the tourist industry, and c and m_5 take the form $Ah_{T1} + B$ (A, B constants).

Further, it is clear from (7·16) that the path of λ is simply

$$\lambda_t = \lambda_{T2} e^{-rt}.$$

Thus in Phase IV the ARI is simply equal to the pure time preference rate. This underlines the lack of alternative physical investment opportunities and the absence of technical progress. The former feature seems to us to be a reasonable reflection of reality in the type of isolated and very small economy exemplified by the Seychelles. The latter is more contentious. It should be possible to reformulate the model with some appropriately specified uniform technical progress in all sectors. Given the nature of the world market for copra, and the method of production, it is not at all apparent that this would be realistic in the plantation sector. As regards the tourist industry, it is unreasonable to expect increases in physical labour productivity in a service sector of this type. A secular rise in foreign exchange earnings per man (and thus rising real income) depends on the one hand on technical progress in the rich countries of the world, coupled with the income elasticity for tourist services; and on the other, on real income trends in the major tourist locations, and hence on the alternative cost of tourist services coupled with the price elasticity for them.

We have not felt competent to pick our way through this maze and hence our (hopefully pessimistic) preliminary assumption of no secular earnings growth.

9.2 *Phase III*

In Phase III, $h=0$, $h=h_{T1}$, $n_1=0$; population grows at a steady rate, n; and the labour force in food production is steady at a level $(\bar{n}_3$, say) determined by:

$$f'(\bar{n}_3)=\frac{W}{p_3}=a_4 \qquad \text{(from 7·8, 7·10, 7·11, 7·13)}.$$

In other words, at a time when it pays to import food and export the plantation crop the marginal productivity in the two sectors should be equated.

Substitution yields:

$$N(c+m_5)=(f(\bar{n}_3)\ -a_4\bar{n}_3)+(a_2\ -a_4d_2\ -d_0\ -k_2)h_{T1}+a_4d_1N$$

$$\text{or} \quad c+m_5=\frac{A_1+A_2N}{N}, \text{ say}.$$

In Phase III, c and m_5 bear a constant ratio to each other, determined by g_0, g_1 and b; so we can write

$$c^b=A_3(c+m_5)^b$$

and similarly for $m_5{}^b$.

With h_{T1} given, the only problem in integrating for V_3 revolves around the terms in c and m_5; for these we have something of the form (taking the case of c):

$$I=\int_{T_1}^{T_2}Ng_0A_3(c+m_5)^be^{-rt}dt$$

$$=N_0{}^{1-b}g_0A_3\int_{T_1}^{T_2}(A_1+A_2N_0e^{nt})^b\,e^{\{(1-b)n-r\}t}\,dt.$$

Provided b is integer valued, and $\dfrac{r}{n}$ is rational, we can employ a series of substitutions to reduce this to the form

$$I=A_4\int_{U_1}^{U_2}U^\alpha(U^\beta+1)^bdU,$$

where α, β, are integers chosen to make I integrable. Indeed, in some particularly simple cases the expression can be integrated as it stands. Thus, if $b = -1$, $n = r = 0 \cdot 02$:

$$I = \frac{N_0 g_0 A_3}{n A_2} \log \left(\frac{A_1 + A_2 N_{T2}}{A_1 + A_2 N_{T1}} \right)$$

If $b = -1$, $n = 0 \cdot 01$, $r = 0 \cdot 02$:

$$I = \frac{N_0^2 g_0 A_3}{A_1} \left[(T_2 - T_1) - \frac{1}{n} \log \left(\frac{A_1 + A_2 N_{T2}}{A_1 + A_2 N_{T1}} \right) \right]$$

Thus the particular form of V_3 depends on the chosen parameter values; for some combinations it runs to a fairly large number of terms. Just as V_4 was a function of h_{T1}, V_3 is a function of T_1 and h_{T1} (via A_1 as well as directly).

9.3 Phase II
Phases I and II present all the real difficulties. In both cases we are unable to obtain exact solutions and have to resort to approximations. To prevent these resulting in artificial discontinuities at the junction of the two phases, they are carried out around T_0.

Phase II yields two differential equations in h and λ.

We have a linear first order differential equation with constant coefficients in λ, $\dot{\lambda}$. From (7·17), using (7·8, 7·9, 7·12, 7·13):

$$-g_2 N_0 e^{(n-r)t} - g_3 e^{-rt} + \dot{\lambda} \left(\frac{a_4}{a_1} + k_1 \right) + \lambda (a_2 - d_0 - k_2 - a_4 d_2) = 0,$$

which has the solution

$$\lambda = Q_0 e^{-q_0 t} + Q_1 e^{(n-r)t} + Q_2 e^{-rt}$$

where $q_0 = \left[\dfrac{a_2 - d_0 - k_2 - a_4 d_2}{a_4/a_1 + k_1} \right]$, Q_1 and Q_2 are constants,

and Q_0 is determined by the initial value, λ_{T0} (derived from Phase I).

The differential equation in $\dot{h}$ is derived from the balance of payments constraint (7·7). After substitution, we have

$$\left(k_1 + \frac{a_4}{a_1} \right) \dot{h} + (k_2 + d_0 + a_4 d_2 - a_2) h + (k_0 - f(\bar{n}_3) + a_4 \bar{n}_3) - a_4 d_1 N + N(c + m_5) = 0.$$

Now from (7·15), we have that $c^{b-1} = \dfrac{\lambda e^{rt}}{g_0 b}$

and similarly for m_5. Given that these are in constant ratio, we can then replace $N(c + m_5)$ by $A_5 \lambda^{\frac{1}{b-1}} e^{(n + \frac{r}{b-1})t}$ where A_5 is a constant. The differential equation can then be written (with the z_i constants) in the form

$$\dot{h} - q_0 h + z_1 + z_2 e^{nt} + z_3 e^{(n + \frac{r}{b-1})t} \lambda^{\frac{1}{b-1}} = 0.$$

We are unable to solve this equation exactly, so we approximate by taking the first three terms in a Taylor expansion of the final term. By this means, we obtain an approximation of the form.

$$\dot{h} - q_0 h + z_1 + z_2 e^{nt} + (v_1 + v_2 t + v_3 t^2) e^{mt}$$

where $m = \dfrac{r - q_0}{b - 1} + n$ and the v_i are functions of λ_{T0}.

This equation has as solution an equation of the form

$$h = S + S_0 e^{q_0 t} + S_1 e^{nt} + (S_2 + S_3 t + S_4 t^2) e^{mt}$$

where S and S_1 are constants; S_2, S_3 and S_4 are functions of λ_{T0}; and S_0 is determined by the initial value h_{T0} (derived from Phase I).

All that remains is to compute the value of the objective function, V_2. The two 'pollution' terms simply involve integrating he^{nt} and $he^{(n-r)t}$ which is straightforward. As regards the consumption terms, we may again illustrate by considering the food good. We have

$$I = \int_{T_0}^{T_1} N g_0 c^b e^{-rt} dt.$$

Once again, we make use of the substitution from (7·15) and write

$$c^b = \frac{\lambda c e^{rt}}{g_0 b};$$

I becomes $\dfrac{N_0}{b} \int_{T_0}^{T_1} \lambda c e^{nt} dt.$

Using Shadow Prices

From (7·2), we have that $c = \dfrac{f(\bar{n}_3) + m_3 - d_0 h}{N}$

and after appropriate substitutions, we obtain an equation of the form

$$c = B_1 h e^{-nt} + B_2 \dot{h} e^{-nt} + B_3 + B_4 e^{-nt},$$

giving $I = \dfrac{N_0}{b} \int_{T_0}^{T_1} (B_1 \lambda h + B_2 \lambda \dot{h} + B_3 \lambda e^{nt} + B_4 \lambda)\, dt,$

which is messy, but again integrates in a straightforward way. The explicit form of V_3 is far too lengthy to write down here, but evidently it is a function of T_0, T_1, h_{T0}, h_{T1}.

9·4 *Phase I*
In Phase I we have the additional complication of change in the food sector.

From (7·10) and (7·11), we have:

$$p_3 = \frac{w}{f'(n_3)} = \frac{\lambda a_4}{f'(n_3)}$$

After appropriate substitutions, equation (7·17) now yields the differential equation

$$-g_2 N_0 e^{(n-r)t} - g_3 e^{-rt} + (a_2 - a_4 d_2 - d_0 - k_2)\lambda$$

$$+ \left(1 - \frac{a_4}{f'(n_3)}\right) d_0 \lambda + (k_1 + \frac{a_4}{a_1})\dot{\lambda} = 0, \tag{7·18}$$

i.e. it differs from the Phase II equations by the term

$$\left(1 - \frac{a_4}{f'(n_3)}\right) d_0 \lambda;$$

in Phase II this vanishes as $f'(\bar{n}_3) = a_4$.
From the balance of payments constraint, (7·7), we now obtain the equation

$$k_0 + k_1 \dot{h} + k_2 h + m_5 N = x_2 + x_4$$

since $m_3 = 0$ in this phase.

224

After substitution, this yields:

$$k_0 + \left(k_1 + \frac{a_4}{a_1}\right)\dot{h} + (k_2 + a_4 d_2 - a_2)h + a_4 n_3 - a_4 d_1 N + m_5 N = 0. \qquad (7\cdot19)$$

In $(7\cdot18)$ and $(7\cdot19)$ there are three terms which are not linear in λ or h, viz.

$$\lambda\left(1 - \frac{a_4}{f'(n_3)}\right) \text{ in } (7\cdot18) \text{ and } n_3 \text{ and } m_5 N \text{ in } (7\cdot19).$$

The next step is to linearize these three terms around $\lambda = \lambda(T_0)$; $h = h(T_0)$; and $t = T_0$. For this purpose we make use of the relations:

$$f(n_3) = cN + d_0 h$$

$$= \left(\lambda \frac{a_4}{f'(n_3)} \frac{e^{rt}}{bg_0}\right)^{\frac{1}{b-1}} N + d_0 h \qquad \text{from } (7\cdot2), (7\cdot15).$$

$$m_5 N = \left(\frac{\lambda e^{rt}}{bg_1}\right)^{\frac{1}{b-1}} N \qquad \text{from } (7\cdot16).$$

These linearizations are accomplished by implicit differentiation, but are too lengthy to describe here. The upshot is that for $(7\cdot18)$ we get an approximation of the form

$$\alpha_0 \dot{\lambda} + \alpha_1 \lambda + \alpha_2 h + f(t) = 0. \qquad (7\cdot18)'$$

And for $(7\cdot19)$ the symmetrical form

$$\beta_0 \dot{h} + \beta_1 h + \beta_2 \lambda + g(t) = 0. \qquad (7\cdot19)'$$

Finally, using operators, it is possible to treat $(7\cdot18)'$ and $(7\cdot19)'$ as a pair of simultaneous equations to yield two second order linear differential equations in λ and h separately. Thus for λ, we obtain

$$[\beta_0 \alpha_0 D^2 + (\beta_0 \alpha_1 + \beta_1 \alpha_0)D + (\beta_1 \alpha_1 - \alpha_2 \beta_2)]\lambda + (\beta_0 D + \beta_1)f(t) - \alpha_2 g(t) = 0$$

and symmetrically for h.

Solution of these equations is straightforward, given the form of $f(t)$ and $g(t)$ that emerges, and is of the type

$$\lambda = B_1 e^{(n-r)t} + B_2 e^{-rt} + B_3 e^{nt} + B_4 t + B_5$$

and similarly for *h*, where all the B_i are functions of T_0.

All that remains is to obtain the value of the objective function. Once again the terms in *h* integrate readily and we need here consider only the consumption terms.

Once again we use the relation

$$Nm_5{}^b = m_5{}^{b-1} m_5 N$$

$$= \left(\frac{\lambda e^{rt}}{bg_1} \right) m_5 N.$$

From the balance of payments constraint, we have

$$m_5 N = (a_2 - a_4 d_2 - k_2)h - (k_1 + \frac{a_4}{a_1})\dot{h} + a_4 d_1 N - k_0 - a_4 n_3.$$

For n_3, we substitute the linearization developed earlier, i.e.

$$n_3 = G_0 + G_\lambda \lambda + G_h h + G_t t$$

The integration of this term then follows in a straightforward, though somewhat inelegant, fashion.

As regards food, we have $Nc^b = c^{b-1} Nc$

$$\text{with} \quad c^{b-1} = \frac{\lambda a_4 e^{rt}}{bg_0 f'(n_3)} = \frac{\lambda e^{rt}}{bg_0} \left[1 - \left(\frac{1-a_4}{f'(n_3)} \right) \right]$$

$$= \frac{\lambda e^{rt}}{bg_0} - \frac{e^{rt}}{bg_0} (F_0 + F_\lambda \lambda + F_h h + F_t t)$$

using the linearization referred to above.

$$Nc = f(n_3) - d_0 h,$$

which may be approximated by

$$f(\bar{n}_3) + f'(\bar{n}_3) \ (n_3 - \bar{n}_3) - d_0 h$$

$$= [f(\bar{n}_3) - f'(\bar{n}_3)\bar{n}_3] + f'(\bar{n}_3)[G_0 + G_\lambda \lambda + G_h h + G_t t] - d_0 h.$$

Hence the integration of Nc^b. V_1 will evidently be a function of T_0, h_{T0}.

10. NEXT STEPS

What remains to be done falls naturally into two parts. In the first place a particular set of parameter values, and a form for $f(n_3)$, must be chosen. Inserting these into the V_i, it will then be possible to obtain optimum values for T_0, T_1, h_{T0}, h_{T1}, and hence compute the path of λ(and the ARI) associated with these values from the Phase I and II formulae sketched above.

The second stage involves detailed assessment of the hotel construction programme, using the standard Little–Mirrlees approach, the empirical data and the computed path of the ARI. At this stage it is necessary to check that the detailed paths for hotel construction and employment in the various sectors should be broadly in line with those embodied in the simplified plan. If they were not, it would be necessary to repeat the whole process described in this section; clearly that possibility places a premium on getting the parameters 'right' first time. To the extent that detailed information is available only for the next few years, this check is only partially available. In this more realistic context a rolling plan would be desirable, with adjustments made whenever the two versions began to diverge.

11. CONCLUDING COMMENTS

An underlying problem in all applications of cost–benefit analysis is that of tying different periods of time together. There are three ways in which an accounting rate of interest might be derived to fulfil this requirement. We might guess a plausible rate; for example, by making reasonable adjustments to the market rate of interest. We might try to predict the future course of the economy under existing policies, and derive a rate from this. Or finally we might try to construct a stylized model of the economy, and derive an optimum path and its associated accounting rate. These options are in increasing order of difficulty. The second seems inappropriate since the very need for an accounting rate presupposes a concern with optimality; if it is the Government which has this concern, then the future course of the economy becomes a matter for choice. The only situation in which the second approach is valid is when an optimizing agent (a Government Department, or an international agency or other donor) is attempting to select projects in a country which as a whole follows non-optimizing rules of thumb.

In what is hopefully the normal case, the choice therefore boils down to the first and third approaches. The first is much simpler but more arbitrary, and is that typically followed. In this paper we have advocated the third. The crucial question is whether the considerable increase in time and effort is justified by the putative gain. It seems to the authors that this is very much a matter of horses for courses. If the economy is relatively large and stable, and the set of investment opportunities seems likely to unroll in a fairly smooth way as time passes, the additional labour of the third approach may well go largely unrewarded. What we have argued here is that in the case of small economies which are in rapid process of virtual reconstruction the first approach is dangerously arbitrary and the additional labour of the third manageable.

It is perfectly true that the present model is both highly simplified from the viewpoint of economic reality, and yet exceedingly complex as models go. Simplification as such is not too serious a defect, given the purpose of the model; what matters is that the simplified model should have, loosely speaking, the right sort of 'shape'. In this sense the present model may be unsatisfactory in several respects. The economy it portrays is effectively under complete state control; there is no secular earnings growth; the treatment of the plantation sector is questionable in itself, and that sector hardly provides a satisfactory surrogate for alternative domestic investment and employment opportunities; and the possibility of lending to foreigners is excluded. The impact on the initial path of the ARI of some at least of these deficiencies will be muted by futurity, but deficiencies they clearly are. Various remedies are feasible, at the cost of further complicating the model. Given the paucity of work in this area, and bearing in mind the likelihood of rather rapidly diminishing returns, it seemed desirable to air the model in its present state.

It is clearly unrealisitic to expect very small economies like the Seychelles to devote the necessary resources to an exercise of this type. But there is no reason to view that as the end of the matter. It would be perfectly feasible for some agency, such as the World Bank, to develop a computer package. Such a package could comprise a wide variety of stylized 'phases' appropriate to different types of circumstance. A particular country could then select, with expert advice if need be, the particular sequence of phases that best described its general intentions, and the appropriate parameter values. The central point is that although models of this type are necessarily complex, the existence of a package of the type outlined would mean that they need not require excessive sophistication on the part of governments using them as policy tools. Such a procedure would not only make it much more likely that detailed decisions were consistent with a government's general intentions; but also provide a check on the consistency of the intentions themselves. Finally, if such a package were to be developed for a large body of potential users, it might be worth while to go rather further than the example here given, and reduce the rather draconian approximations used, both in the structure of the model, and its solution.

This whole argument rests on the presupposition that there is sufficient similarity between groups of economies to allow them to be modelled using parts out of a common kit. We would argue that small tourist economies are one such group. In any event the deployment of optimizing models will depend on the likely gain from using them. We hope eventually to throw some light on this by comparing the putative optimum path derived from our model with the actual long-term plan adopted by the Seychelles.

CHAPTER EIGHT

Practical Problems of Implementing Accounting Prices*†

Ian G. Heggie

The preparation of a set of accounting prices is a reasonably manageable affair, provided they are prepared for a whole sector, or for a whole range of public sector activities, and are not developed on a 'once-off' basis for use on specific projects. The difficulty with the once-off approach is that it substantially increases the number of man-hours required to carry out an evaluation or, if the number of man-hours available to carry it out are fixed (as it often is), it diverts a significant proportion of the available resources away from other aspects of the evaluation. It also makes it more difficult to ensure consistency between the assumptions used in each project. For example, it is not uncommon to find different firms of consultants using quite different shadow wage rates in the same country. Indeed, it is even possible to find different teams from the same firm using different shadow wages in the same country.

Another difficulty with the once-off approach is that it often results in the accounting prices being produced *after* the initial engineering design has been completed. In most evaluations a mixed team of engineers and economists works in parallel, so that the adjusted factor prices only become available part way through the engineering design. Indeed, -they usually only become available after the conceptual part of the design process (e.g. the activity during which major alternatives are specified) has taken place. The accounting prices are therefore only really used during the evaluation and not during the design—thus negating their major purpose (i.e. to increase labour intensity, etc.).

It is therefore preferable, for reasons of efficiency as well as of economy, to prepare sector-wide matrices of accounting prices in advance of any specific evaluations. This clearly reduces the amount of effort involved and ensures that all projects are designed and

*I am most grateful to Ian Little and Maurice Scott for having commented on an earlier draft.

†The substance of this article was originally presented at a conference on Subsidies held at the University of British Columbia, Vancouver, in 1973.

evaluated using consistent prices. It likewise makes revision much easier, ensuring that changes in circumstances and assumptions can be speedily reflected in an amended matrix.

A system of accounting prices does seem to deal reasonably effectively with most of the disadvantages associated with distorted market prices (at least as far as they affect public decisions, or private decisions amenable to public directives): if one cannot get rid of market distortions, the least one can do is to ensure that all public planning and policy decisions are based on a set of prices that exclude these distortions.

In some cases the arguments in favour of accounting prices are almost overwhelming. This is most apparent when major investment decisions are evaluated. The use of accounting prices then enables the decision between capital-and labour-intensive alternatives to be objectively evaluated taking full account of any effects—whether temporary or permanent—on employment; it spells out, in a way that market prices can never do, what the net effect of alternative policies is likely to be on the entire national economy; and it gives considerable insight into the relative scarcity of each factor input and hence suggests (in a production engineering sense) potential planning solutions that might otherwise be overlooked.

However, in spite of these admitted advantages, there remain unresolved difficulties which are generally encountered only when considering the day-to-day management of public facilities. Investment and management decisions cannot easily be separated and yet, as will become apparent, sets of adjusted prices are really suitable only for investment appraisal. This was well illustrated by the difficulties encounted in setting up a new tariff structure for Port Louis,[1] Mauritius, after a master plan for the port had been prepared using a detailed matrix of accounting prices. These difficulties likewise suggested that the conflict between investment and management decisions is not peculiar to ports. It will be argued in the conclusion that the problem is a general one and that the evaluator ignores it at his peril.

In Mauritius the use of these accounting prices generally led to the selection of a different set of facilities than if market prices had been used. For example, the economics of handling bulk sugar was significantly affected by the reduction in unskilled wage costs, the net

---

[1] Sir Alexander Gibb & Partners and Freeman Fox and Associates, *Port Louis Master Plan,* unpublished, 1973.

effect of which was to encourage the selection of a different labour-intensive method of handling cargo. The use of accounting prices thus resulted in the selection of projects which, when valued at market prices, were relatively *less* expensive in terms of capital costs and *more* expensive in terms of current operating expenses. The overall costs of operation (capital and current expenses at market prices) were also generally, though not always, higher. In some cases the use of accounting prices also resulted in *additional* investment (e.g. a new lighter quay) that might not have been justified using market prices; just as certain other investments (e.g. heavy capital intensive cargo handling methods) were rejected for similar reasons.

The first question that arose in connection with the new tariff structure was how to reflect the newly acquired assets (e.g. quays, tugs, etc.) in the port's capital account. This would clearly affect the amount of depreciation debitable to the services provided (regardless of the way in which it was calculated and apportioned) and would hence affect the overall level of dues and charges. The second question was how to deal with current expenses. These were generally higher than they would have been, both relative to capital costs as well as in absolute terms, if valued at market prices. In the following discussion it will therefore be assumed that capital costs were lower, and that both variable and total costs were higher, if valued at market prices, than they would have been if the entire evaluation had been carried out using market prices throughout. Now there are three basic ways of dealing with these issues. To an economist only the last is satisfactory, although the discussion which follows will argue that all three are imperfect.

One can either:

1. Insist on strict financial accountability and require the port to cover all its costs at market prices (including depreciation and a reasonable return on capital).

2. Provide the port with a set of 'dummy accounts' that show the value of all capital assets at an 'agreed' price, but preserve the requirement of strict financial accountability (i.e. adjust the port's capital account but require it to cover all costs so adjusted, including depreciation and a reasonable return on capital and including variable costs at market prices).

3. Fix tariffs and manage the port facilities using accounting prices throughout (i.e. for both capital as well as current operating expenses).

Several variations and combinations of the above methods are also possible. The three methods selected nevertheless include the obvious alternatives generally suggested when a new set of management accounting procedures are being designed and also serve to illustrate the potential difficulties associated with any method which attempts to reconcile the differences between accounting and market prices.

Each of the above three methods must now be evaluated from two points of view: how can they be implemented and what indirect effects are they likely to have?

1. STRICT FINANCIAL ACCOUNTABILITY

This is the most popular solution, since it is clearly the easiest to implement. As far as the government treasury is concerned, it is usually the 'ideal' solution. Once the investment decision has been taken—or in this case once the Master Plan had been approved—the management of the new facilities could simply be dealt with by the well-tried and familiar procedures of government accounting. The inter-departmental transfer of funds would not be affected (since all assets would be valued at their *actual* cost); the principle of strict accountability would not be violated so that, except for unforeseen losses, there would be no need for recurrent subsidies, and any financial transactions between the port department and third parties (whether other government departments or members of the private sector) could take place without interfering with the normal procedures of government accounting.

There is nevertheless some resistance to this concept. This generally comes from port users. As already explained, the use of accounting prices for investment decisions often leads to the selection of facilities which, when valued at market prices, have a lower capital cost, a higher running cost and a higher total cost (allowing for depreciation and interest charges) than if the whole scheme had been designed using market prices. Under these circumstances port users are clearly somewhat reluctant to pay higher port dues because the government, in its widom, bases its planning decisions on 'funny' prices. Why, for example, they will argue, should they have to continue using expensive lighter operations—particularly when this involves the construction of new lighter quays—when it would cost them less to use alongside quays, particularly for handling bulk cargoes?

There is no simple answer to this dilemma. Port users generally feel, probably quite rightly, that the government is not justified in singling them out and making them bear the costs of a social policy (as reflected in the shadow wage) which should more properly be borne by the nation as a whole! The use of strict financial accountability would be tantamount to raising a special tax on port users to finance part of the government's employment policy.

The use of strict financial accountability might therefore be resisted by port users. But the method also has other disadvantages, since it has widespread implications that are often not fully appreciated by those responsible for planning new facilities (e.g. consultants or government planning agencies). The first, which clearly follows from the antipathy felt by users, is that private operators who are not bound by accounting prices will increasingly offer selective port services in competition with the public authority. This might start with transit shed facilities and gradually extend to cargo handling equipment and even to private quays.

Such developments are generally undesirable. They lead to the unnecessary duplication of facilities, to under-utilization and hence to port services that are unduly expensive (at either accounting or at market prices). The government might therefore have to resort to a system of restrictive licensing to give them a monopoly over the provision of port services—except at their discretion. This, of course, has implications of its own, but it will not be examined within the confines of the present chapter.

The second disadvantage is that strict accountability has a direct effect on the day-to-day management decisions of the port. Any competent manager who is faced with a set of current expenses that are higher, when valued at market prices, than they would be if the facilities had been designed using market prices will probably try to adapt his operating system to reduce these current expenses. This is particularly true if he is being pressed by disenchanted port users to reduce dues to a 'reasonable level' (corresponding to what they would have cost if they had been designed using market prices). 'Expensive' labour-intensive methods of cargo handling might therefore be replaced by 'cheaper' capital-intensive ones: hand carts may quickly give way to fork lift trucks and to tractors with trailers.

This difficulty can be overcome within a framework of strict accountability only by resorting to some form of restriction. All purchases over a relatively small figure (e.g. perhaps £200–£300) would have to be subject to planning agency approval, as would all reductions in the normal dock labour force. This would not only tie up staff in the government planning agency on a continuing basis, which destroys one of the original arguments for preferring strict accountability (i.e. the method can be dealt with by the normal procedures of government accounting); the need to secure prior approval for anything but trivial payments would also hamper the efficient management of the port.

The third disadvantage is that this method is likely to distort some transactions between the port and third parties. If the port is compelled to handle cargo by a given set of labour-intensive techniques, it will be under a certain amount of pressure to contract selected services out to private operators. The handling of cargo in the transit shed, and its delivery to hauliers, is an example of the kind of service that could either be provided by the port or by a private contractor. The whole stevedoring operation is likewise a service that, in most ports, is done under private contract. When accounting prices are used for planning purposes, in conjunction with the use of strict financial accountability for management purposes, a clear dividing line therefore has to be drawn between those services that will (and must) be provided by the port and those that may (and almost certainly will) be provided privately. Whenever a service can be provided in several different ways—differing only in terms of the relative combinations of labour and capital—the method selected at accounting prices will generally be more expensive than that selected at market prices when both are priced in accordance with strict financial accountability. The port will then be able to provide labour-intensive services only when such services are 'protected'. This has quite widespread implications. Not only does it mean that all port services have to be classified into public or private sector activities, giving the public sector a complete monopoly over all the services it is expected to provide, the port must also be prevented from 'contracting out' any of the services thereby assigned to it.

2. USING DUMMY ACCOUNTS

The second method is a natural extension of the first. Although, as already discussed, a framework of strict accountability has many attractions for government, it generally finds little favour with port users. They generally find that the use of accounting prices, coupled with strict financial accountability in all management and pricing matters, leads to a higher overall level of dues and charges than if market prices are used throughout. This naturally leads to the demand for an accounting procedure that does not 'discriminate' against port users by requiring them to subsidize the government's social policies on employment, etc. Although a new lighter quay might thus be justified on the basis of accounting prices, port users are likely to argue that such investments are 'unnecessary' in operational terms and should not be financed out of regular dues and charges. The expenditure is justifiable only on social grounds and it should—in the interests of equity—be treated on the same basis as any other public works project or social security payment: its should be directly financed from government revenue.

Such arguments can be quite persuasive. If the private sector (and probably all other government departments as well) are allowed to continue trading at market prices, why should the existence of market imperfections (e.g. unemployment, institutional constraints, etc.), most of which are wholly beyond the control of the average port user, be allowed to increase the cost of port services on a discriminatory basis?

Emotive arguments like this are clearly not always justifiable. Such beliefs are nevertheless quite widely held and usually result in a serious—and generally successful—attempt to get accounting prices abandoned or to have the port accounts so constructed that no overt discrimination results from the use of the government's 'funny' prices. This leads to the pressure for 'dummy' accounts. Although the port may therefore decide, on the basis of accounting prices, to construct a new lighter quay it might pretend, for both overall financial as well as cost-accounting purposes, that it has constructed a modern, well-equipped, alongside quay.

The concept of dummy accounts does have some attractions and is the sort of compromise solution that often emerges from protracted negotiations between civil servants and business interests. However, the concept is easier to articulate than to apply. It suffers from three major difficulties. The first is that the dummy alternative must nearly always be hypothetical and its estimated costs, both initial as well as recurrent, will not only be subject to quite wide margins of error (for example, it might not be possible to estimate what a new alongside quay would cost without sinking a series of expensive trial boreholes); the unit prices themselves are also liable to be the subject of considerable disagreement (as the variation between tender prices confirms). The problem of deriving an agreed set of dummy prices should not therefore be underestimated.

The second difficulty relates to the quality of the port services rendered. Lighter working can sometimes be faster than an alongside quay, but the cargo is subject to more damage and pilferage, and interruptions due to bad weather and labour disputes are generally more frequent. How can such differences be incorporated into a set of dummy accounts?

The final difficulty is that port users might occasionally try to get the dummy accounts based on a new and untried technology. For example, before the widespread adoption of containerization, port users might have pressed for a set of dummy accounts based on widely accepted estimates of the cost of this new technique. In the absence of any experience to the contrary, such estimates might very well have been accepted and, as recent experience has shown, would have been wildly optimistic. The fathers of containerization did not anticipate, or adequately allow for, the enormous institutional problems involved in changing from loose stow to palletized or containerized cargo, and for the heavy cost of organized redundancy schemes and the new restrictive labour practices precipitated by the new technology.

When all the above factors are considered, it is clear that dummy accounts, while representing a neat compromise to the otherwise intractable conflict between port planners and port users, are simply unworkable. It is almost impossible, in a real-world planning situation, to conceive of the two sides agreeing on a common basis for constructing them. Indeed, part of the difficulty in the conflict is that neither side can—by definition—have access to complete and accurate information about the substance of the negotiations. The dummy accounts have to be largely based on a set of hypothetical estimated costs which, with the best will in the world, will rarely achieve an accuracy of more than $\pm$ 30% (this is particularly true of current expenses).

The use of dummy accounts likewise does not avoid all the indirect effects likely to result from the use of a non-standard tariff structure, although it does prevent some of them. For example, if a common basis of valuation can be agreed between port planners and port users, the latter will have less incentive to offer private port services in competition to those provided by government. The uneconomic duplication of facilities should thus be prevented without the need for any form of restrictive licensing.

The effect on the possible adaptation of facilities by the port management is more problematical. The dummy accounts used for pricing purposes will generally earn less revenue than that required to replace the port's capital assets. Unless the central planning authority thus exercises some measure of control over the port's day-to-day management decisions, or meets this difference by an explicit subsidy from the treasury—tied specifically to those items whose values have been 'adjusted'—the port management will face a number of choices that would enable it to reduce its overall operating deficit. In other words, if its revenue is determined by one set of accounts and its expenses by another, there will be a continuing incentive to adapt facilities until the two accounts coincide. Since the port's revenue account is fixed by negotiation, it is thus the expense account (reflecting a technology that was carefully chosen on the basis of accounting prices) that will be gradually adapted. To prevent this the government will either have to resort to the same form of planning approval suggested under 'strict financial accountability', or will have to resort to the payment of explicit subsidies (discussed in Section 3, below).

The method of dealing with the possible adaptation of facilities will clearly also affect transactions between the port and third parties. If no explicit subsidies are paid, and if the planning authority does not exercise control over day-to-day management decisions, the port management will again have some incentive to contract out as many functions as possible. This can only be avoided by the payment of explicit subsidies (to make the port management indifferent between in-house and contracted-out services) or by a clear definition of which activities the port may and may not contract out.

3. USING ACCOUNTING PRICES THROUGHOUT

One of the most popular solutions suggested for dealing with the above difficulties, and that generally advocated by the supporters of accounting prices, is to base all decisions—both planning and day-to-day management decisions—on a consistent framework of accounting prices. All planning, pricing and management decisions will then be based on a uniform set of criteria (at least with respect to prices) so that no undue distortion should arise.

This is certainly an attractive solution. Since all facilities and services will now be priced in relation to accounting costs, the overall level of dues and charges will generally be lower than if the port based all decisions on market prices. There will be exceptions, of course, and some isolated charges might increase (this is particularly true when incorrect methods of capital recovery are used: for example, when the government effectively 'subsidizes' its own interest rate). However, in general, they will tend to decrease particularly in situations involving a low shadow wage rate. Port users are therefore likely to welcome the use of accounting prices as a 'progressive move'.

In this instance the difficult problems of implementation lie on the side of the government. It is fairly easy for them to adjust the cost of capital items. These are only infrequently incurred and are usually readily identifiable. It is therefore relatively easy for the government to pay a subsidy—or levy a special tax—each time a capital item is acquired to ensure that the costs appearing in the port's accounts correspond to their computed accounting prices.

It is far more difficult to deal with current expenses. They are not only incurred on a day-to-day basis; they are more numerous and cover a very wide range of bought out (or contracted out) goods and services. It is therefore quite difficult to conceive of a system of explicit subsidies able to cause the prices of all goods and services facing the port—both those they already buy as well as any substitutes they might switch to —to coincide with their appropriate accounting prices. It is a quite different exercise from that of computing a matrix of accounting prices for use in project appraisal. In the latter case one deals in generalities and can get away with 'standard conversion factors' covering categories as broad as 'all consumption goods'. This is not true of the price matrix needed for efficient management purposes which has to be far more specific and must not only deal fairly accurately with the cost of different types of labour (to prevent the substitution of one class of labour for another), but must also cover the cost of services of accountants (which can either be bought from outside or provided internally); the cost of utilities; the cost of fuel; and the cost of a wide range of materials and equipment. It is difficult enough to see how these can be computed; let alone incorporated into a system of manageable subsidies. In practical terms the government can probably therefore do little more than calculate the appropriate prices for the principal items of expenditure appearing in the port's accounts and pay explicit subsidies on these.

The other prices will simply have to look after themselves, perhaps by using a uniform *ad valorem* subsidy on all miscellaneous items. Indeed, it would be interesting to know, on an empirical basis, how many accounting prices would have to be calculated to cover, say, 80% of the port's costs.

But assuming that a manageable system of subsidies can be devised, how is it likely to affect overall port operations? It clearly is not going to affect them in the same way as the other two methods. Provided an effective subsidy structure can be erected, (a) there will be little incentive for port users to offer private port services in competition with the port; (b) there will be no reason for the port to adapt its capital facilities to reduce its current operating expenses; and (c) except for odd items not covered by explicit subsidies (to reduce the cost of administering the system) the port should have no incentive to contract any of its functions out as a means of reducing its costs. A completely new set of potential distortions nevertheless arises.

Since the use of accounting prices means that the cost of certain port services are lower than at market prices, it follows that a number of transactions with third parties are bound to be affected. The two most important are as follows. First, in areas where the port competes with private enterprises (e.g. when it hires out equipment or leases land), it will be able to undercut them—because of the generally lower cost structure based on accounting prices—and put them out of business. This could happen even if the cost of the competitive private sector activity, when valued at accounting prices, was lower than that of the port. This is likely to lead to a misallocation of resources since the lowest cost operator (lowest cost to the nation) will not always secure the business.

The second potential distortion arises in areas where port services can be substituted for activities that are normally provided by the private sector. For example, the charge for the use of port-owned warehouses will generally be lower than the cost of operating a private warehouse at market prices. All port users will therefore attempt to have all warehousing functions performed by the port. The same will apply to the provision, and operation, of special handling facilities (e.g. handling equipment for bulk cargoes), to the provision of special purpose quays and moorings, to the provision of special storage equipment (e.g. reefer sheds and L.P.G. tanks), and so on. In many ports these facilities are provided by the users, who simply rent the site from the port. As soon as accounting prices are used, users will have every incentive to hand all such facilities over to the port, whether or not the final solution is cheaper or more efficient than it was before. The only thing that will concern them is whether the port dues are lower than their own costs at market prices. This is clearly a side-effect that could be prevented, but only at the cost of a further set of regulations and controls again defining explicitly which services the port may, or may not, provide.

CONCLUSION

The principal advantages and disadvantages of using either of the above three methods for planning port facilities are summarized in Table 8·1. This clearly indicates that, although accounting prices are desirable in principle, they are extremely difficult to apply in practice. What is quite clear is that accounting prices cannot simply be used for investment decisions, leaving the questions of pricing and financial management to look after themselves. Any investment decision based on accounting prices has widespread repercussions on a large number of other aspects of the evaluation and these must be clearly recognized, and allowed for in one way or another, if the use of accounting prices is not to lead to a less optimal solution than straightforward market prices.

In the case of Port Louis, for example, which is by no means an atypical port, the cost of port services at market prices differed significantly from the same costs calculated using accounting prices. The average cost of fixed facilities, e.g. quays and sheds, when valued at accounting prices were 12% lower than at market prices; the initial cost of mechanical equipment was roughly the same (running costs were lower because of the exclusion of fuel taxes and the effect of the shadow wage on the cost of labour used for maintenance and operation); while labour costs were substantially lower on the basis of a shadow wage rate that varied from 0·37 to 0·62 times the market wage, depending upon the type of labour involved.

Such marked differences clearly posed a number of serious questions for tariff policy. These questions fell into two broad categories: in the first case the use of accounting prices altered the relative cost structure between the port and the rest of the private sector of the economy; in the second, the revaluation of factor costs

Table 8·1 *Principal Advantages and Disadvantages of the Three Main Ways of Implementing Accounting Prices*

	Problems of implementation		On provision of competitive services	Possible side effects	
	For government	For private sector		On day-to-day management decisions	On transactions with third parties
Strict financial accountability	'Ideal' solution. Can be dealt with using conventional methods of government accounting	Since this method generally leads to higher* port dues, it is resisted by port users who regard it as discriminatory	Because dues are generally higher* port users seek to provide competitive private services	Because the cost of operation is generally higher, there is an incentive to adapt facilities, in the light of market prices, to reduce costs	Because the cost of operation is generally higher, there is an incentive to contract out as many functions as possible
Using dummy accounts	Difficult for government and port users to agree on a common basis for constructing these accounts		Should eliminate incentive for port users to provide competitive services	Since the revenue earned differs from the cost of providing port services, there will be an incentive to adapt facilities to reduce costs	Since the port's revenue will differ from its expenses there will be an incentive to contract out as many functions as possible
Using accounting prices throughout	Extremely difficult to design an explicit subsidy structure to ensure that all the costs facing port management correspond to their accounting prices	Since the level of dues will generally fall, port users will welcome this method	No incentive for port users to provide competitive services. Strong possibility that the port will undercut—and eliminate—private operators offering competitive services. Great incentive for port users to pass their own internal costs on to the port management by contracting out (to the port) as many internal functions as possible.	No incentive for the port to adapt its facilities to reduce costs	No incentive for the port to contract out any functions

* Higher = more than if port was designed using market prices.

altered the relative attractiveness to the port of using different methods of handling cargo.

(a) Altered relative cost structure. The cost, at accounting prices, of providing fixed facilities like quays and sheds was roughly 12% lower than at market prices. When the costs of operation were included, the difference increased to between 15% and 20%. Even allowing for any reduced efficiency on the part of the port, there thus remained an important difference between the two cost structures. If the tariff of dues and charges had been based on accounting prices, the private sector would therefore have had every incentive to offload all warehousing, quay and other ancilliary activities on to the Port Authority.

(b) Technical substitutability. The effect of basing investment decisions on a different set of factor prices naturally favoured labour-intensive methods of handling cargo. It clearly encouraged the use of hand carts and men instead of fork-lift trucks and tractor-trailer combinations. It also affected the overall cost of using lighters for general cargo instead of using alongside quays: in Port Louis, the cost of alongside quays turned out to be cheaper in both cases; in other ports accounting prices have favoured the retention of lighters (e.g. this would have been true in Port Swettenham[1] had accounting prices been used). The different factor prices finally also affected the overall cost of handling sugar in bulk instead of manhandling it in lighters. The former was cheaper at market prices; the latter at accounting prices.

It was therefore quite clear that the use of accounting prices for planning purposes posed a number of serious problems for the management and operation of the port that could not be avoided, or which could be avoided only in part, by basing the tariff on any of the three cost concepts described above. But are ports in any way special, or do the above reservations about the use of accounting prices apply equally to other parts of the transport industry or, indeed, to any other part of the economy?

Although many of the above difficulties appear to be specific to port investments, there are sufficient similarities between ports and other transport facilities, and between projects in other sectors, to suggest that they might be common to most types of project evaluation. Turning first to other transport facilities, it is clear that the effects of

---

[1]Coode & Partners and The Economist Intelligence Unit, *Port Swettenham Feasibility Study,* unpublished, 1968.

altering the relative cost structure between the project being evaluated using accounting prices and the rest of the economy, and the scope for technical substitutability, apply to most of the sector. All that differs with other transport facilities is the relative, and in many cases also the absolute, importance of these effects. Where there is mixed ownership in a sector—as in shipping, airlines, airports (municipal versus national), road haulage and distribution—the use of different cost structures will invariably lead to some potential distortion. It is only really in the case of roads, which are almost universally owned and operated by a public authority, that this conflict is avoided. Even there, however, one often finds public and private toll bridges competing, or a bridge competing with a private ferry (or vice versa). It is usually only in the area of substitutability that the conflict is less. Aeroplanes and steam ships offer little scope for substituting labour for equipment, although airports, rather like ports, offer many such choices. Road haulage likewise offers similar choices (e.g. speed versus driver costs), as do most terminal activities in which handling equipment can be almost continuously substituted for labour.

The pattern in other sectors is similar. There is tremendous scope for mechanizing agriculture, mining, forestry and other resource industries and there is also usually some scope for the increasing or decreasing mechanization of most industrial processes. A change in the cost of labour relative to plant and machinery will thus automatically alter the comparative advantage of different production processes and lead to a change in emphasis in the employment of the different factors of production. Technical substitution, and the effect of direct and indirect competition between firms using different cost structures, should therefore be a fairly widespread phenomenon not exclusively confined to ports. Indeed those sectors, or industries, which are immune from these effects seem more like exceptions. The general rule seems to be that the use of accounting prices for planning purposes cannot avoid having an important impact on whatever provisions are made for the management and operation of facilities.

But what was done in Mauritius? Given that the above problems existed, was any compromise evolved which avoided any of the potential distortions referred to above? Hopefully it was, although the solution itself seems to have generated a further set of problems. The solution adopted was based on strict financial accountability, accompanied by a suggested provision in the tariff structure entitled a 'subvention due':

> The Director of Marine may, upon written *instruction* from the Minister of Commerce, declare a 'Subvention due' payable under Schedule A, B or C for a specific type of ship, for a specific type of cargo, or for a particular type of user. This due shall then supersede any other dues payable under these schedules and the Ministry of Commerce shall reimburse the Director of Marine for the annual cost, measured by the difference between the due provided in these Regulations and the Subvention due, at the end of each financial year.

Provided this due can be used in a flexible way, it can deal with nearly all the objections listed in Table 8·1. Dues can be adjusted to meet the objections of port users; a quick response to obvious differences in private/public port costs can be dealt with to prevent the private sector providing competitive port services; a quick response by the central planning agency can forestall—and prevent—the adaptation of facilities; and transactions with third parties can be dealt with on a similar basis.

However, in spite of these potential advantages, the method has three serious shortcomings:

(i) It is difficult to ensure that a due like this does not simply become a convenient way of giving in to selected pressure groups.

(ii) If used too frequently, the subvention due might simply evolve into a comprehensive explicit subsidy system, but the *ad hoc* nature of the provision may not lead to a very efficient structure. Only experience will show if it does.

(iii) A system like this can work efficiently only if it is operated in a businesslike way. This is unfortunately not likely to happen when government departments are involved. Government treasuries show a universal reluctance to get involved in paying explicit subsidies; in many instances the port is likely to be indifferent whether dues are calculated using accounting prices or straightforward financial costs (it will receive the same unit revenue either way); central planning agencies are likely to avoid getting involved in inter-departmental arguments about subsidies; and the poor port users, who stand to gain most from the declaration of the subvention due, do not generally have enough knowledge of the relevant accounting prices (will it increase or reduce the regular due?) to be able to argue effectively for its use.

Let us hope, however, that these objections are more imaginary than real and that we can look forward, after a few years of operating experience, to the evolution of a system of dues and charges that do effectively reconcile the enormous difficulties associated with the use of accounting prices and a real-world management system.

Index

Foreign Loans, 76-7, 216-7, 228
Foreign Investment
  (*see* Investment)
Freeman Fox and Associates, 127,
  231n

GEORGE, K.D., 160, 201
Gerakis, A., 41
Ghana
  balance of payments, 98-9
  effective exchange rates, 98-100
  forest concessions, 104-6
  government economic policy, 88,
    98-101, 104-6, effect on efficiency
    of firms, 116-23
  National Development Bank, 101,
    102
  Tariffs, 98-100
  Timber Co-operatives Union, 101,
    102, 104
  Timber Marketing Board, 101, 104
Ghana – Timber Industries,
  accounting ratios, 109-11
  capital finance, 101-2
  capital–labour ratios, 102-3
  efficiency of firms, 116-23
  exports, 89-90
  forest concessions, 104-6
  management, 92-7
  sample characteristics, 123-5
  shadow wage rates, 109, 111
  social profitability 112-6, and
    private profitability, 114-6, rates
    of return, 114-6
  structure and ownership, 90-2
Gibb, Sir Alexander, 127, 231n
Government plot charges, 65, 70, 71,
  78-9

HARBERGER, A.C., 159, 201
Harewood, J., 38
Heggie, I.G., viii, 128
Henry, J., 41
Heyer, S., 154
Hotels
  (*see* Trinidad Hilton and Tourism);
Housebuilding Costs, 57-9

Household size, 140n, 143,
  (*see also* Equivalent Adults)
Housing Research and Development
  Unit, 69, 87
Hilton International Corporation,
  16-17, 19
Hughes, G.A., vii, 12, 45n, 49n, 87,
  155, 201

ICOR, 180, 181
  (*see also* capital–output ratio)
Import Controls
  Mauritius, 128
Import Goods, 211-2, 215, 217
Income Distribution and Shadow
  Pricing, 3-5, 48-9, 81, 132-7, 140-
  3, 146-9 (*see also* consumption,
  social value of)
Indian National Council of Applied
  Economic Research, 141n, 153
Industrial Development
  Corporation, Trinidad, 16-17,
  26, 32
Inflation, 178, 179, 184, 193, 212-3,
  218
Infrastructure, Social, 55-6, 72, 85-6
Interdependent Projects, 208-9
Interest Rates, 159, 164, 194-5
Intermediate Technology, 52-3
Internal Rate of Return,
  Trinidad Hilton, 30-32
International Bank for
  Reconstruction and Development,
  76-7, 228
International Labour Office, 14, 87,
  153, 173, 175, 176, 179, 190, 192,
  201
International Union of Official
  Travel Organisations, 41
Investment
  by companies (*see* Balance Sheets)
  foreign, 7-9
  foreign private, 162, 168, 191-2,
    200-1
  functions, 159
  private, appraisal of 7-10
  social value of, 154, in Kenya,
    196-201, valuation, 156-69

rates of, 180
tax deductions, 164, 193, 194

JAEGER, I, 144n, 153
Jolly, R., 14
Joshi, H.E., 12
Joshi, V.R., 12

KENYA
  accounting prices for private
    companies, 196-201
  accounting rate of interest, 168, 200
  accounting ratios, estimates of, 48-
    59, 74
    for capital goods, 170
    for profits in manufacturing, 170-7
  balance of payments data, 189-92
  balance sheets of companies, 182-9,
    193
  census of industrial production,
    172-7
  convertibility of currency, 187
  exchange rate, 172n
  manufacturing investment and
    growth, 179-81
  profits in distribution, 179
  stock exchange, 159, 182-5
Keynes, J.M., 161
Khan, A.R., 12, 161, 201
King, J.R., 164, 186, 201
Kitchen, R.L., 12

LABOUR
  casual, 139-40, 144, 145
  female, 142, 145-7
  relief, 130, 138, 144, 145
  skilled, 47-50, 59-60, 61-3, 85, 149
  supply, 213, 215-6
  unskilled, 47-9, 61-3, 130-2, 138-
    42, 145
Lal, D., 1n, 3n, 5n, 7, 9n, 12
Lall, S., 1n, 14
Lancaster, K., 64, 87
Landlords, 65-6, 71, 73, 79
Leibenstein, H., 119n, 125
Leith, J. Clark, 88n, 99n, 100n, 125
Leverhulme Trust, 1, 13
Little, I.M.D., vii, 1, 3n, 4n, 7, 13,

14, 36, 41, 43, 88n, 157, 201, 230n.
Little, I.M.D. and Mirrlees, J.A., vii,
    1, 3n, 8n, 10n, 14, 21n, 35, 36, 37,
    41, 106, 108, 125, 128n, 135n, 153,
    154, 156, 157, 162, 201, 209-10

MACARTHUR, J.D., 43n
    (see also Scott, M.FG., MacArthur,
    J. D. and Newbery, D.M.G.)
MacDougall, G.D.A., 159, 201
McDougall, I.A., 125
McNamara, R.S., 3n, 14
Management
  efficiency of, 9, 95-7, 117-9
  experience, 9, 92-5, 118
  Ghana, timber industries, 92-7,
    118-9
  of housing, 59-60
  Trinidad Hilton, 17
March, J.A., 160, 201
Marginal Utility of Income
  Mauritius, 136-7
Marx, K, 161
Matrix
  of direct and indirect inputs,
    Trinidad Hilton, 17-18, 20, 39-40
  housing in Kenya, 45-7
Matthews, 41
Mauritius
  distribution of household incomes,
    140-3
  import controls, 128
  outdoor relief, 133
  population, 127
  shadow wages, 129, 131-49
  subsistence income, 133, 135, 138
  sugar, price of, 4-5, 128, 148
  unemployment, 129-30
  wage rates 130
Mauritius, Government of, 128, 153
Meade, J., 128n
Mirrlees, J.A., 12
    (see also Little, I.M.D. and Mirrlees,
    J.A.)
Mitchell, F., 41
Monopoly, 51, 161n, 193
Monte Carlo Analysis, 83-4
Moral Hazard, 159, 160

250